BEYOND THE STREAM

Comparative Studies on
Muslim Societies
General Editor, Barbara D. Metcalf

BEYOND THE STREAM

ISLAM AND SOCIETY IN A WEST AFRICAN TOWN

ROBERT LAUNAY

University of California Press
Berkeley · Los Angeles · Oxford

University of California Press
Berkeley and Los Angeles, California

University of California Press, Ltd.
Oxford, England

© 1992 by
The Regents of the University of California

Library of Congress Cataloging-in-Publication Data

Launay, Robert, 1949–
    Beyond the stream : Islam and society in a West African
town / Robert Launay.
        p.   cm.—(Comparative studies on Muslim societies ;   15)
    Includes bibliographical references and index.
    ISBN 0-520-07718-0 (cloth : alk. paper)
    1. Dyula (African people)—Religion.   2. Muslims—
Ivory Coast—Koko—Religious life.   3. Islam—
Customs and practices.   I. Title.
II. Series.
DT545.45.D85L37   1992
306.6'97'0899634—dc20
                                                    92-2893
                                                    CIP

Printed in the United States of America
9 8 7 6 5 4 3 2 1

*To the memory of my sister Marianne,
and of my brothers in Koko, al-Hajj Valy Cisse,
al-Hajj Mory Kounandy Cisse, and Ladji Cisse,
and of their wives, Rokiya Coulibaly and
Gogo Maiga*

Contents

Preface

My wife Catherine and I first stumbled into the neighborhood of Koko in 1972. We had just arrived in the town of Korhogo, in northern Côte d'Ivoire, where I was looking for a field site to conduct research for a dissertation on the Dyula, Muslim traders who have been living as a minority in the region for several centuries. My intention had been to study contemporary patterns of trade. As the title of my first book—*Traders without Trade*—might suggest, my plans had to be revised, if not entirely scrapped. I wrote my dissertation on the subject of marriage, a practice that, unlike trade, was not on the decline.

Whether I chose to study trade or marriage among the Dyula, I could not afford to ignore Islam. Religion is central to fundamental Dyula notions about their own identity: to be Dyula is to be Muslim. For example, I witnessed attempts to introduce a new, and in principle a specifically Muslim, wedding ceremony among the Dyula.[1] At the same time, a controversy was raging among Muslims in Koko about whether (among other points of dispute) one ought to pray with arms crossed or outstretched. While the controversy had no obvious bearing on the subject of my research, it was difficult—and would have been foolish—to ignore it.

In short, I had a general interest in Islam among the Dyula, if only because it was a critical feature of Dyula culture and society, one that—as Jack Goody, my supervisor at Cambridge, rightly hammered into my skull at every appropriate occasion—I had better not, at the peril of my doctorate, if not my soul, disregard. But I also had several quite specific and puzzling questions to answer. Why would anyone bother trying to introduce a new wedding ritual? Why—more to the point—would anyone agree to have it performed, thereby adding to the already considerable expenses involved in weddings? Why did it matter so much to virtually everyone in the community whether one prayed one way or the other?

However interesting these questions seemed, they were relatively far removed from the highest priorities on my research agenda: determining patterns of trade in the region in the nineteenth century as best possible, or understanding the bases for the heavy Dyula preference for in-marriage, for example. Beyond this, my ethnographic interests tended to be broad rather than focused. I was trying to understand who the Dyula were, what they did, and why. Islam was only one part, albeit an integral one, of the picture.

It was the process of writing about the Dyula, in the form of a dissertation, and later of articles and a book, of attempting to formulate this "picture" of a society in words, that focused my attention increasingly on Islam. Both the thesis and the book attempted to understand the Dyula in historical perspective, and centered, in one way or another, on processes of change; the word *change* appeared in the (entirely different) subtitles of both the thesis and the book. Islamic issues were a part of these processes of change. Dyula were acutely aware of important ways in which their practice of Islam had changed within living memory. What else were questions about whether or not to adopt a new wedding ceremony, or whether or not to pray in a different posture, if not questions about "change"? Of course, Islam was hardly the only domain in which change was taking place, and Dyula were just as acutely conscious of many (perhaps not all) of these other changes, too.

Still, it was while I was writing my accounts of change that I had the acute sensation of an *occasion manquée,* a lost opportunity, as far as Islam was concerned. This sensation had to do with Muslim sermons, delivered, in Dyula, on a variety of occasions, but most frequently in connection with funerals. I had, in the course of my residence in Koko, attended a number of such sermons, just as I attended any other kind of public ceremony. Anthropologists, by and large, attend other peoples' ceremonies as assiduously as they avoid their own. At the time, the sermons tended to last until the early hours of the morning, owing less to the stamina of the preacher than to the frequency of interruptions. I usually excused myself before the conclusion. In fact, I was often invited to record the sermon on my cassette recorder. I recorded snippets of sermons on a few occasions, but by and large I declined such invitations. I was, quite frankly, not all that interested in what was going on. On occasion, either the scholar preaching or members of the audience expressed mild disappointment when I declined to tape a sermon. My few attempts at taping sermons, on the other hand, met with unanimous approval and instant cooperation on the part of everyone involved.

After I returned from the field, as I was writing, I looked back with horror at what I had done, or rather, not done. I had been offered "data" on a platter, and I had turned it away. The sermons would have been "mine" for the taping. When I wanted to ask who was married to what kind of cousin, whether they had ever been divorced and how many children they had, alive or dead, people were suspicious and sometimes frankly unwilling to cooperate. There were sound reasons for such suspicions. Forced labor had only been abolished in France's African colonies in 1946; older people associated census taking and other attempts to "count heads" with the process of establishing quotas for recruitment. People were naturally puzzled about my reasons for collecting survey data of any kind, and quite reasonably wanted assurances that it would not be used against their interests. Taping sermons, on the other hand, fell within the purview of normal human behavior, the kind of activity whose motives are so obvious that no sensible person would think of questioning them. I resolved that when I returned to the field, I would tape sermons and use them as a vehicle for better understanding Islam among the Dyula.

For a variety of reasons, personal and professional, I did not actively pursue the possibility of such a return to the field for a decade. I was spurred into action when colleagues of mine at the Program of African Studies at Northwestern University—John Hunwick, John Paden, and Ivor Wilks—decided to apply to the National Endowment for the Humanities for a multi-year grant to study "the changing role of the *'ulama'* in Africa." My plans for research among the Dyula fitted the rubric perfectly, and I jumped at the chance to associate myself with the project.

Specifically, my intentions were to collect and analyze sermons in order, broadly, to examine the relationship of their content to their context. Briefly, I hypothesized that the religious preoccupations of Dyula Muslims in town would be somewhat different from those of the people in the surrounding villages. To the extent that sermons might provide a vehicle for understanding the preoccupations of the audience, as well as of the preacher, they might shed light on such differences. In 1973, I had the impression that such differences were to be found. When I returned in 1984 for a stay of about a year, I was quickly convinced of the contrary: that variation reflected the different styles, if not idiosyncrasies, of preachers much more than any clear distinction between town and village. My earlier impressions were probably mistaken. However, it should also be noted that the availability of cassette recorders and their use in disseminating taped sermons throughout all of Côte d'Ivoire had vastly increased in the course of a decade. Arguably, the popularity and easy availability of such cassettes has contributed to a relative standardization of style and content, erasing differences I might have been able to measure in the past.

One way or the other, I concluded that there seemed to be little point in chasing down sermons in villages, and that I should concentrate my research in town, in Koko. In fact, while I continued to tape sermons and to borrow tapes from the collections of Dyula friends, I began to question how much they were really telling me about Islam in Koko. I never doubted the soundness of my original premise, that the sermons reflected real preoccupations of both the scholars and their audience, but I felt that other, equally real preoccupations were, for whatever reason, left out; that the sermons, taken by themselves, constituted a very incomplete—perhaps even somewhat distorting—image.

On the other hand, there is no doubt that the very act of taping the sermons was in and of itself extremely useful. I developed an unchallenged reputation as the most pious unbeliever in all Korhogo. My regular attendance at sermons, tape recorder in hand, made it clear to scholars and to their audiences that I was specifically interested in, and serious about, learning about Islam and matters Islamic. Scholars were always happy to have their sermons taped, though, this time, I usually found five or six other cassette recorders taping the sermon at the same time as mine.

I had no need on this second trip to establish my identity. In 1972, Catherine and I had been the only Europeans living in Koko (for nearly two years) among Africans. Koko is a close-knit community, and even after a decade, far more people remembered us than, I regret to admit, we ourselves remembered. The fact that we came with our two daughters this second time made us more human. In 1972, we had constituted a puzzling couple, not because we were childless, but rather because we were apparently quite content to remain so for the time being. Now that we had children, we were on our way to becoming fully adult in a culture where, in some contexts, fifty-year-old men may categorize themselves as *den-misen*, "infants." Once I recovered a passable level of fluency in Dyula—a process that, to my surprise and delight, took only about a month—I could speak with virtually anyone in the community without needing either an interpreter or an introduction. I was able, most particularly, to interview people, and specifically Muslim scholars. Such interviews, where I set out to ask specific people specific questions, tended by and large to be relatively informal and open-ended. I did not record these interviews on tape, a process that makes me feel uncomfortable and that would, unlike the taping of sermons, have constituted a highly unconventional and conceivably unsettling use of tape recorders.

It is important to point out that most of the people I interviewed were also people I saw regularly, sometimes almost daily, in a variety of contexts. I knew them as friends and neighbors—people I would chat, joke, and sometimes quarrel with—rather than merely as "informants." More important, I also saw them interacting with one another. These days, anthropologists have become self-conscious about the influence that their very presence may have on the situations they are presumably "observing." This self-consciousness is sometimes quite justified, but sometimes it can be carried too far, paradoxically inflating the anthropologist's sense of his or her own importance. People in Koko would talk with, joke with, complain about, and argue with one another without necessarily paying undue attention to my being there. My presence was not, I suspect, more disturbing than that of many other visitors—and among the Dyula there are always visitors around. I was "around" too often and too long for people to put on a show for my benefit.

Within this framework of the flow of everyday life in Koko, I participated in, or was privy to, a multitude of "conversations." Unlike "interviews," I did not set the agenda for conversations. They happened. Sometimes my presence was incidental; sometimes, people were specifically speaking to (or with) me, or concerned to include me in a wider discussion. Like all normal conversation (and sometimes even, I daresay, interviews), they were highly context-related. Consequently, they were sometimes in French, sometimes in Dyula. Many Dyula—particularly, but not exclusively, men—are fluent (often highly fluent) in French. French colonial policy, largely continued after independence, dictated that all formal schooling, even at the most elementary levels, be conducted entirely in French. French is—along with Dyula—very much a lingua franca in Côte d'Ivoire. I happen to be a native speaker of French, and even if I pride myself, all things considered, on as good a command of Dyula as might reasonably be expected, many Dyula are far more competent in French than I am in their language. When one or several people fluent in French were specifically speaking with me, conversation normally tended to be in French. It is equally true that many Dyula, indeed virtually all Muslim scholars, have a very limited command of French, and would invariably speak with me in Dyula. It is an anthropological convention (or fiction?) that fieldwork be conducted in "the native language." It should be clear from certain passages of this book that this was not always the case, but it would be equally misleading to conclude that my fieldwork was conducted exclusively in French. At any rate, French is not a foreign language for me or, in important respects, for many Dyula.

These conversations, in French and in Dyula, provided me with insights into Islam among the Dyula that I could have gotten neither from sermons nor from interviews. A chance remark often suggests new ways of looking at phenomena, challenging complacent certitudes about what one is looking for or likely to find. The insights such remarks provide are, by their very nature, unsystematic. One cannot seek them out; rather, one must be open to them, receptive to the implications of what people have to say, of how they react, not so much to the questions one sets out to ask, as to the many concrete situations that constitute the ebb and flow of everyday life and, as part of that, of everyday religion. I have learned as much from stray sentences as from whole sermons. Both are part of Dyula discourse about religion and its importance in everyday life.

The picture I have attempted to present here of Islam among the Dyula of Koko is consequently, if not unsystematic, at least not entirely systematic. Rather than constituting a series of steps in a logical argument, the various chapters represent my attempts to come to grips with specific issues I find central to or puzzling about Islam among the Dyula of Koko. Taken together, they are not intended to form a complete picture—as if such a thing really exists—but rather represent parts of a process of understanding the religion of people I have come to know relatively well and about whom I have come to care, personally, a great deal. The chapters grow out of the concrete questions I felt I had to ask myself, questions stemming from remarks, from attitudes, from actions, questions like the ones I have already mentioned. Why invent a new ceremony? Why might people come to blows

XVI   *Preface*

about praying with crossed arms? To the extent that these questions grow out of conversations, they reflect Dyula preoccupations about Islam, and not simply my own.

This book would never have been possible without the cooperation, patience, and generosity of Muslims, scholars and lay persons, young and old, men and women, especially in Koko but also in other parts of Korhogo, as well as in villages in the region. I owe a heavy debt of gratitude to all of them, consider many of them as friends, and love some of them deeply, as family—my adoptive Cisse elder brothers and sisters, who took us in in 1972 and have ever since been unwavering in their support and their affection.

This second trip to the field, for the duration of the academic year 1984/1985, was made possible by grants from the National Science Foundation and the National Endowment for the Humanities, and by a leave of absence from Northwestern University. I am deeply grateful for the generous assistance and cooperation I received in Côte d'Ivoire from the University of Abidjan, and especially from Moriba Toure and Félicien Dédi Séri at the Institut d'Ethno-Sociologie. In Korhogo, I was most fortunate to be able to benefit from the fellowship and advice of Father Pierre Boutin. His personal library of works, published and unpublished, on Korhogo and its region is unsurpassed anywhere. I am also grateful for the friendship and support of other colleagues of mine who were in Korhogo at the time: Nicole Sindzingre, Albert Kientz, and Marcia Tiede.

After our return from the field, I was privileged to receive an invitation to present a paper to a conference, organized by the Committee for the Comparative Study of Muslim Societies of the Social Science Research Council, on "Movement and Exchange in Muslim Societies." Participants were to compare societies in two distinct parts of the world, and in the first version of what is now chapter 4 of this book, I elected to contrast Koko with Java. In the process, I spent two months reading and thinking about Islam in Indonesia, about which I knew virtually nothing. Although I can now claim to know at least a little, I was mercifully spared the embarrassment of further pursuing, much less publishing on, the subject. Nonetheless the experience turned out to be invaluable, precisely because it wrenched me away from specifically African (or "Africanist") preoccupations and forced me to confront more global issues concerning Islam. It was really in the process of writing that paper that the idea of this book took shape. I am particularly grateful, not only for having had the opportunity to participate in the conference, but for the comments and encouragement of my colleagues on that and subsequent occasion, and especially those of Dale Eickelman and James Piscatori, the editors of *Muslim Travellers: Pilgrimage, Migration, and the Religious Imagination*, which grew out of the conference.[2]

I am also indebted to my colleagues at Northwestern, especially Ivor Wilks, John Hunwick, Karen Hansen, and Caroline Bledsoe, as well as to Barbara Metcalfe, the editor of this series, to John Bowen, and to Charles Stewart for their suggestions, their criticism, and, most of all, their support. I have presented versions of many of these chapters at various scholarly meetings and seminars, and cannot begin to list, much less thank individually, all those whose comments have helped me see more clearly. If, in spite of everything, I have not seen clearly enough, it is entirely my fault and not theirs.

In the department of anthropology at Northwestern, Andrea Dubnick and Michael Culhane helped me with the manuscript at every stage, not least by patiently guiding me through the steps of using a word processor. Kim Hirschman generously volunteered to prepare the kinship diagram in chapter 6, as well as another diagram that has since disappeared from the text. Through the good offices of my colleague John Hudson, Elizabeth Hoog kindly drew the map.

Lynn Withey, at the University of California Press, has been invariably helpful and encouraging.

I apologize to all those whom I have not mentioned by name, but whose assistance, encouragement, and kindness have helped make this book possible.

1

The One and the Many

THE "ANTHROPOLOGY OF ISLAM" IN A MUSLIM COMMUNITY

This book is about Islam in a single neighborhood of a relatively large town in the West African country of Côte d'Ivoire. As a description of a small community in a corner of the globe remote from North America and Western Europe, it is typical of the work that anthropologists tend to undertake. Admittedly, the ethnography of small communities—communities non-anthropologists might even be tempted to label "insignificant"—might seem a curious approach to the study of a phenomenon of such global spread and significance as Islam. Yet it is the premise of this book that analysis of the religious beliefs and practices of Muslims in the neighborhood of Koko constitutes a reasonable, valid, and significant way of contributing to the understanding of the religion of Islam. Of course, that premise underlies, not only this work, but the whole of the burgeoning field of the "anthropology of Islam."

The "anthropology of Islam," as a deliberately constituted field of academic inquiry, has only emerged within roughly the past twenty years. Its birth was heralded in 1968 by the publication of Clifford Geertz's book *Islam Observed.* Of course, anthropologists had not previously ignored Muslim societies, much less the importance of religion in those societies. E. E. Evans-Pritchard's study of the Sanusi of Libya (1949) and Geertz's monograph of religion in a Javanese town (1960) are among the most prominent, although hardly isolated, examples of prior anthropological interest in Islam. Yet even the titles of these two books—*The Sanusi of Cyrenaica* and *The Religion of Java*—are revealing. Both titles end with the

1

name of a specific locale, yet neither refers to Islam by name, but only obliquely: the Sanusi, a Sufi order, are ipso facto Islamic; and the majority of Javanese do claim, in one way or another, to be Muslim.

As their titles indicate, such works fall within a well-established monographic tradition. Anthropologists were expected to study specific "cultures" or "societies" situated in some precise, and usually exotic, corner of the globe. "Religion" in one form or another was conceived to be an essential component of such a culture or society. If some or all of the members of this culture happened to be Muslim, it was likely that the anthropologist would have something to say about Islam in that particular locality. Indeed, such a discussion might be essential to any comprehensive description. Thus, for example, Horace Miner's *The Primitive City of Timbuctoo* (1953) devotes an entire chapter to Islam, sandwiched between chapters on "Elementary Economics" and "Genii and Witches." A monograph might even focus quite specifically on the religion of a particular culture, as Geertz's 1960 book does on that of Java, or, more precisely, of the town of Pare, alias "Modjokuto." Geertz had to concern himself with Islam in it because it was, to one extent or another, "the religion of Java."

In short, until relatively recently, anthropologists did not set out to study Islam per se, but rather the religion of some particular culture, society, or locality. To a certain extent, there were informal biases against studying Islam, and even Muslim societies. In the first place, the "anthropology of religion" had, since its origins in the nineteenth and early twentieth centuries in the writings of Spencer, Tylor, Frazer, and Durkheim, been concerned first and foremost with "primitive" religions, or, as they are now more euphemistically labeled, "traditional," "nonliterate," or "nonscriptural" religions. The nature of religious texts posed another problem for anthropologists who might choose to study Muslim societies, particularly outside the Arabic-speaking world. Anthropologists were usually too busy acquiring minimal competence in the local vernacular to have time to learn classical Arabic, the language in which Islamic texts are written. The study of these texts, and consequently of Islam, was by and large left to "Orientalists," whose expertise lay precisely in their exegesis.

Such reticence about studying Muslims and, a fortiori, Islam, notably in parts of the world such as sub-Saharan Africa where both anthropologists and Muslims might be found in relative abundance, was not, as we have seen, an absolute barrier to the production of books, chapters, and articles by anthropologists dealing with Islam and things Islamic. Nevertheless, it was only with the publication of Geertz's *Islam Observed* that Islam in and of itself became an explicit object of anthropological study. The central problem raised by the book, and indeed by the "anthropology of Islam" as an academic discourse, is the diversity of religious beliefs and practices in the Islamic world. Geertz approaches this problem by contrasting two national Islamic traditions— Indonesian and Moroccan—at the symbolic antipodes of the Muslim world. This explicitly comparative perspective also characterizes subsequent books such as Ernest Gellner's *Muslim Society* (1981) and Michael Gilsenan's *Recognizing Islam* (1982), as well as various theoretical articles surveying the field of the "anthropology of Islam" (e.g., Zein 1977, Asad 1985). As one might expect among anthropologists—a fractious lot, overall—there is not a great deal of obvious consensus among these various authors about how exactly one ought to go about the business of developing an "anthropology of Islam." Yet their very real theoretical differences have obscured the extent to which they are all engaged in a common enterprise and grappling with a common set of questions that had not previously troubled the community of anthropologists, even those who studied Muslim societies and who wrote in one way or another about religion.

Perhaps the most fundamental assumption these authors share is the conviction that the "anthropology of Islam" is, in itself, a meaningful enterprise. This assumption is not entirely self-evident; it presumes the reality of "Islam." These writers postulate that "Islam" is more than simply a label for

a variety of phenomena that have little, if anything, intrinsically in common—in other words, that the concept of "Islam" is not, epistemologically speaking, analogous to, say,
the concept of "totemism." In the nineteenth century, and for
part of the twentieth, there was widespread academic consensus that certain kinds of beliefs and practices constituted
"totemism," and that examples of "totemism," if not "totemic
religion," could be found in Australia, Polynesia, North
America, and Africa among other places. In retrospect, it is
clear that "totemism" was really an invention of anthropologists, an amalgam of unrelated traits that tended to occur separately more often than together. It was an artifact of academic discourse rather than of the exotic cultures the
anthropologists purported to describe.[1] Obviously Islam, unlike "totemism," is not an invention of Western academics.
Real people all over the world freely identify themselves as
Muslims; few, I daresay call themselves "totemists."[2] Even
so, such self-identification does not in itself justify the analytical usefulness of the label. People have also identified themselves as "members of the Aryan race," a fact that would
hardly in and of itself justify an "anthropology of Aryans."

Admittedly, anthropologists have not, by and large, challenged the reality of Islam, as they have challenged the reality of "totemism" and of "the Aryan race." But, until recently, Islam was simply taken for granted, precisely because
it was not itself an object of study. For example, Islam could
be conceptualized as a reality initially external to the culture
an anthropologist was studying, as in Joseph Greenberg's
monograph on *The Influence of Islam on a Sudanese Religion*
(1946). Seen in this way, Islam would appear to be an externally constituted set of beliefs interacting with some other,
internally constituted, set of beliefs to produce a syncretic
synthesis. It was the task of the "Islamicist" to describe Islam, and the task of the anthropologist to describe its "influence" at the "periphery" of the Muslim world, if not its local
peculiarities within the Muslim "core."

Paradoxically, it is only with the emergence of an "anthropology of Islam" that anthropologists have no longer been

able to take "Islam" for granted. The problem that has emerged is, how can the very diverse—if not diverging—religious beliefs and practices of Muslims be comprehended within a single idea of "Islam"? Perhaps the most obvious solution to the question would be to posit the existence of, not one, but multiple "Islams."[3] Anthropologists sometimes seem to lend credence to this idea by using national or ethnic qualifiers to write about local Islamic beliefs and practices, implying by their use of terms that there exist both an "Indonesian Islam" and a "Moroccan Islam," a "Dyula Islam" and a "Hausa Islam."[4] Such a formulation is theologically unacceptable to most Muslims, who assert that there is, and can only be, one Islam. This assertion is by no means a sign of naïveté. Muslims are as aware as Western academics of the diversity of beliefs and practices within their own religion. In the first place, the idea of a single and unitary Islam can nevertheless leave conceptual room for variability, exemplified for example by the notion of the four Sunni *madhhab*, or "schools" of jurisprudence. In the second place, Muslims may hold that particular groups and individuals, whether in error or through malice, label as "Islamic" certain beliefs and practices that are inconsistent with the one true Islam. Of course, Muslims disagree about what is or is not acceptable, about what is or is not Islamic, but this very disagreement assumes the existence of a single true Islam. For anthropologists to assert the existence of multiple Islams is, in essence, to make a theological claim, one most Muslims would not only deny but, they rightfully argue, anthropologists have no business making.

In any case, the empirical diversity of the religious beliefs and practices of Muslims is not only of significance to anthropologists. Aside from Muslims themselves—who, after all, are most directly concerned—this diversity has not escaped the notice of historians, Islamicists, and other academics interested in one way or another in Muslims around the world. However, anthropologists, precisely because their discipline is rooted in the ethnography of small-scale local communities, tend to approach the problem of diversity somewhat differently from other scholars. Typically, anthropologists are inclined to interpret the phenomena they study as quasi-organic products of the particular, if not peculiar, features of a specific locality. Seen in this light, the "religion" of a community may be analyzed as an integral component of its overall "culture," or as a reflection of its underlying network of social relationships. When the religion in question is a so-called "traditional," nonscriptural religion, such an "organic" approach to its analysis seems less self-evidently problematic.[5] However, Islam is obviously not a "product" of any specific local community, but rather a global entity in itself. The problem for anthropologists is to find a framework in which to analyze the relationship between this single, global entity, Islam, and the multiple entities that are the religious beliefs and practices of Muslims in specific communities at specific moments in history.

Certainly the easiest, but perhaps the least satisfactory, way to resolve this tension between the local and global aspects of Islam as practiced is to posit a neat theoretical dichotomy between a universal Islam on one hand and local culture or society on the other. Seen in this light, local practices would in fact constitute some sort of syncretic synthesis between an organically constituted "pre-Islamic" culture and a coherent, unitary, and preestablished Islamic faith. Alternatively, one might attempt to distinguish between constant and variable components of Islamic belief and practice in different communities. Constant features would constitute the essential "core" of Islam, whereas variable features could be explained in terms of local social and cultural peculiarities.

The "anthropology of Islam" has emerged out of a common refusal to accept such solutions, however acrimoniously its practitioners may debate one another on other grounds. In the first place, Islam does not exist apart from the specific beliefs and practices of diverse individuals in particular communities at precise moments in historical time. This undoubtedly seemed less self-evident to earlier anthropologists who studied Muslims on the "periphery" of the Islamic world, notably in sub-Saharan Africa. However, as anthropologists turned increasingly to the study of Islam in its putative Middle Eastern "core," the range and nature of variability simply refused to melt away. In short, there was simply no place on earth where one could observe "pure" Islamic practice divorced from local "syncretic" accretions or deviations of one form or another. It was equally clear that, despite tremendous variability, Islam as practiced could not be reduced to a virtually infinite series of purely local idiosyncrasies. Practices initially judged "atypical" of Islam, and consequently deemed to be products of local culture or society, often turned out on closer inspection to have a far broader distribution within the Muslim world than initially imagined.

From this dilemma, the "anthropology of Islam" has carved itself out a specific theoretical space, between the particularities of the specific local communities anthropologists study intensively and the global features of a universalizing religious discourse, Islam. Explicitly comparative studies, such as those of Geertz, Gellner, and Gilsenan, represent one way of mapping out this space. However, even such explicitly comparative works are ultimately based on ethnographic fieldwork in specific locations, and so monographic studies of Islam in specific communities are now, virtually of necessity, part of an essentially comparative enterprise, an enterprise that seeks to reconcile, analytically rather than theologically, the one universal Islam with the multiplicity of religious ideas and practices in the Muslim world.

In any case, this multiplicity is not a feature of Islam that emerges only through the comparison of one local community with another. On the contrary, Muslims—not only clerics, but ordinary believers—are often acutely aware of alternative ideas and practices among other Muslims, either within their own communities or outside. This was precisely the case in Koko, the neighborhood that constitutes the subject of this book. It was not simply that individual Muslims were conscious of other ways of thinking or acting. More precisely, individuals defined their own religious practices with explicit reference to the religious practices of others. In the first place, Muslims, a minority in the region, contrasted

Islam to the religion of their "pagan" neighbors. More recently, within the context of the colony, and later independent nation, of Côte d'Ivoire, Christianity, the religion of the former French rulers, and nowadays of a sizable number of Africans, also furnishes an explicit point of reference. By and large, these contrasts with other, non-Muslim religions tend to be made complacently enough. For committed Muslims, differences between their own religion and the religions of others constitute a series of grounds for asserting the superiority of Islam over its immediate rivals.

However, the variability of religious ideas and practices in Koko was by no means limited to the contrast between Islam on the one hand and "paganism" and Christianity on the other. Rather, the beliefs of Muslims were just as often, and perhaps more saliently, contrasted with those of other Muslims. In the first instance, the practices of Muslims nowadays were contrasted with those of the past. Muslims in Koko were acutely aware that the practice of Islam in their neighborhood had changed in fundamental respects within the past fifty years. Certain quite specific features had been abandoned, and others had been adopted. It was universally acknowledged, at least in public discourse, that these changes were for the better. Thus the contrast between the present practice of Islam and its past practice—but only in certain, highly specific respects—was ultimately reassuring, much as was the contrast between Islam and other religions practiced in town.

There existed yet a third, and more troubling, sort of contrast, the contrast between discrepant notions about whether specific ideas and practices are or are not fully consistent with Islam. The changes that had occurred some fifty years ago were the product of just such a controversy, but since then other terrains of disagreement have taken their place. Muslims may rest assured about the superiority of Islam over other religions; they may have no doubts that they know better than to repeat the religious errors of their ancestors (or perhaps only of the ancestors of their next-door neighbors). However, Muslims can never be quite so assured that their own conception of Islam is correct, and that challenging views are in error. Koko was—and remains—a terrain where discrepant conceptions of Islam confronted one another in competition for the allegiance of the Muslim community. Muslims in Koko must ultimately decide to commit themselves to one point of view or another. Such challenges do not, by any means, always take the form of militant confrontation, of factional strife. Nonetheless, the existence of alternatives remains present in the consciousness of Muslims, even if these alternatives are largely identified as the practices of "other" Muslims in "other" communities, for in any case some of these "other" communities can generally be found on the other side of town.

What I wish to suggest is that, at one level at least, the multiplicity of religious beliefs and practices emerges only in the context of salient oppositions: Islam is opposed to non-Muslim religions; the religious errors of the past to the practices of the present; one's own conceptions of what is or is not proper Muslim practice to the conceptions of others who explicitly disagree, or who may, more quietly, seem to doubt. In a sense, multiple conceptions of Islam are defined, not so much by consensus among their adherents, as by the cleavages that distinguish them from other recognized and rejected alternatives. Muslims, I would suggest, are acutely conscious of the differences between their beliefs and practices and the beliefs and practices of others, Muslim or not, past or present—perhaps even real or imagined.

In other words, the empirical variability of Islam is not simply an analytical problem for anthropologists, historians, or other academics concerned with comparing Islamic beliefs and practices in different places and/or times. Most Muslims, I strongly suspect, are aware of the existence of different conceptions of Islam from the ones they hold, of alternative ideas and practices that also lay claim to the name of Islam, but that are, to some degree, if not radically, inconsistent with their own. At the center of these conceptions are questions about what it means to "be Muslim"—in other words, about what ideas and, especially, what practices are acceptable, desirable, or obligatory, or else objectionable, if not prohibited. Conceptions of Islam, as opposed to one another in

specific places and times, revolve around disagreements over
the status of specific practices, about the ways in which Muslims ought to act and the religious significance of different
forms of action.

It might seem reasonable to assimilate these different conceptions of Islam to so many different "interpretations" of Islam. After all, Islam is not only a scriptural religion but, compared with other scriptural religions, a highly textual one.
Answers to these questions are to be found in the texts; indeed, that is the very purpose of many, if not most, of these
texts. However, like all texts, they are not free of ambiguities,
and so they can be read in different ways. Western scholars
(and probably many non-Western scholars) are inclined to explain different doctrines and practices in terms of different
"readings" of the texts. However, this is not at all how Muslims in Koko explain such differences or, more critically, con-
ceive of their own beliefs and practices in the light of poten-
tially contradictory ones. For example, the standard textbook
of Maliki *fiqh*, the *Risala* of Ibn Abi Zayd al-Qayrawani (1968:
173), states that the minimum marriage portion must be
one-fourth of a dinar. The Muslims of Koko and surrounding
communities are aware of and respect this stipulation, so that
one of the prestations involved in any marriage transaction is
the *robon dinari*, the fourth of a dinar. The problem is that di-
nars have never been used in the region as a unit of currency.
This is not in itself insurmountable, as long as some standard
equivalent—in gold, cowrie shells, colonial or post-colonial
currency—is socially recognized. Indeed, when I was inquir-
ing in the field about marriage practices in 1973, I easily
found such standardized equivalents. However, while it was
certainly not the case that each particular village had its own
unique equivalent, it became obvious that such equivalents
were subject to local variation. The point is that these specific
equivalences, and the fact that they might in fact vary, were
never conceived as specific "interpretations" of the general
rule. Indeed, to speak of an "interpretation" in the first place
is to recognize, at least tacitly, that the text in question is
ambivalent, that it can in fact be "read" in different ways,

even if only one of these readings is deemed to be "correct." On the contrary, informants asserted that the rule was perfectly straightforward: a valid marriage had to include the payment of one-fourth of a dinar. Individual informants not only stated that this was the case in their own community, and in every other Muslim community in the area, but even went so far as to assert that the standard equivalents were everywhere the same. In other words, it was flatly denied on principle that the text might be "interpreted" in more than one way.

There are a number of objections that might be raised to this example. The first is that the issue of the *robon dinari* is a trivial one. It is, however, extremely dangerous for outside observers to make a priori assumptions about which particular issues are or are not trivial. The very fact that equivalents did exist in every community suggests, on the contrary, that Muslims in these communities took great pains to observe this particular stricture as scrupulously and conscientiously as possible. A more powerful objection would be that informants were not always answering in perfectly good faith. Despite high rates of endogamy, not only within villages but also within descent groups, marriages between members of different villages certainly occur nowadays, as they did in the past. Those discrepancies in rates of equivalence that did not escape my notice must, from time to time, have come to the attention of local Muslims. To assert that the rule could be applied one and only one way was a convenient legal fiction, rather than a statement of fact. Even if this is the case, the fact that a legal fiction is necessary to protect the notion that texts can have one and only one interpretation is itself significant. This is apparent in the way in which Muslims spoke about openly recognized differences of opinion. Such differences included outright doctrinal controversy, for example in disputes between the majority of the Muslims of Koko and adherents of the so-called "Wahhabi" movement. On the other hand, Muslims who share the same overall doctrinal perspective may yet disagree about whether certain acts in specific contexts remain religious obligations, or whether their performance is in fact an ostentatious pretense of piety. In all such cases, when it was clear that there were different opinions about specific issues, not to mention radically different conceptions of Islam as a religion, no one ever suggested to me that there might be two interpretations of specific texts, much less of "Islam" as a whole. On the contrary, different viewpoints were always characterized as "ignorance." Disagreement never implied the logical possibility of an alternate (if misguided) "reading" of the same texts, but rather the notion that one party to the dispute (one's opponent) possessed an incomplete knowledge of otherwise unambiguous rules.

The fact that Muslims in Koko may contrast their own conceptions of Islam to those of others in terms of "knowledge" versus "ignorance" might seem to suggest that such conceptions are doctrinally coherent systems of Muslim religious thought, systems that may be more or less perfectly known by the individuals who subscribe to them. Seen in this light, the aim of the investigator—anthropologist, historian, Islamicist, or whatever—would be to reveal, as fully as possible, the component elements of such a system and their interrelationship. The most obvious way to undertake such an enterprise would be to focus on the teachings and writings of those individual adherents of any conceptions acknowledged as the most "knowledgeable"—prominent ʿulamaʾ and Sufi *shaykhs*, for example. Such a strategy is more typical of Islamicists than of anthropologists, for whom such teachings and writings constitute only one element (albeit frequently, though not inevitably, an extremely important element) of broader systems of meaning. Unlike the discourse of the "knowledgeable," such systems are not consciously articulated by their followers, just as the rules of grammar may be totally unknown to the native speaker of a language. The role of the anthropologist, if one accepts the premises of such a semiological approach, is to uncover the hidden logic behind such systems of meaning.

Those who assume that the key to the system is to be found in the discourse of the most "knowledgeable" assume, at least implicitly, that specific conceptions of Islam are not fully comprehended by the mass of believers, but only by those few who are able to articulate them. Conversely, semi-ologically minded anthropologists imply that all adherents comprehend the underlying system of meanings at one level, but that only academics such as themselves—generally out-siders—are capable of articulating it. Both perspectives, how-ever, posit the existence of an internally consistent, logically coherent system of meaning, whether in the form of state-ments of doctrine or of shared, if tacit, understandings. I hardly wish to suggest that neither doctrine nor tacit under-standings are relevant to the understanding of various con-ceptions of Islam, but I would definitely call into question the assumption that such conceptions necessarily entail a fully developed internal consistency. To the extent that such con-ceptions are most consciously articulated with respect to one another, Muslims, not only the learned but also ordinary be-lievers, are able to express the salient points of difference be-tween Islam as they understand and practice it and alterna-tive practices or ideas. On the other hand, there may be considerable variability among ideas and practices within a single conception of Islam, and not only between differing conceptions. In other words, from the point of view of an outside observer, beliefs and practices within one single con-ception of Islam may appear inconsistent, if not contradic-tory. The anthropologist, after all, constructs a representation of a given conception of Islam out of a welter of individual statements, actions, and events observed and recorded in the field. The extent to which this representation reflects an underlying coherence is as much a testament to the anthro-pologist's ingenuity and his or her commitment to identify-ing such a scheme as it does the "nature" of that conception of Islam.

If the quest for coherence is, taken too far, illusory, how, then can one talk about, much less characterize, a specific "conception" of Islam? This book is an attempt to answer this question, taking as its center the conception of Islam held by the majority of Muslims in Koko in the 1970s and 1980s. The first part of the book is concerned with the ways in which dif-ferent conceptions of Islam have emerged and confronted one another in the community of Koko. These chapters attempt to situate conceptions in history, and consequently center on the themes of change as well as on controversy. However, I am not going to present a historical overview of Islam in Koko in conventional chronological order, with different chapters focusing on different periods of time. Rather, I wish to explore the themes of change and of confrontation between different conceptions of Islam from a variety of vantage points, which constitute the organizing themes of different chapters: for example, the sources of scholarly authority, or the centrality of different kinds of ritual. The second part of the book focuses on ideas and practices within a single conception of religion at a single moment in time. From the vantage point of an external observer, these ideas and practices are characterized by certain inconsistencies. For example, most Muslims in Koko state that it is highly meritorious to belong to a Sufi order, and yet, to the apparent despair of Koko's few Sufis, very few bother to join. In principle, the authority of local scholars is based on how much they know compared to their colleagues, yet it is next to impossible to formulate any clear system for ranking scholars in terms of who knows more than whom. Unlike those points of contention that serve to demarcate one conception of Islam from another, such inconsistencies, such points of ambiguity, are not of great concern to local Muslims. Rather, they appear inconsistent and ambiguous only to the extent that one attempts to fit a variety of observed statements and events into a single coherent, consistent system.

AFRICAN TIME, AFRICAN SPACE

Within the "anthropology of Islam," the problem of multiplicity tends to pose itself in either the most global or the most localized terms. On one hand, Islamic ideas and practices in geographically and socially disparate localities can be compared and contrasted with one another; or, alternatively, analysis may focus on variability within the confines of a single community. However, any such opposition of "local" and "global" space is obviously too crude; between a single neighborhood of a single town and the worldwide community of Muslim believers, there are a variety of "middle grounds" to be taken into account. Nations constitute perhaps the most obvious of these middle grounds, and indeed anthropologists have not hesitated to write about Islam in Morocco, Indonesia, and Iran, for example. However, such a national approach is clearly inappropriate to studying of Islam in sub-Saharan Africa in any historical depth. Nations like Côte d'Ivoire are very recent creations. Koko quarter is literally older than Côte d'Ivoire. In an African context, it makes more sense to speak in regional than in national terms. In other words, one can analyze Islam in Koko in the more general framework of Islam in West Africa as a whole.

Curiously, anthropologists have had very little to say about Islam in West Africa in general. By and large, the "anthropology of Islam" has bypassed sub-Saharan Africa,[6] despite the large number of anthropologists who have studied African societies. Indeed, anthropologists have made noteworthy contributions to the study of Islam in specific West African communities,[7] contributions that have exhibited a considerable knowledge of and sensitivity to issues in Islam. Nevertheless, the focus of these studies has been on issues other than the study of Islam per se, and anthropologists have by and large left the field of discourse on Islam in West Africa to specialists in other fields, for the most part Islamicists and historians.

However, in studying Islam within a specific local community such as Koko, it is essential to situate it within the broader context of Islam in West Africa. The way in which this broader context is characterized becomes crucial. In particular, change over time—the conversion of non-Muslims to Islam, the abandonment by Muslim communities of certain conceptions of Islam in favor of others—is hardly a phenomenon peculiar to Koko. The most obvious way of characterizing such changes in West Africa has been in terms of progressive stages of Islamization. Seen in this light, competing conceptions of Islam, locally as well as regionally, can be

identified as representing different stages. The problems
with such an approach are legion. At its worst, this kind of
developmentalism is easily combined with an explicitly or implicitly racist evolutionary discourse. Islamic civilization is
contrasted to the intrinsic savageness of the generic African,
who is only capable of assimilating Islam gradually, bit by bit.
The following passage (published as late as 1959!) exemplifies
this kind of thinking:

> The difference between Islam as a developed civilization with
> a body of religious doctrine and the African religio-social sys-
> tems with which it is in contact is so profound that the psycho-
> logical shock of conversion would seem as great as with Chris-
> tianity. It is not so in practice. The reason is that African Islam
> in contact with animists is characterized by a series of gra-
> dations which act as insulators passing Islamic radiation on,
> diminuendo, to animist societies. Thus the form in which Is-
> lam first makes its impact upon the animist seems little re-
> moved from animism. This gives Islam the advantage of rarely
> finding itself in direct contact with animists in a form whose
> cultural level is too high to render mutual understanding
> possible.
>
> (Trimingham 1959: 33)

The author goes on to identify three stages "in the assimilation of Islamic culture": first, "the infiltration of elements of
Islamic culture into animist life"; second, "conversion, characterized more by the break with the old order than the adoption of the new"; and, only finally, "the gradual process by
which Islam changes the life of the community" (ibid.: 34).
Different conceptions of Islam in West Africa are hierarchi-
cally evaluated in terms of their degree of Africanness; the
less "African," the better. The purity (at least the relative purity) of Islamic civilization is directly contrasted to the essential animism of Africans.

Such crude characterizations, typical of some schools of
colonial discourse about Islam in Africa, have fortunately and
most justifiably fallen into disrepute.

However, there are still scholars who continue to conceptualize Islam in West Africa in terms of a series of progressive

stages of Islamic development. The leading exponent of such a view is Humphrey Fisher (1973), who, like Trimingham before him, has identified three stages of Islamization: "quarantine," where the presence of minority Muslim communities is tolerated, but these communities remain spatially and socially distinct from the majority; "mixing," where rulers declare themselves to be Muslims, but where religious practices are a syncretic amalgam of Islam and of traditional African religions; and finally "reform" in an attempt to purge Islam of such supposedly syncretic accretions. At one level, Fisher's stages can be taken to represent a chronological sequence that can be applied without much difficulty to West African history. The empire of Ghana, which flourished roughly between the eighth and eleventh centuries, was indeed characterized by what Fisher calls "quarantine." Although the empire was heavily involved in trans-Saharan trade, a trade that remained in Muslim hands, the rulers did not convert to Islam, and Muslims lived in a separate area apart from the neighborhood of the palace. On the other hand, the rulers of later medieval West African empires, notably of Mali and Songhay, but also of Borno and of the Hausa kingdoms, adopted Islam as the official religion of state. Finally, the late eighteenth and nineteenth centuries saw a series of militant jihads launched by Muslims against these states or their successors, whose rulers were accused of being Muslims in name only, if at all. However, it must be pointed out that, seen in such chronological terms, these stages correspond, not to religious beliefs or practices, but rather to their role in the ideology of specific states. "Quarantine," "mixing," and "reform" are distinguished by the extent to which the legitimacy of rulers is couched in specifically Islamic terms. In Ghana, rulers made no claims to be Muslim. The adoption of Islam as the official religion of the court, in Mali for example, was intended to supplement rather than to replace other principles on which the rulers based their legitimacy. The jihads of the eighteenth and nineteenth centuries, on the other hand, were justified precisely by the identification of such courts as fundamentally un-Islamic. However, whatever the ideology of rule, religious practice in any of these states and empires was essentially heterogeneous. Rather obviously, the characterization of a certain polity as in a stage of "quarantine" tells us strictly nothing about the nature of the beliefs and practices of the Muslim minority. Conversely, the leaders of jihads were generally unable to impose their views and practices on important segments of the population, notably much of the peasantry, not to mention dispossessed members of the former ruling class.

In any case, Fisher intends these stages to represent something more than a chronological sequence. The sequence is explicitly teleological; in Fisher's words, "the basic underlying progression has been towards a *purer* faith" (ibid.: 31; emphasis mine). In the first place, such a Whig interpretation of Islamic history matter-of-factly takes an intrinsic tendency to progress for granted, without explaining why this should be so. (In a sense, once one takes such assumptions about progress for granted, only cases of backsliding need to be explained.) More disturbingly, such a teleological sequence implies not only that not all Muslims are equal, but that Western academics can determine which ones are more Muslim than others. In fact, notions akin to "purity" and "mixing" are categories of Muslim discourse, rather than objective categorizations of religious practice. Not infrequently, adherents of rival conceptions of Islam accuse one another of "mixing." In some circumstances, one party definitively gains the upper hand, as was the case in the successful jihads of the eighteenth and nineteenth centuries, where the adherents of one type of conception took over the apparatus of state power. To accept the "reformist" notions of "purity" and "mixing" at face value is to vindicate the jihadists, ignoring or dismissing the fact, for example, that large numbers of 'ulama' supported the other side. Any teleological approach implies that, in any fundamental debate among Muslims, one side represents a "purer" Islam than the other, and, what is more, that in the long run that side will win out. I must point out that nothing could be further from Fisher's intentions than such an assertion. However, it is the only logical conclusion than can be drawn from an attempt to categorize different conceptions of Islam in terms of any developmental, much less teleological, sequence.

In all fairness, most recent scholarship on Islam in West Africa has avoided teleological assumptions that explicitly privilege one concept of Islam over another. To the extent than one can legitimately speak of bias at all, it emerges not so much in the work of individual scholars but in the choice of subjects that have received the most scholarly attention in the study of West African Islam. One of the principal foci of historical studies have been the eighteenth and nineteenth century jihad movements and the states they established. ʿUthman dan Fodio's jihad in what is now northern Nigeria has undoubtedly attracted the most attention, but jihad movements in Senegal as well as the jihads of ʿUmar Tall and Ahmadu Lobbo in the Middle Niger have also been the subjects of considerable study.[8] A second, and often related, area of focus has been the Sufi brotherhoods or orders: their diffusion to West Africa in the eighteenth and nineteenth centuries, their relationship to jihad movements, and their institutional forms, particularly where these have been highly structured and developed, as, for example, in the case of the Mouride brotherhood in Senegal, which has in and of itself received considerable scholarly attention.[9]

Associated with these topical foci has been a regional focus on Senegal and on northern Nigeria, areas where jihad movements played a very prominent historical role and where Sufi brotherhoods continue to thrive and play a major role in local Islam. It would, of course, be churlish, and in any case unreasonable, to reproach individual scholars for choosing to devote their energies to such topics, which are as valid subjects of study in their own right as any others. Such studies have contributed greatly to the Western scholarly understanding of Islam in West Africa. I feel equally uncomfortable in suggesting that such studies might be the result of some sort of collective bias, as if there could be some conspiracy in the disciplines involved in the absence of conspirators.

However, it is easy to see why such subjects of study are attractive to scholars, for the jihad movements as well as the Sufi brotherhoods have, in the areas where they have flourished, made Islam very "visible" as a subject of study. The implications of this focus are most apparent in recent works surveying West African Islamic history as a whole (Clarke 1982, Hisket 1984), the bulk of whose discussions of West African Islamic history since the eighteenth century are devoted to jihad movements, to the spread of Sufi brotherhoods, and to the reactions of Muslims and Muslim societies to colonial rule (a subject described largely in terms of the continual spread of the Sufi orders and the rise of nonviolent, but militant, Muslim reform movements).[10] A recent edited volume on *The Cultivators of Islam* (Willis 1979) highlights the same trends; the majority of the essays (if not, in certain respects, all of them) deal with the leaders either of jihad movements or of Sufi orders. Reading these works, one cannot help drawing the conclusion that reform movements of one sort or another on one hand, and highly organized Sufi orders on the other, have been the central features of Islam in West Africa since the beginning of the nineteenth century, and that anything else (except perhaps among recently converted "pagans," who cannot be expected to know better) is peripheral. I must stress, however, that such a bias, if it exists, has never to my knowledge been openly formulated. Indeed, I can perhaps justly be accused of reading it into works where it was never intended. In a sense, therefore, this criticism is distinctly unfair to authors who have attempted broad surveys. They have had to rely, for the most part, on secondary sources, and such sources are far more available about northern Nigeria and Senegal than about other parts of Muslim West Africa. However, one cannot simply assume that northern Nigeria and Senegal are in any sense "typical." More important, "typical" cases (whatever they may be) do not tell us any more (or any less) than atypical ones. The reform movements and the Sufi orders represent certain conceptions of Islam, but so do varieties of so-called "mixed" Islam where they exist and have existed, as well as yet other kinds of conceptions which may not fit neatly into any of these categories.

The fact is that such apparently "atypical" Muslim societies have not only existed in West Africa in the past, but that
they continue to exist. The majority of members of these societies have been indifferent to, if they have not actively resisted, Muslim "reform" movements (though they have by
no means been unaware of them). While certain members of
these societies label themselves Qadiris or Tijanis, Sufi orders
have never played a very central role in their conceptions of
Islam. A whole belt of such Muslim societies, stretching from
parts of Senegal to northern Ghana (including parts of Côte
d'Ivoire, Mali, and Burkina Faso), are characterized by what
Ivor Wilks (1984) has called the "Suwarian tradition," tracing
its intellectual roots to the teachings of al-Hajj Salim Suware.[11]
(This is not to say that the Suwarian tradition constituted the
only or even the major West African alternative to a stress on
Islamic reform and/or highly structured Sufi orders; for example, Charles Stewart's [1973] study of the career of Shaykh
Siddiyya al-Kabir in Mauritania does not focus on militant reform and consistently downplays the importance of Sufi orders, despite the fact that the *shaykh* was a Sufi leader.) If I insist on the existence of such alternate traditions in Islam in
West Africa, it is not simply in order to demonstrate that the
Muslims of Koko are not a "freak" of West African Islamic
history, or that studies of such traditions are essential in the
name of some criteria of exhaustiveness or of fairness.
Rather, studies of Islam in such societies are theoretically important, not only in their own right, but also as a means of
placing studies of Islamic reform and of Sufi orders in perspective. In the first place, a bias in favor of studying Muslim
societies where reform movements have taken hold tends, as
I have tried to argue, to give credence to the teleological notion (which does not follow) that such movements are historically inevitable, or at least that they represent the logical development of the process of Islamization (and by implication
that Muslims who resist these movements are in some intrinsic way "out of step" with history). Secondly, and more important, there are epistemological limits to the kinds of gen-
eralizations one can make about phenomena such as reform
movements simply by accumulating instances of cases where

they occur and take root. For example, one strategy for explaining such movements is to compare known instances and to attempt to determine the features they have in common. However, it may well be that some features that characterize societies where reform movements have been successful may equally characterize societies where such reforms have failed, or perhaps not even been attempted. To put it another way, one essential (but sometimes overlooked) component of the study of reform movements is to consider cases where reform movements have not met with success. Such cases constitute, if I may be permitted to use the experimental sciences as a metaphor, a kind of "control," a means of circumscribing the conditions under which Islamic reform movements will or will not take hold.

CHOICES AND COMMITMENTS

In one way or another, both anthropologists and historians have had to cope with the problem of the multiplicity of conceptions of Islam. Very crudely, one might suggest that each discipline tackles a different dimension of the problem. History stresses the dimension of time, examining the succession of conceptions of Islam; anthropology, conversely, considers the question in space, contrasting different conceptions of Islam coexisting in the present, whether these be as remote from one another as Indonesia and Morocco or as proximate as different neighborhoods of a single city. Of course, this contrast between "history" and "anthropology" is caricatural, and as artificial as the division of fields of inquiry into the subject matters of various disciplines. In actual practice, as Ernest Gellner (1981: 214) has aptly pointed out, it is often hard to distinguish between the work of anthropologically minded historians and that of historically minded anthropologists. In a real sense, however, the problem remains the same whether one considers the dimension of space or of time: why do groups and individuals adhere to one conception of Islam rather than another? What constitutes a set of alternatives at any one time may emerge, in hindsight, as part of a process of change, as groups abandon certain conceptions in favor of others.

One way of conceptualizing either the coexistence of alternatives or the process of change over time is in terms of the choices of individual actors. In a purely formal sense, religious commitments—like any other kinds of "decision"—are the outcome of individual choices. As long as individuals are aware of alternatives in the religious domain, whether this be between different (though not inevitably competing) religions or between different conceptions of a single religion, it follows that individuals have "chosen" the beliefs and practices to which they adhere. However, to frame the process in terms of choice is to imply that individuals engage self-consciously in making decisions about religious beliefs and practices. This is clearly the case in certain instances, and such decisions may involve a great deal of agonizing and soul-searching. Conversion, for instance, and indeed any deliberate act of change in religious belief and practice, can reasonably be labeled a "choice." On the other hand, it is one thing to be aware of, and indeed deeply concerned by, the existence of alternative religious beliefs and practices, and quite another to engage deliberately in weighing these alternatives in order to decide one's own commitments. For example, some of my Muslim friends in Koko would, from time to time, contrast their own Muslim practices to the practices of Christians as they understood (or misunderstood) them. What is more, they cited one—very isolated—instance of a fellow Muslim in a neighboring village who converted to Christianity (to evangelical Christianity no less!). In short, they were not only willing to consider the abstract possibility of Muslims converting to Christianity, but went so far as to acknowledge that this actually took place. Yet I am deeply convinced that the possibility that they themselves might convert to Christianity had never once occurred to my friends. Their arguments about the superiority of Islam over Christianity were not the outcome of any reasoned process of weighing alternatives, but rather a foregone conclusion from the very beginning. It would be thoroughly misleading to say that they "chose" Islam in the same sense that the lone convert they mentioned "chose" Christianity.

Even when the outcome of individual commitments is not predictable from the outset, it does not necessarily follow that the actors are always conscious of making a deliberate act of choice, of weighing one alternative against others. It is often the case that individuals find certain arguments, certain points of view, more persuasive than others. Certain beliefs may make sense to certain individuals, while other beliefs appear to be nonsensical; certain practices are imbued with self-evident meaning, others appear as but empty gestures. It may not seem to make much difference whether individuals are persuaded by, rather than choose, one alternative or another. However, I would suggest that individuals both experience and verbalize "choice" differently from "persuasion," even though the outcomes may be the same. If choice is the outcome of rational decision-making—if individuals, in other words, behave like "economic men" even in the religious domain—then actors ought to be able to explain the costs and benefits of each alternative. On the other hand, it seems rather silly to ask individuals why they do not choose beliefs they find nonsensical or (unless they are in some way constrained to do so) they engage in practices they deem meaningless. This hardly implies any inability to verbalize the differences between various alternatives; quite the contrary. Such verbalizations, while they may certainly yield insights into the nature of people's commitments, are hard to take at face value, particularly if one tries to force them into a "rational choice" model.

The question remains: how can we best understand the real commitments of groups and individuals, particularly when, as we well know, change really does occur? Robin Horton's (1971, 1975a, 1975b) theory of African conversion probably remains the most systematic approach to this kind of question. Briefly, Horton argues that African cosmologies have a two-tiered structure, with a single supreme creator at one pole and lesser spirits at the other. (Horton never explains why this should pertain specifically to "African" cosmologies; there is no reason a priori why Horton's explanatory scheme should be more or less applicable in Africa than anywhere else in the world.) In particular, lesser spirits are associated with events within the social "microcosm," that is to say, the local community and its immediate social environment. The supreme being, on the other hand, governs the "macrocosm," and in particular relationships that transcend the immediate horizons of the community. To the extent that groups and individuals are critically involved in relationships beyond the "microcosm," they will consequently emphasize explanations of events that invoke the supreme being, rather than lesser spirits. In other words, polytheism and monotheism constitute poles along a single continuum, varying along with the degree to which social relations are internally or externally directed.

Clearly, Horton's scheme is far too mechanistic, but it is precisely the extent to which it focuses attention on social relations that makes it a useful point of departure. Unfortunately, Horton conceptualizes both social relations and types of religion in terms of single continua, from "microcosmic" to "macrocosmic" and from "polytheistic" to "monotheistic." It is by no means obvious that individuals and groups, much less "societies" as wholes, can be unambiguously or even meaningfully placed along a single "micro/macro" scale. The urban beggar and the bureaucrat both depend on the "macrocosm," but they live in very different worlds. Rating religions, or conceptions of religions, in terms of their degree of monotheism is an even more perilous enterprise in certain respects. After all, reform movements in both Christianity and Islam sometimes attack their opponents for harboring implicitly polytheistic beliefs or practices. According to Horton, a belief in the efficacy of saints, to take only one example, is relatively polytheistic in the emphasis it places on "lesser spirits" as opposed to the "supreme being." A great many Muslim and Christian theologians would take issue with, just as others would take comfort from, Horton's characterization. But is this a matter for secular academics to decide? In fact, Horton's scheme, like any other unilineal scheme of development, is by implication teleological. Movement can occur in only one of two directions: forward or backward. While oscillation is clearly possible in the short and even the medium term, the long-term outcome is in no doubt.

What is more, such unilineal approaches are in the fullest sense reductionist, reducing everything to one single dimension. One feature of Horton's reductionism is that, for the purposes of his argument, he reduces religion to cosmology, and in particular to systems of "explanation, prediction and control." The central premise is both attractive and convincing: people will be attracted to a system of explanation that both makes sense of their environment and suggests ways of acting within it. However, such a reasonable assumption is only relevant to the study of religious change if cosmology, or at least system of explanation, is the major feature differentiating alternative religions or conceptions of religion. Horton's paradigm of conversion, adapted from John Peel's (1969) study of Aladura churches in Nigeria, revolves around the initial confrontation of mission Christianity and the traditional religions of converts or would-be converts. In many respects, this represents an extreme case. Early missionaries were, by and large, totally contemptuous of African cosmologies, generally dismissed as "heathen superstitions," and deliberately set out to replace local beliefs as well as practices.[12] As long as missionaries insisted on the strict incompatibility of African and Christian cosmologies, Africans had no choice but to decide between one or the other, or else—as was ultimately the case with the Aladura—to devise their own alternatives.

However, cosmology was hardly the only factor differentiating Christianity from traditional African religions, and it is by no means obvious that it was the deciding factor in accounting for the preferences of all the groups or individuals who converted. Often enough, cosmological concerns are quite secondary. When I was first in Koko in 1972, a religious controversy was raging within the Muslim community. The most heated discussions revolved around whether or not one should cross arms in prayer. All told, Islamic controversy in Koko tended to concern ritual—which rituals were proper or improper for Muslims to perform, and how. Such questions of ritual, much more than of cosmology, distinguished (and continue to distinguish) the Muslims of Koko from their "pagan" neighbors. Nor is it possible to argue that ritual is essentially a mirror of cosmology; the position in which one prays is certainly not, in any straightforward way, related to any particular explanation of the world. It would be much more to the point to argue that arguments about ritual are also arguments about morality—that is to say, about how one should or should not act in specific situations.

Indeed, issues of ritual and morality are just as salient as cosmology in discussing the differences between mission Christianity at the turn of the century and traditional African religions. Horton's self-styled "intellectualist" approach assumes that ordinary people behave rather like Western academics (or perhaps as Western academics would like to believe that they themselves behave), and that their primary concerns are with finding the best possible way in which to explain the world. Seen in this light, controversies about how to pray are either entirely irrational or else simply smokescreens for some more "fundamental" debate about explanatory principles. Intellectual concerns are simply one of several dimensions that allow one to contrast different religions, or different conceptions of the same religion, and it cannot be assumed that they are more important than the spiritual, aesthetic, ritual, or moral dimensions of religion. Rather than prejudge the question, as Horton does, it is essential to determine, in the first instance, the specific nature of the controversies that oppose one viewpoint to another. If the groups and individuals involved insist that ritual is of crucial importance, we must assume that this is so and accept this assertion at face value. What still needs to be explained, of course, is why arguments arise over specific issues, and why groups and individuals commit themselves to one side or the other.

I would suggest that one can be even more directly sociological than Horton without necessarily being nearly as
reductionist. Religious conceptions are not only conceptions
of the world but conceptions of society, or, to phrase it in a
less Durkheimian manner, of how individuals ought to behave toward one another, as well as toward God and/or toward spirits. These moral and social dimensions of religion
cannot be reduced to abstract moral rules such as "Thou shalt
not steal," and "Love thy neighbor as thyself," let alone to
the prescription that one pray five times a day in the direction of Mecca, though such rules are obviously important,
too. Rather, questions about how individuals should behave
toward one another frequently require that one ask the subsidiary questions "Who?" and "Toward whom?" In other
words, rules of behavior are formulated in terms of social
identities: "senior" and "junior," "male" and "female," "in-
sider" and "outsider," and so on. Two truisms need to be
stressed: first, that all individuals have multiple social identities; second, that specific social identities are only salient in
contrast to other possible identities, although these do not
necessarily (as the very partial list above might imply) have
to come in pairs. I would like to suggest that the choices
individuals make between different conceptions of religion,
or for that matter between different religions, have a great
deal to do with the relationship between religion and social
identities.

In the first place, religions (at least monotheistic ones) entail the adoption of specific social identities. For example, to
be a "Muslim" means, among other things, not to be an "unbeliever," though whether an unbeliever is Christian or "pagan" also makes a difference. Different conceptions of Islam
may draw the distinction between "Muslim" and "unbeliever" in different ways. Indeed, during the jihads of the
eighteenth and nineteenth centuries, it was not unusual for
the battle lines to be drawn according to the ways in which
"Muslim" and "unbeliever" were to be defined. In any case,
"Muslim" and "unbeliever" are not the only social identities
defined in obvious ways by conceptions of Islam. Other iden-

tities may distinguish a specific subset of Muslims from ordinary believers, and in some cases from one another; "scholars," "sufis," "saints," and "sharifs" are examples. The importance accorded to any such category, the kinds of behavior expected from individuals who belong to them, the ways in which individuals may lay claim to belong to them, and the way in which such claims are likely to be accepted or rejected by their fellow Muslims may all differ from one conception of Islam to another. In short, one can reasonably ask questions like: What does it mean to be a scholar or a sufi in Koko? To what extent has this meaning changed over the past fifty years? To what extent is this meaning challenged in one way or another by alternate viewpoints within, or at least known to members of, the community?

In important respects, such identities are specifically Islamic, even if they are not common to all conceptions of Islam and if analogues can be found within other religious traditions. They can all be labeled, in some commonsense if not theoretical way, as "religious" identities, and any reasonably complete description of Islam in any particular community or society, inside or outside of West Africa, can at the very least be expected to record their presence, if not their absence. However, specifically "religious" identities obviously do not exhaust the realm of relevant social identities in any society. Individuals also have specific ethnic, political, and kinship affiliations. They are male or female, slave or free, elder or junior, warriors, traders, or farmers, and so forth. The list of such relevant identities obviously varies from place to place, time to time, and even context to context. More important, not only the nature of such identities, but the ways in which they are defined, the implications of claiming one identity (or being ascribed it) rather than another, may also differ. Many of the discussions of subjects such as ethnicity, class, and gender in modern social science hold these propositions about identities to be self-evident. However, such identities are also directly relevant to the study of religions such as Islam. Conceptions of religion do not necessarily reflect, in any mechanical way, "nonreligious" social identities, but rather

have in one way or another to come to terms with them, as
features of the social universe that cannot simply be ignored.
An obvious example is the relationship between different
conceptions of Islam and notions of political legitimacy. At
one extreme, in a theocracy, a leader's legitimacy may be defined in exclusively religious terms. The modern Iranian regime is an example.[13] More commonly, conceptions of Islam
may legitimize a ruler's authority, even though this authority
may not be defined exclusively in religious terms. The West
African "theocracies" established by various jihad movements are examples; succession to authority was determined,
in these polities, by various hereditary principles. In a very
different vein, other conceptions of Islam uphold the legitimacy of the Sharifian dynasty of Morocco. Even the dynasty's most fervent supporters would not argue that descendants of 'Ali are the only legitimate rulers of Islamic states,
but only that, all other things being equal, they are especially
qualified to rule. On the other hand, certain conceptions of
Islam may simply tolerate political authority, perhaps as a
necessary evil. Even here, there is room for important differences, depending on whether or not it is important or indeed
necessary for the ruler to be a Muslim (and, if so, on how one
decides whether or not he is in fact a Muslim). Finally, of
course, conceptions of Islam may deny the legitimacy of particular rulers, though again it matters whether this denial
ought to be translated into a stance of quietism, of passive resistance, or of active revolt. One way or another, every conception of Islam must adopt one such stance. Seen in this
light, professed indifference to principles of political legitimacy is not the absence of a position, but simply one possible
position among others.

The issue of political legitimacy comes, of course, as no
surprise to students of Muslim societies. The study of Islamic
theories of the state is a reputable and firmly established
scholarly subspecialty. However, I wish to suggest that ethnic
differences, class differences, age differences, gender differences, and the like are all equally relevant to different con-

ceptions of Islam wherever such differences are socially salient. Different conceptions of Islam must either in some ways
legitimize these distinctions, refuse to acknowledge that such
distinctions can legitimately be made by Muslims, or pass
over these distinctions in silence on the grounds that they are
ultimately irrelevant to Islam. Different conceptions of Islam
are consequently not simply different explanations of the universe per se, but rather different ideologies of the social universe. By calling such conceptions "ideologies," I merely
wish to underscore the point that they either confer or deny
legitimacy to specific social distinctions. Even silence about
such distinctions confers a sort of provisional legitimacy, for
such silence implies that any present state of affairs is at least
tolerable as far as Islam is concerned, although at another
level it may also free Muslims to contest such distinctions
without necessarily running the risk of violating religious
principles.

By suggesting that conceptions of religion are, in this
broad sense, ideological, I certainly do not wish to advocate a
narrowly instrumentalist approach to understanding religion, either by implying that individuals deliberately choose
a religion or conception of religion that is in their own best interest or, even more cynically, by suggesting that religion fos-
ters the interests of the powerful by gulling the powerless
into accepting their inferiority. Such approaches to religion
are modeled on one variety or another of economic theory,
classical or Marxist as the case may be. The classical model
does not explain how individuals actually decide what is in
their own best interest; the Marxist model leaves us with the
mystery of why the oppressed are so often and so easily
hoodwinked by their exploiters.[14] This is hardly to deny that
there is any relationship between religion and the "interests"
of individuals in society (though these interests are more
usually identified by academics than by the individuals
concerned). However, the relationship is a more complex
one than simple instrumentalist explanations would lead us
to believe.

Rather, I hold that different conceptions of religion define
and express the ideal nature of communities and consequently the proper place of individuals within them. Hierarchies of one sort or another are legitimated or contested, the
responsibilities (or lack thereof, in some instances) of different categories of individuals toward one another are delin-
eated, principles of authority of various kinds are established. Religions provide one, though by no means the
only, category of answers to questions about who individuals
are, who they ought to be, and whom they can aspire to become with respect to one another. Religion does not "reflect"
society but rather makes sense of it, morally as much as
intellectually.

Precisely because moral issues, in the most general sense,
are so central to the differences between conceptions of religions, a model of choice based on a deliberating rational actor
is inappropriate. Only cynics are conscious of "choosing" in
such matters. Individuals adhere to one position or another
because they are convinced that it is "right." Such "rightness" entails first of all that an ideal of a community or communities be salient within the social environment of the
groups and individuals concerned. For example, an emphasis
on genealogy may simply be irrelevant in a heterogeneous
and relatively anonymous urban setting; it makes little sense
to define oneself with reference to one's ancestors if no one
else knows who they are. On the other hand, "rightness" is
also related to an individual's sense of his or her own worth.
Individuals will more likely be attracted to a vision or a moral
universe that vindicates them for being who they are rather
than relegating them to a relatively marginal moral existence.

It follows from such an approach that religious controversies revolve in fundamental ways around different ideals of
"community" as they apply to concrete communities of real
groups and individuals. Different social categories of individuals, then, are more likely to be attracted to one point of view
or another. The stakes, in a very real sense, are the communities in which they live, for these communities are not
simply "given," but rather are socially constructed entities

predicated precisely on the collective recognition of some common moral framework. This common moral framework is always subject to renegotiation; it can always be called into question in one way or another. Such processes are virtually inevitable; communities do not exist in isolation but are parts of wider social environments subject in their own right to processes of short- and long-term historical change. The vision of "community" at stake in religious controversy is not simply the web of relationships between its members, but equally the nature of the relationship of the community as a whole, as well as of its individual members, with different institutions, groups, and communities in the outside world.

This is broadly the perspective from which I shall analyze religious controversy and change within the confines of a single community over roughly the past hundred, and especially the past fifty, years. The key question informing my analysis is, quite simply, what is at stake? In the first place, the question needs to be taken absolutely literally: what, specifically, are the issues of controversy or of disagreement within the Muslim community? For example, does one pray with arms crossed or outstretched? The matters over which people disagree are also those they consider to be the most important. It is not up to academics to decide which issues are trivial and which weighty. However, by asking what is at stake, we need to understand not only what the source of disagreement is, but ultimately "To whom?" and "Why?" The way I address such issues necessarily reveals my own methodological and theoretical biases. In the first place, as I have argued above, it is misleading to understand individual commitments as the outcomes of processes of deliberate choice—that is to say, as formally equivalent to decisions about which breakfast cereal to purchase. This is certainly not to imply that such decisions are irrational; they are neither more nor less rational, I suspect, than most other decisions humans have to make in the course of their lives. However, I would argue that the justifications that people give for their commitments to one side or the other are not necessarily identical to their underlying reasons, reasons they may not necessarily

articulate either to anthropologists or to themselves. Justifications are context-bound; they depend on who is providing
them, and to whom. Clerics are likely to give different kinds
of answers than ordinary believers, and indeed to frame an
answer differently if addressing a colleague rather than a lay
Muslim seeking counsel, or an adherent of an opposing point
of view. Gender, the relative seniority of the speakers, the
presence or absence of an audience, all of these are among
the factors that may influence the justifications any individual may or may not provide in a given situation. Needless to
say, answers to the prodding questions of anthropologists or
other outside observers are even more problematic. This is
not to say, of course, that one should ignore the justifications
individuals provide for their own religious commitments, but
rather that such justifications may raise as many questions as
they answer.

In the last resort, I have looked for underlying patterns in
terms of the categories of persons—in terms, for instance, of
age, class, gender, ethnicity, and level and nature of education—who tend to commit themselves to one side or the
other of any controversy. There is no preestablished list of
relevant categories, nor is there any a priori way of decoding
in any particular case which categories will be salient. This is
precisely because the controversies revolve around the religious relevance or irrelevance of certain social distinctions,
around the legitimacy or illegitimacy of different hierarchies
and of different forms of authority. Different conceptions of
Islam, by the ways in which they confer or deny legitimacy to
social relationships, provide individuals with different possible ways of defining their own identities and the identities of
others. It is presumptuous for an outside observer to decree
which of these ways is ultimately in anyone's best interest,
and virtually impossible to determine whether, much less
how, individuals have attempted any such calculations themselves. The best one can do, perhaps, is to try to show why
they might find either one side or the other more persuasive,
more in keeping with a vision of the social universe where
they have more than a marginal place.

   Admittedly, this view of religion is a variety of sociological reductionism. In focusing explicitly on the social dimension of Islam, I certainly do not wish to deny the importance of its other dimensions—intellectual, spiritual, and aesthetic. The commitments of specific individuals may be informed by any or all of these concerns, rather than by the nature of the legitimacy one conception or another of Islam confers on specific visions of "community." However, my analytical concerns are ultimately not with the religious commitments of individuals per se, but with those of a community as a whole. Certain very real changes have taken place, changes of which members of the community are fully conscious, and with which they are able to identify. Others have equally really been attempted and have failed to win support, and these failures are perhaps as significant as the successes, for they show that while changes of one sort or another are inevitable, it is impossible to predict with certainty of what sort they will be, and to identify a single "direction" in which Islam is heading. Any teleological scheme accounting for change—and all directional schemes involving some notion of development as an explanatory principle are teleological—is ultimately reductionist, whether or not it is sociological. If real historical changes in specific communities at specific times are not simply the expression of intrinsic and inevitable forces pointing in a single direction, neither are they simply the aggregate of individual "decisions" made in isolation. These are issues of concern to everyone in the community. The actions of individuals tend to generate opposite, though not always equal, reactions. The adoption or rejection of changes by groups and categories of persons, whether they represent an abrupt switch from one conception of Islam to another or rather a more gradual shift in the orientation of any specific conception, are "social facts," and I would argue, with Durkheim, that as such they are to be understood in social terms.

2

Beyond the Stream

The town of Korhogo in northern Côte d'Ivoire looks very much like the other middle-sized towns in that country. The resemblances are owing, in large measure, to government policy dictating the private ownership of land in towns, which has established a system of rectangular plots, with rows upon rows of rectangular little cement houses with corrugated iron roofs along reasonably wide, if not always level, streets. The center of Korhogo is marked out by its large, partly covered marketplace and the street leading from the market past the banks and the poshest hotel to the prefecture. Away from the center, in the shade of "Mount Korhogo"—a lone promontory that dominates the flat, wooded savanna landscape only by default—lie the wealthier residential neighborhoods, with spacious villas peopled by expatriates and by upper- and middle-level civil servants from other parts of the country. The rest of town is more densely packed with buildings, though occasional villas are juxtaposed with more modest structures, as well as with rectangular blocks of one- or two-room flats for the multitude of residents who cannot afford more elaborate accommodation. The circular mud huts with thatched roofs that still characterize most villages of northern Côte d'Ivoire have entirely disappeared from the urban landscape, though only twenty years ago pockets of them still existed in parts of town. Unlike most other towns in northern Côte d'Ivoire, Korhogo continues to mushroom. New rows of cement houses, and bit by bit new neighborhoods, are constantly springing up on the outskirts of town. The relative prosperity of Côte d'Ivoire has until now ensured a certain semblance of order; by and large, Korhogo has not yet seen the proliferation of shantytowns.

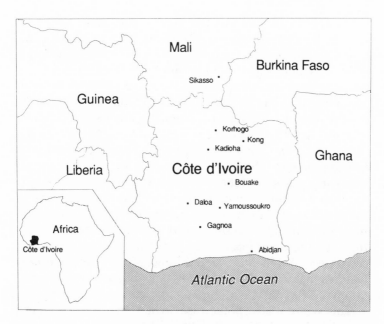

Map of Côte d'Ivoire

Korhogo is, for most intents and purposes, a new town. When I first came to Korhogo in 1972, its estimated population was about 35,000; in 1984, I was told that it had jumped to about 85,000. Even if one takes such figures with a grain, if not a tablespoon, of salt, it is absolutely clear that the overwhelming majority of the town's population are recent arrivals. The two-storey "palace" of Korhogo's late chief, Gbon Coulibaly, is the nearest equivalent to a historical monument—and this, too, is in fact a twentieth-century construction. Little if anything that meets the eye of the casual visitor would suggest that the town is anything other than a modern, colonial and postcolonial creation, like so many other African towns, in Côte d'Ivoire and elsewhere.

Yet there is at least one part of town that is, in a very real sense old—the neighborhood of Koko. The name "Koko" means "beyond the stream" and in fact, if one travels to Koko from the central marketplace, one must cross a little bridge over a tiny brook just past the cinema. Continuing just a bit further, the visitor cannot help noticing the brand-new, enormous, and imposing mosque, in the purest Ali Baba Gothic style, a cement pastiche of a Middle Eastern mosque and also—or so I was told—an exact replica of the mosque at Yamoussoukro, the birthplace of Côte d'Ivoire's president, Félix Houphouët-Boigny, and a national center for monumental architecture. This is no mere local mosque, but serves the whole town for Friday worship and for the major religious festivals. To the right, but some distance away from the road, the visitor may even notice a patch of virgin forest, seemingly adrift in a sea of cement houses. This is the sacred forest of the *poro*, the initiation society, where rituals take place that none but initiates are allowed to attend, and from where, from time to time, masked dancers will emerge. These two sacred establishments, "pagan" and Muslim, are the only features that mark Koko as in any way different from the rest of town.

This was not always the case. When, in 1903, the French colonial administration decided to make the village of Korhogo the administrative center of a *cercle*, the little stream served as a boundary between two quite distinct halves of the same community. Such split villages were by no means uncommon in the region around Korhogo. Sometimes, as in Korhogo, a stream would mark the boundary between one part of the village and the other; in other cases, the two halves of the village might be as much as a kilometer apart. Such halving of village communities was symptomatic of the social heterogeneity of the region. Quite commonly, the inhabitants of each half of the village spoke a different language. The majority of the inhabitants of the region were native speakers of one dialect or another of Sienar, a Gur or Voltaic language. These are the people who are known in the ethnographic literature, as well as by connoisseurs and historians of African art, as "Senufo." However, a substantial minority of the region's population—at least one-tenth, and substantially more in certain chiefdoms, including Korhogo—were native speakers of dialects of Manding, a northern Mande language en-

tirely different from Sienar. These Manding-speakers called
themselves "Dyula," which in their own language means
"traders."

As their name implies, these "Dyula" were part of a vast
Manding-speaking trade diaspora. Most Dyula trace their origins back to the land of "Manden" and to the great medieval
West African empire of Mali, which flourished from the thir-
teenth to the sixteenth centuries (Levtzion 1973). The breakup
of the Malian empire accelerated the movement of trading
communities southward, closer to the forest, and into regions
such as Korhogo. Kola nuts, in great demand as a mild stim-
ulant throughout the West African savanna and sahel, grow
exclusively in the forest. The north, in turn, was a source of
salt, slabs of rock salt mined in the Sahara desert. Of course,
precolonial patterns of trade were a great deal more complex,
involving a variety of other goods—cloth, livestock, iron,
slaves, and weapons to name a few—with east-west routes
crisscrossing the major north-south axis. Even so, this trade
of salt for kola nuts was so central to trading patterns that the
very terms used by the Dyula for the directions "north" and
"south" were *worodugu*—literally "the land of kola"—and *ko-
godugu*, "the land of salt." The frontier with the forest, which
occupies most of the southern half of Côte d'Ivoire, acted as
a magnet, drawing Manding-speakers toward all of what is
now northern Côte d'Ivoire, either as a majority (in the
northwest) or as a sizable minority, around Korhogo and to
the east. However, Korhogo was peripherally located relative
to the major north-south routes, which passed either to the
east or to the west. As a result, the Dyula of Korhogo and the
surrounding region depended more heavily on local trade
with their Senufo neighbors than on participation in the in-
terregional north-south trade.[1]

Perhaps because of their involvement in local trade, Dyula
were not averse to living next to their customers, and split villages—one half consisting of Muslim Dyula "traders," the
other of "pagan" Senufo farmers—were thus a common,
though hardly the only, pattern of settlement. However, because the village of Korhogo was also the capital of a small

chiefdom, its social composition was more than usually complex. The side of the stream across from Koko was first and foremost associated with the chiefship itself. It was where the chief and his people resided, and as such was relatively homogeneous, linguistically and ethnically. On the other side, "beyond the stream" in Koko, lived a heterogeneous assortment of miscellaneous "others": Dyula; but also various hereditary groups of artisans (often labeled "castes"); Senufo who spoke the Fodonon dialect of Sienar, quite distinct from the Tiembara dialect spoken by the chief and the majority of the chiefdom's population; and even some Tiembara speakers who, for whatever reason, chose to live on the "other" side rather than on the chief's side of the stream. In one sense, Koko was the Muslim quarter of Korhogo before the colonial period. All the Dyula—and consequently all the Muslims—lived in that half of the village. On the other hand, non-Muslims lived side by side with Muslims.

In any case, the socio-spatial division of the community was hardly restricted to the partition of Korhogo into two discrete halves. On the contrary, Koko was divided and subdivided into neighborhoods and sections corresponding to a host of groups and categories of various order. In the first place, each of the constituent "ethnic" groups, the Dyula, both Senufo groups (Tiembara and Fodonon), and each of the different artisan groups, occupied a different part of the quarter. Each of these neighborhoods, if large enough, was further subdivided into its constituent units. The organization of the Dyula community was particularly complex. In the first place, it was divided into *kabila*, or clan wards. Members of each ward (with the notable exception of descendants of slaves) acknowledged a common origin and in principle a common ancestor. The ideology of descent was distinctly patrilineal, or agnatic. Children—except, in past times, the children of slaves, and nowadays sometimes children born out of wedlock[2]—belong to the clan ward of their father. Given stated preferences for, and in fact high rates of, in-marriage within the clan ward, many individuals can trace membership through both parents. Still, the patrilineal ideology of the Dyula, however imperfectly realized in practice, contrasts sharply with the matrilineal ideology of their Senufo neighbors. Each ward was identified by its patronym: Cissera, the Cisse ward; Fofanara, the Fofana ward, and so on. Many of these patronyms are widely distributed throughout the Manding-speaking world, and so certain unrelated wards shared the same patronyms. Large clan wards were in turn segmented into constituent subunits along more or less genealogical lines, though few clan wards were large enough for such segmentation to make much sense. Individual families of "strangers"—affines, friends, relatives—could easily attach themselves as clients to any "host" clan ward. The "host/stranger" relationship was in principle perpetual; client families who grew numerous enough to constitute a clan ward in their own right continued to acknowledge another ward as their "host." Only the "original" occupants of Koko were not "strangers" to anyone else. However, the "host/ stranger" relationship was used to group clan wards together in loose associations called *makafo* or *makafu*, with one ward acting as "host" to the others in its cluster.[3]

Less than a decade after their conquest of northern Côte d'Ivoire, the French decided to move their administrative headquarters to Korhogo. This choice undoubtedly rested on two factors. First of all, the village was located in the center of a relatively densely populated zone, which only encompasses about 2,200 km^2 (SEDES 1965, 1: 20); by contrast, the area surrounding this zone is much more sparsely populated. Secondly, the chief of Korhogo was not only willing to cooperate with the French but, even more important, able to make himself useful to the new rulers. These two factors were not necessarily unrelated. Well before the French arrived, throughout the latter half of the nineteenth century, the area around Korhogo had been prey to the expansionist tendencies of neighboring states and empires. The French were neither the first nor the most ruthless colonial power in the region. Korhogo escaped many of the ravages of war because its chiefs judiciously allied themselves with whichever power held the upper hand in the region, at least partly explaining why it was relatively densely populated. The alliance with the French represented a successful continuation, and not a break, with past policy.

Despite the fact that Korhogo became the capital of a *cercle* much larger than the chiefdom overnight, the nature of the village community was hardly transformed immediately. In 1931, the total population of the town—if town it could be called—was only 4,350 (SEDES 1965, 1: 87). Initially, colonial rule had the effect of drawing people away from Korhogo. The various efforts of the colonial administration to develop the production of commodities for export ultimately succeeded in the forest, in the southern half of Côte d'Ivoire, with the establishment of the cocoa and coffee plantations, which, for better or for worse, still remain the backbone of Côte d'Ivoire's economy. Until 1946, when the French abolished forced labor in their African colonies, men were forcibly recruited in the north, especially in the Korhogo region, for work in the south. In any case, the plantation economy led to the proliferation of urban centers in the southern half of the country, which, until then (unlike the north) had little if any history of urbanization. These new towns seemed to offer far more prospects for enterprising traders than sleepy district headquarters like Korhogo in the north, and Manding-speaking traders flocked there, whether from Koko, from elsewhere in northern Côte d'Ivoire, or from neighboring French colonies. The whole of northern Côte d'Ivoire was effectively transformed into a backwater, economically and educationally underdeveloped compared to the south, a source of labor for the southern plantations and food for the southern cities, whose residents could hardly nourish themselves on the coffee and cocoa grown on nearby plantations.

Precolonial north-south trade routes had, as we have seen, tended to bypass Korhogo to the east or to the west. The colonial transportation network was to do exactly the same. The railway running north from Abidjan to Ouagadougou passes through Ferkessédougou, some fifty kilometers to the east of

Korhogo, as do the major roads leading to Burkina Faso and to Mali. In spite of all of these obstacles, Korhogo began to grow into a veritable urban center, and to become the capital in more than a purely administrative sense of northern Côte d'Ivoire. Migrants of various origins began to settle in Korhogo in ever larger numbers: people from the villages and quasi-towns—the *sous-préfectures*—of northern Côte d'Ivoire, who could thus attempt to reap the benefits of urban living without moving too far from their families; from neighboring countries to the north, for whom all of Côte d'Ivoire—even Korhogo—constitutes a relative haven of wealth and ease; from the south, mostly as civil servants, in part because the south has a longer history of Western education, in part because of government policy that posts people away from "home."

Not surprisingly, the colonial administration had chosen the chief's side of the stream as the site for the district headquarters. The new urban migrants followed their example, moving to the loci of political and economic power. Initially, it seemed as if one half of the village of Korhogo grew into a town, while the other half remained a village as it had been. However, as the town continued to expand, it was obvious that Koko would not remain untouched, whatever the wishes of its residents. Its residents, in any case, were anxious to benefit from the real amenities of town living: electricity, running water, modern medicine. On the other hand, Koko, like the rest of town, was subjected to division into privately owned, regularly shaped plots of land, the sine qua non for transforming the neighborhood into a series of rectangular grids indistinguishable from the rest of town on the other side of the little brook.

Astonishingly enough, this urban transformation did not entirely destroy the social composition of the neighborhood of Koko. As plots were being portioned out, whole ethnic and clan wards managed with relative success to stay together, even if they had to relocate within the quarter. The process was not quite perfect, but by and large Koko quarter managed to reproduce itself. The "casted" artisans, the

Dyula clan wards, and the Senufo families whose ancestors had lived in Koko in the nineteenth century all managed to stay, and even, grosso modo, to replicate the various socio-spatial divisions and subdivisions that had characterized Koko in the past. As a result, while Koko now looks more or less like most other neighborhoods in town, its social fabric is virtually unique in Korhogo. Most residents of Koko are descended from the nineteenth-century inhabitants of Korhogo, whereas the majority of their fellow townsmen in other neighborhoods are new, if not brand-new arrivals. Most residents are, if not members of, at least attached as "strangers" to co-resident corporate kin groups of one sort or another. For this very reason, Koko is "home" to its residents in a much fuller sense than are most urban neighborhoods. For most inhabitants of Korhogo, "home" is somewhere else, outside of town, whether in a nearby village or in another country. "Home" is where one comes from (not necessarily where one was born), where one's kin reside (in principle, even if many are dispersed). Koko is "home," not only to its residents, but to numbers of individuals and whole families who live in the capital or in other towns of southern Côte d'Ivoire.

In certain respects, Koko still bears a very real resem-blance to a village community. It is very closely knit; face-to-face relationships are of primary importance. People know one another, not only by name, but as members of specific kin groups and in terms of their particular status within those kin groups; they know to whom other residents are married, whose patron or client a resident may be, and with whom their neighbors are on good terms or quarreling. A dense network of ties links Koko to the villages of the region, resembling the ties the villages have with each other. These ties do not simply involve isolated individuals, but rather whole kin groups in town and in villages. Nevertheless, Koko is not a village that has been engulfed by a town, but rather a very real part of the town itself. A variety of ties bind residents of Koko to individuals on the other side of the stream. People cross the stream to work, to buy most of the commodities they need and sell most of the commodities they produce or in which they deal. Doctors and pharmacies are all on the other side. While a neighborhood school provides primary education for Koko's children, they must cross the stream to pursue their studies beyond the elementary level. Local politics turns residents of Koko into supporters, opponents, or sometimes only tactical allies, of politicians from across the stream. It might seem, at first glance, that these ties between individuals in Koko with others elsewhere in town are purely instrumental. Admittedly, this is often enough the case, but it is equally true that there often exist deep affective bonds linking individuals in Koko with others across the stream, and not only between residents of Koko quarter. Koko may be a very unusual part of Korhogo, but it is, in every sense, a part of town, and not a world apart from it.

Koko's mosque is in many ways an appropriate symbol of the community. It is, in one sense, the whole town's mosque, the site of Friday midday prayers, though daily mosques have proliferated throughout the rest of town. The new mosque was erected thanks to a grant from the national government, a deliberate goodwill gesture to Korhogo's Muslim community and, in an even more general sense, to the entire Muslim community of Côte d'Ivoire. Before that, an insignificant-looking tiny rectangular building on the same site served as the town mosque. For a while—constituting an even greater embarrassment to Korhogo's Muslim community—a few, uncompleted cement brick walls had stood prominently beside the main road, bearing witness to an earlier, aborted project to build a proper mosque. In fact, Friday prayers have always been held in Koko, testimony to the time when Koko housed Korhogo's only Muslim community. Rights to the office of imam to the Friday mosque are still vested in Koko, a monopoly shared by only two specific Dyula clan wards. Most of the time, it serves Koko's inhabitants, the more pious among them using it for their daily prayers. For Koko's Dyula Muslims, it is really their mosque, one in which they take real pride in proprietorship. Once a week, throngs of Muslims come to Koko from across the stream, reversing the usual flow. On one hand, the presence in Koko of such a monument to Korhogo's Muslim community can only be understood with reference to the past, to the history of Islam in Korhogo and the former status of Koko as the Muslim quarter. On the other hand, the building is equally a tribute to the involvement of the world across the stream—the Muslim community of the entire town, local politicians, and ultimately the national government.

Like the mosque, Islam in modern Koko can only be fully understood with reference both to the past and to the world across the stream. This is owing in large measure to the unusual, if not unique, nature of Koko, which is simultaneously a tightly knit local community comprised of corporate kin groups and a modern urban neighborhood. It is precisely this dual nature that makes the study of Islam in Koko so rewarding. It is truly possible to examine changes in religious beliefs and practices in a single community from the mid nineteenth century up to the present day. Such time depth is often inapplicable to African towns, many of which are colonial creations. Of course, it would have been possible to study religious change over the course of a century or so in any of the numerous Dyula villages or village halves in the vicinity of Korhogo. However, whatever takes place in Koko—not only in the domain of religion, but in terms of marriages, funerals, local politics, or simply gossip—rarely if ever escapes the attention of surrounding Dyula villagers, and vice versa. Changes are likely to be initiated in Koko, rather than in the villages. This is hardly to say that the villagers automatically emulate their own cousins, but it is fair to say that they look to Koko in the same way that the residents to Koko look to Abidjan, the capital, or even to some of the other large towns of the south, for possible examples to follow.

More crucially, the nature of the villages' involvement with the outside world, and particularly with the wider community of Muslims both within and beyond the frontiers of Côte d'Ivoire, is quite different from that of townspeople. In the first place, Dyula villagers are spatially removed, even if they are hardly isolated, from the outside world. They are generally freer to arrive at consensus about religious practices away from the watchful eyes of outsiders. Most often, it is the towns that are the battlegrounds of Muslim religious controversy. Of course, many "villagers"—those who define the village as "home"—are in fact living in urban communities, either in Korhogo or in the towns of the south. However, many of these urban residents from the villages are quite willing to stay on the sidelines, to wait to see which side gains the upper hand in the towns before deciding whether such changes ought to be imported into the home village.

The nature of the villagers' involvement in the national and international economy, whether at "home" or as migrants to one town or another, is also rather different from that of Koko's residents. This is owing, in no small measure, to the educational backwardness of northern Côte d'Ivoire as compared with the south. Western education was very late in reaching the Dyula Muslims of Koko, and even later in reaching Dyula villagers. When, shortly after independence, positions opened up, particularly in the government sector, for qualified workers, Western education was essential. The north, as a whole, was underrepresented, and the villages particularly so. Such opportunities have, in any case, been steadily shrinking. On the other hand, the large numbers of migrants from Côte d'Ivoire's poor sahelian neighbors, Mali and Burkina Faso, constitute a vast reserve of unskilled workers. More recently, dramatic increases in the price offered for cotton have led to a cotton boom in northern Côte d'Ivoire, a boom that has drawn Dyula villagers much more heavily into the agricultural sector, and, I also suspect, closer to their Senufo neighbors, with whom they share common interests in controlling cotton prices, and so on.[4] One way or another, many of the religious issues or controversies that have, in the past fifty years, impassioned if not divided the Muslims of Koko have not impinged very heavily on religious concerns in village contexts. Those villagers who have been most concerned with such questions are precisely those who have integrated themselves most fully into the life of the towns—though these are not, it should be emphasized, a negligible category. Even so, they have tended to leave their religious concerns behind when paying visits "home." The attitude of Dyula Muslims from Koko when they visit their village relations is hardly any different. Practices certain townspeople might frown upon or even condemn at home are easily tolerated in the villages, on the rather supercilious grounds that the villagers "don't know any better."

Koko, on the other hand, is a perfect arena for religious controversy, or at least questioning, precisely because of the way in which it partakes simultaneously of the worlds of town and village. Its residents are as fully involved in the economic and political life of the town as are inhabitants of virtually any other neighborhood. On the other hand, every family has extensive networks of kinship and of friendship in nearby villages, and, as we have seen, the very socio-spatial structure of Koko replicates the model of a typical village community in the region. For most Ivoirians, "town" and "village" are spatially and socially separate arenas, between which individuals can move back and forth, committing themselves in greater or lesser degrees to one arena or the other. For those who live in Koko, such movement is impossible. The arenas of "town" and "village" are only symbolically separated by a bridge over a little rivulet that the people of Koko cross every day to go to work, to shop, to seek medical attention, to attend weddings and funerals, or just to visit with friends; and over which Muslims from across the stream pass, every Friday at midday, to pray at the mosque.

3

A Muslim Minority

In one sense or another, the Dyula have been a Muslim minority since their arrival in northern Côte d'Ivoire in the seventeenth century. Such a statement can easily foster the illusion of historical continuity. The problem is that Muslim minorities can only be defined with reference to some other group or groups of people who constitute the non-Muslim majority. In the case of the Dyula, both the specific nature of the non-Muslim majority and the way in which the distinction between Muslim and non-Muslim is conceived have changed radically since the beginning of the twentieth century. This change in the context of what one might (awkwardly) call "minorityhood" has had far-reaching effect. The very notion of "being Muslim" no longer means the same thing in Korhogo as it did in the past.

It was the gold trade that first attracted Muslim traders from "Manden," the heartland of the empire of Mali along the Niger river, south toward the tropical forests. A major center of this gold trade was the town of Begho, in what is now northwestern Ghana, conveniently situated near the Lobi gold fields and on the way to the more important Akan deposits (Wilks 1962). This early (fifteenth- and sixteenth-century) trade in gold spawned the development of subsidiary trade in a variety of other commodities, creating demands in one region for products only found in another. In particular, kola nuts became a major export of the Akan forests.[1] This north-south trade between the savanna and the forest attracted increasing numbers of Manding-speaking Muslim traders, who settled along the various routes throughout all of what is now northern Côte d'Ivoire. As it happened, the north-central part of Côte d'Ivoire, including

49

the region of Korhogo, was placed at a considerable disadvantage in the north-south trade as compared to either
the northeast or the northwest. Due south of Korhogo, the
savanna extends further, in a U-shaped depression; the kola-
producing regions of the forest were thus either to the southwest or to the southeast. Even so, by the seventeenth century, the earliest Dyula settlements in the region, Dyendana
and Faraninka, were established as outposts on one of the
trade routes leading southwest. To the east of Korhogo, the
town of Kong developed into a major trading center, but also
into a centralized state.[2] By the beginning of the eighteenth
century, a Dyula, Seku Wattara, seized power in a coup d'état.
Kong not only became the dominant power in the immediate
area, but a force, both commercial and military, to be reckoned with well beyond its borders. At its apogee, it dis-
patched raiding parties as far away as the Niger river, and
was able to hold off, if not to defeat, the armies of Ashanti.

Kong remained a major commercial center until its destruction at the end of the nineteenth century, but its military preeminence was relatively short-lived. Nonetheless,
this burst of military activity was to have important consequences in the vicinity of Korhogo. Several chiefdoms trace
their origins to bands of warriors setting out from Kong, if
not always firmly under its control. These armies carved out
little dominions among the acephalous, Sienar-speaking
Senufo peoples to the west. In the early eighteenth century,
one such band, under Jangarawuru Wattara, settled in the
village of Pundya, along the route to the kola-producing forests of western Côte d'Ivoire. The Senufo villagers were
rapidly driven off to a new site, a few kilometers away, as Jangarawuru's village, renamed Kadioha, established its hege-
mony over its immediate hinterland.[3] Oral traditions indicate
that the chiefdom of Korhogo was founded at about the same
period and in a similar manner.[4] However, Nanguin Soro,
the warrior who founded Korhogo, was Senufo. The region
saw the emergence of a number of small chiefdoms, some
(but not all) tracing their origins to Kong, and most, with
the notable exception of Kadioha, under Senufo rule. Kong,

at the height of its power, thus provided the impetus for the beginnings of political centralization of the Korhogo region, less than 150 kilometers away. Surprisingly enough, Kong never exercised any direct control over a region so close by. In any case, this process of centralization, either in Korhogo or among its neighbors, remained minimal until the mid nineteenth century, with the expansion of the nearby state of Kenedugu, whose capital, Sikasso, lay just north of what is now the border between Côte d'Ivoire and Mali. The reigning chief of Korhogo, Zwakonion Soro, chose to ally himself with his powerful northern neighbor as a means of consolidating his own power in the region.[5] The village of Korhogo thus became the capital of a chiefdom that, though relatively small by absolute standards, was, if only by default, one of the major political centers in the region. As such, the village attracted Dyula settlers in increasing numbers.

By the end of the nineteenth century, both the chiefdom and the village of Korhogo were characterized by a matrix of ethnic categories and subcategories corresponding broadly to a system of division of labor and allocation of political authority (see table on p. 52). Most of the population consisted either of Sienar-speaking "Senufo" agriculturalists or of Mandingspeaking Dyula traders. However, each of these categories was subdivided in significant ways, and there were several other groups who did not fit neatly into either category. In any case, the very name "Senufo" is a Dyula phrase, *siena fo*, "to speak Siena[r]." The majority of Sienar speakers, those whose primary occupation was agriculture, called themselves *senambele*. The *senambele* were in turn divided along linguistic lines: the Tiembara, speaking a northern dialect of Sienar, were the politically dominant group in the chiefdom and alone accounted for the majority of its population; the Fodonon, speaking a southern dialect of Sienar, were an encapsulated minority. Socially distinct from the *senambele* were the *fijembele*, members of hereditary (though not endogamous) groups traditionally associated with specific crafts: the *fonombele*, "blacksmiths"; the *kulebele*, "sculptors"; and the *kpeembele*, "brass casters." The *kpeembele*, I was told, once

Ethnic Categories and Subcategories of Precolonial Korhogo

Group	Category	Native Language	Occupation	Muslim/ Non-Muslim	Initiation Societies
Tiembara	Senambele	Sienar ("Senufo")	agriculturalists	non-Muslims	present
Fodonon	Senambele	Sienar*	agriculturalists	non-Muslims	present
Fono	Fijembele	Sienar	blacksmiths	non-Muslims	present
Kule	Fijembele	Sienar	woodcarvers	non-Muslims	present
Kpeem	Fijembele	Sienar	brass casters	non-Muslims	present
Dieli	?	Dieli	leatherworkers	non-Muslims	present
Milaga	?	Manding	blacksmiths	non-Muslims	present
tun tigi	Dyula	Manding	warriors, traders, weavers	Muslims	present
mory	Dyula	Manding	Islamic scholars, weavers, traders	Muslims	absent

*The Fodonon speak a dialect of Sienar that is quite different from Tiembara and incomprehensible to native Tiembara speakers.

spoke their own distinct language. According to Dolores
Richter (1980: 15), "Kulebele and Fonombele support their
oral tradition that they originated in Mali and migrated
southward." Whatever the case, these craft groups now
speak as a native language one dialect or another of Sienar,
depending on where they are settled. In Korhogo, they all
speak Tiembara. However, the Dieli, "leatherworkers,"
whom oral traditions identify as the oldest occupants of the
site of Korhogo village, still have their own language distinct
from either Sienar or Manding.[6] Finally, the Milaga "blacksmiths" were native Manding speakers like the Dyula. The
Dyula, in turn, were divided into two hereditary categories:
tun tigi, "possessors of quivers"—that is to say, "warriors,"—
and *mory*, "scholars." In principle, these hereditary categories were occupationally and linguistically defined. Reality,
of course, was less static and more complex than such a neat
system of divisions might suggest. Bilingualism was quite
common, especially among members of linguistic minorities.
Although Tiembara and Fodonon *senambele* might define
themselves as "agriculturalists," agriculture was in fact an activity common to members of all groups. Various minority
groups enjoyed monopolies, or quasi-monopolies, over certain occupations. Depending, in part, on the demand for
their goods or services, members of such an occupational minority might practice their trade full time, seasonally, or not
at all.

The relationship between occupation and hereditary status was particularly complex among the Dyula, who represented a substantial proportion—perhaps as much as one-
sixth—of the chiefdom's population. Long-distance trade
was effectively a Dyula monopoly, made possible by their
links with other Manding-speaking trading communities outside the region. However, as we have seen, major north-
south trade routes tended to bypass Korhogo either to the
east or to the west. Weaving was another Dyula monopoly;
indeed weaving, rather than trade, was a ubiquitous occupation among the Dyula. Cloth was, for the most part, traded
to the Senufo, as were imported luxury goods, whose local

distribution the Dyula controlled. Yet the Dyula themselves
were further subdivided, as we have seen, into the hereditary
categories of *mory* and *tun tigi*. These categories applied to
entire *kabilas*, or clan wards. The domains of warfare and especially politics were the preserve of *tun tigi kabilas*, Islamic
scholarship the domain of the *mory*. Unlike other hereditary
distinctions in the region—between Dyula and Senufo, between *senambele* and *fijembele*—the division between *mory* and
tun tigi was of greater ideological than economic significance.
The real units of economic specialization among the Dyula
were the individual *kabilas*. Only a few *mory kabilas* were devoted to advanced Islamic scholarship, and only those *tun tigi*
kabilas with rights to chiefly office in a village or chiefdom
were specifically concerned with politics. Aside from such
specialized *kabilas*, the distinction between *tun tigi* and *mory*
involved no monopolies; a *mory* individual might well take
up arms as a profession, just as a *tun tigi* might devote himself to study. Rather, this division reflected the notion that
warfare and politics on one hand, religion and scholarship
on the other, were antithetical careers. Both, however, were
compatible with trade and weaving, which were ultimately
the economic mainstays of the Dyula community.

The distinctions among all of these various categories—
Dyula and Senufo, *senambele* and *fijembele*, *mory* and *tun tigi*—
were reflected in the religious domain. Within the village of
Korhogo, where each of these categories was represented,
every group—with the significant exception of the Dyula
mory, the Islamic scholars—had its own separate initiation
society, known as *poro* in Sienar, *lo* or *jolo* in Manding. Each
society initiated its own members separately. Each had its
own distinct set of masks and ritual paraphernalia (though a
certain amount of borrowing could and did occur) associated
with both funeral and initiation ceremonies. In other words,
the religious practices of a significant proportion of the Dyula
population—the *tun tigi* or "warriors"—did not differ significantly in many respects from those of their *senambele* or
fijembele neighbors.

One might be tempted to conclude that precolonial Korhogo
was characterized by the coexistence of two clearly distinct

religious systems: an initiation-society complex on one hand and Islam on the other. Other aspects of *tun tigi* behavior would lend credence to such a view: the offering of animal sacrifices to "fetishes" (*jo*), the material embodiments of various spirits; drinking alcoholic beverages; nonobservance or irregular observance of Muslim prayers and of the fast at Ramadan. Nevertheless, the *tun tigi* were considered to be Muslims, not "pagans."[7] In effect, the distinction between Muslims and non-Muslims, at least within the confines of the region, coincided exactly with the distinction between Dyula and non-Dyula. Non-Muslims in the region were collectively known as *banmana*, literally "refusers," that is to say, "unbelievers," "those who refuse Islam."[8] In ordinary speech, the term *banmana* was generally used to refer to the Senufo; Sienar was called *banmana-kan*, "the unbelievers' language," as opposed to *Dyula-kan*, or Manding. However, language itself was not the determining criterion for religious identity; the Milaga blacksmiths, who spoke Manding, were classed as "unbelievers" rather than as Muslims, as were the Dieli leatherworkers. These distinctions were reflected in marriage patterns. *Tun tigi* and *mory* groups could give and receive wives to and from one another; they could also receive wives from "unbelievers," but not bestow their own women in marriage to them, since Muslim women ought only be given in marriage to Muslim men. The Muslim identity of the *tun tigi* was publicly expressed, not by their observance of the strictures of Islamic law, but rather by their participation in festivities associated with Muslim calendar holidays: *donba* (Arabic *mawlud*), *tabaski* (Arabic ʿ*id al-kabir*) and *sun kalo* (Ramadan).[9]

In short, religion in precolonial Korhogo very neatly mirrored the local system of hereditary social categories. The distinction between Muslim and non-Muslim corresponded to that between Dyula and non-Dyula; among the Dyula, in turn, only the *mory* were obligated in principle to follow the strictures of Islamic law diligently. This correspondence between the categories "Dyula" and "Muslim" made perfect sense in terms of the local monopoly held by the Dyula in long-distance trade. The long-distance trade network of which Korhogo was a part was entirely in the hands of a

Muslim diaspora; one could not participate in such trade without being a Muslim.[10] However, to demonstrate one's identity as a Muslim outside the region, one had to be reasonably familiar with the basics of Islamic ritual: at the very least, one had to know how and when to pray. Precisely because both the prayers and the instructions for their proper use were transmitted in Arabic written documents, the preservation of such knowledge implied the existence of a body of persons literate in Arabic. The maintenance of this tradition was the responsibility of the *mory*, although by no means all *mory* individuals had to be literate in Arabic. Relatively few could read and write Arabic with any degree of fluency; many more were capable of reciting a written text, although not necessarily of understanding its precise meaning.

If the practice of Islam distinguished one category of Dyula from the other, allegiance to Islam, more than anything else, served as the defining criterion of Dyula identity. Only Islam distinguished Dyula unambiguously from all of their neighbors. After all, some Dyula participated in initiation-society activities. Like the *fijembele*, the Dyula enjoyed a hereditary monopoly over craft production—namely, weaving. Even language was hardly an unambiguous marker of identity, for the Dyula shared a native language with "pagan" Milaga blacksmiths (admittedly not a very numerous group).[11] In any case, Manding-speaking *banmana* were to be found in large numbers in regions to the north and to the west of Korhogo. Religion, rather than language, linked the Dyula of Korhogo with the whole community of Muslim traders in the Western Sudan. Indeed, a Hausa quarter existed as close by as Kong (Binger 1892: 297), and several families of Koko's Dyula community in Korhogo trace their origins to immigrant Hausa traders who were able to assimilate without difficulty.

In short, by distinguishing the Dyula from their immediate neighbors and linking them with Muslims outside the region, Islam was crucial to their maintenance of a monopoly over long-distance trade. Since trade and weaving were locally associated, it served equally to preserve the even more crucial monopoly over the production of cloth. It follows that the Dyula had no particular interest in converting their neighbors to Islam; on the contrary, in order to protect their monopoly, they had, if anything, an interest in discouraging such conversions. One could argue that the Dyula scholars, whose Arabic literacy furnished them with a lucrative monopoly on written magical charms,[12] did not even have an interest in reforming the religious practice of their *tun tigi* coreligionists. An early colonial administrator in Côte d'Ivoire related an anecdote that, while it pertains to a community outside the Korhogo region, equally reflects the attitude of Korhogo's Dyula scholars.[13] A "pagan" chief had decided to convert to Islam, and learned the prayers and the rudiments of Arabic, as well as observing the tenets of Islamic law with all the enthusiasm of a neophyte. The local scholars apparently found this rigor disquieting, if not embarrassing. When epidemics decimated both the cattle and the human population of the village, they reportedly addressed the chief in the following terms: "Do not be astonished if the village is subjected to Allah's wrath. He has done well by putting everyone in his place. You have transgressed His orders, and have abandoned the faith of your fathers, whom God manifestly commanded to drink palm wine, to eat unclean meat, and to worship only stones, mountains, and trees. Do not be astonished if your ancestors, and God himself, are punishing your village. This is what God has revealed to us." The story is perhaps apocryphal, a caricature, but not necessarily a radical misrepresentation, of what was the attitude of some, if not all, scholars. There is no evidence that the scholars of Korhogo actively discouraged conversions among the "unbelievers," or reform of the religious practices of their *tun tigi* cousins—nor, for that matter, is there evidence that they had occasion to do so. Rather, they not only tolerated but fully accepted the status quo. In fact, they apparently winked at the limited participation of *mory* youths in the initiation-society rituals of their *tun tigi* kin. Of course, such youths were neither formally initiated nor involved in any blatantly unorthodox activities, such as the offering of sacrifices or drinking beer. However, some of my older *mory* friends in Koko confidentially—but with unabashed nostalgia—recounted to me how they had entered the sacred forests of their *tun tigi* relatives, stripping off their Muslim robes and dancing with the initiates during various masquerades. Scholars must have been aware of such goings on; that they condoned such behavior, even among *mory*, is a sure indication that they were not characterized by any particular zeal to reform the system.

If Dyula scholars so readily accepted such a dual standard of religious practice, it is also because the hereditary division into *mory* and *tun tigi* reflected a deep-seated principle, the separation of religion from politics. This principle was a cornerstone of Dyula policy, and a reflection of their status as a Muslim minority. In keeping with this policy, it was the responsibility of religious leaders openly to proclaim their support for whatever regime happened to be in power, provided that the regime tolerated the free exercise of Islam as a religion. Such moral support included the provision of charms and prayers, when solicited, to ensure the success of the regime's enterprises. It is easy to misrepresent such a stance as quietist (at best) or collaborationist and opportunistic (at worse). On the contrary, such behavior was a moral obligation on the part of religious leaders, but for that very reason was not binding on the Dyula community at large. Ordinary Dyula were free to support one faction or party or another, in or out of power, while scholars were expected to endorse whomever happened to be in power at the time. The regime in place, in other words, was not to be opposed on religious grounds—which is not to say that it was not to be opposed by anyone under any circumstances. The principle placed both religious leaders and Islam in general outside the political arena.

The arrival of the French did not in any way alter this principle of the separation of "religion" from "politics." Colonial rule came late to northern Côte d'Ivoire. It was only in 1895 that the French established a post on the Bandama River, in the vicinity of the region; in 1903, they chose to move the district headquarters to the village of Korhogo, which was to

remain the "capital" of the north. The last decade of the nineteenth century had been a turbulent one, as three rival empires vied for control of the region: Kenedugu, whose capital,
Sikasso, lay north of Korhogo; the empire of Samory, a con-
queror, whose home base had been to the west, in Guinea,
but whose armies, driven eastward by a revolt, subjected vast
areas; and finally, of course, the French. Each of these
armies, in turn, exercised their dominion over Korhogo. In
the early days of French rule, administrators reported that
their subjects fully expected their dominion to be as short-
lived as those of their predecessors, and that the French, like
the others before them, would soon go away or be driven
away by some, yet more powerful, army. In a sense, these ru-
mors were not entirely false. The reign of Gbon Coulibaly,
chief of Korhogo, who had been installed by the king of
Kenedugu, and who had submitted to Samory and later the
French, outlasted the entire period of French rule. He died in
1963, three years after Côte d'Ivoire became independent.
Colonial rule was but a long episode in Gbon's reign.

It became the responsibility of Muslim clerics to declare
open and enthusiastic support for the French, just as they
had declared their loyalty to previous African rulers. Indeed,
an early colonial study of Islam in Côte d'Ivoire (Marty 1922)
cites in its entirety an address from the "Muslims of Korhogo
to the people of Mecca," written during World War I, which
demonstrates the lengths to which such a principle could be
taken:

> The present document, written by Mamadou Soumare, son of
> Brahima Soumare, of Korhogo, is destined to be sent to the
> Muslims of Mecca through the intermediation of the governor
> of Côte d'Ivoire, so that they understand that we, the Muslims
> of the post of Korhogo, are very happy to hear that they are
> now allied with the French to fight the Germans.
>
> Moreover, we are very unhappy to see the Germans make
> war on the French.
>
> Whoever does not wish to see the French in our colony
> [Côte d'Ivoire] is also held in contempt by us Muslims, since
> our prosperity depends entirely on the arrival of these latter
> in our colonies.

It is moreover thanks to the French that we are spared the ravages and pillages of Samory, slavery, and wars between one village and another.

At present, we are free, we can live, work in peace, *and perform our prayers in tranquility* [emphasis added].

Since we have learned that all the Muslims of the Holy City have allied themselves with the French against the Germans, our concern has been to pray to God that the Allies annihilate Germany.

Let Germany be annihilated.

Let the Germans (poor, rich, princes, kings) surrender and submit themselves to the French.

We note that the French race is better than all the others.

When you give a chicken to a Frenchman, he pays you the price of a sheep; one day of work for him is paid by a month's salary (unlike other races).

Which explains why we consider His Excellency the governor as our father and mother. . . .

Needless to say, these words are not of our own invention, but follow qur'anic rules and the point of view of Islam.

Moreover, Muhammad (our master), during his existence in the Holy City, was very fond of the French race. This explains why we Muslims should continue to love the French as he did.

(Marty 1922: 486–87; my translation)

This document, originally written in Arabic, is nevertheless reproduced by Marty in its African author's French translation, replete with mistakes in French usage. Its inclusion as such in the book is intended quite obviously as a rather supercilious testimony to the loyalty of Korhogo's Muslim community to France. To modern readers, it seems either contemptibly and embarrassingly sycophantic or else crassly hypocritical, in either case a pure product of "collaboration" in the worst sense of the word. Such an interpretation, however, rests on a fundamental misunderstanding. The author of this missive was in fact acting precisely in the way Muslim clerics were (and are still) expected to act. The letter stresses the loyalty of Korhogo's Muslim community to the regime in place, and goes so far as to imply that this loyalty is a religious obligation. Its inclusion, in its entirety, in Marty's volume demonstrates that certain colonial administrators accepted such declarations at face value—an implicit, if unintentional, testimony to the efficacy of the policy. But the letter is hypocritical only if its rhetorical excesses are accepted too literally, although of course such a literal interpretation served Muslim interests all the better. Rather, such declarations served the more fundamental purpose of reassuring the French that the Dyula, as Muslims, were not opposed to the regime on *religious* grounds, precisely, as the letter indicates in no uncertain terms, because the French permitted Muslims to pray in all tranquility.[14] Such a stance did not prevent individuals, as long as they were not Muslim clerics, from opposing the regime on other, more purely "political" grounds, provided that the issue of "religion" remained above the fray. Indeed, a number of Dyula from Koko quarter in Korhogo were active militants in the early years of the independence movement. By diligently separating "religion" from "politics" and by expecting religious leaders to affirm loyalty to those in political power, the Dyula, as a Muslim minority, successfully avoided any political repression of the religious community. In effect, they affirmed that there could be no "Muslim opposition" as such. On the other hand, ordinary Dyula were free to join forces with the opposition as long as it was defined in explicitly "political" rather than "religious" terms. This, too, was to the advantage of the Dyula community, should the regime be overthrown. In other words, the continued toleration of the Dyula presence as a Muslim minority involved their continued loyalty, in principle, to "the" political regime, without requiring individuals to commit themselves firmly to any particular regime. This ambiguity was only possible as long as "religion" and "politics" remained conceptually separate domains.

Neither colonial rule nor the postcolonial regime have changed these fundamental attitudes about the relationship of religion and politics among the Dyula. However, colonial rule was to bring other changes, which deeply affected Dyula conceptions about who they were and about the relationship between "being Dyula" and "being Muslim." In the first place, the *pax colonia* irreversibly altered trade routes by

opening up the forest to Muslim traders who had previously
had to obtain the kola produced there from frontier markets.
Muslim traders and would-be traders rapidly emigrated to
the south of Côte d'Ivoire, and the Dyula from Korhogo were
no exception. Here, the Dyula found themselves lumped together as "immigrant strangers" along with Muslims from
other parts of Côte d'Ivoire and from neighboring countries,
and were more systematically exposed to different conceptions of Islam. At the same time, manufactured goods were
increasingly coming into competition with locally produced
items, to the detriment of most traditional craftsmen, including Dyula weavers.

Early in the colonial period, partly as a result of some of
these changes, groups and individuals in Korhogo began
converting to Islam. The most spectacular conversion, about
1920, was that of the Senufo chief of Korhogo, Gbon Coulibaly. If we are to judge by Gbon's political career, this conversion is unlikely to have stemmed from deep moral con-
victions; throughout his entire reign, Gbon managed to
convince those in power—Samory, the French, the RDA independence movement—of his loyalty, never switching allegiance too early or too late. Whatever his motives for conversion, it is clear that Gbon, much to his own convenience, was
able to model his observance of Islam on the practices of the
Dyula *tun tigi*. In other words, as French observers noted
(Marty 1922: 173), he prayed irregularly and inaccurately,
drank beer, and, most important of all, continued to participate in *poro* activity. Gbon's conversion was apparently wel-
comed by the Dyula scholars of Koko, his neighbors, with
whom he had always been on good terms, and who now
served, formally or informally, as his religious advisors. At
the time, the conversion may have seemed essentially a symbolic gesture, one that did little to change the status quo. Yet
it set a precedent that was to rock the foundations of the
Dyula conception of their place in the local social universe.

At the same time, Islam was attracting quite another sort
of convert in Korhogo. These were members of those hereditary craft groups who occupied a sort of liminal position in

local society, those who did not speak Sienar as a native language—that is to say, the Milaga blacksmiths and the Dieli
leatherworkers—and were consequently neither "Dyula"
nor "Senufo." As long as the crafts with which these groups
were associated remained a principal basis of their liveli-
hood, such a liminal status was, if anything, an advantage.
However, the colonial economy, by freeing the movement of
people and goods both within Côte d'Ivoire and across its
borders, opened up new economic opportunities by undermining many traditional monopolies. A new Muslim Mande
diaspora was forming communities in the south of Côte
d'Ivoire. The Milaga were, after all, native Manding speakers. As for the Dieli, since no one else could understand their
language, virtually all of them acquired a native fluency in either Manding or Sienar, and often in both, early in life. In order to assimilate themselves into these new diaspora communities, Dieli and Milaga needed only convert to Islam. Not
surprisingly, they began to do so, assimilating themselves to
their Dyula neighbors in the process. Unlike their Senufo
chief, such individuals did not have the luxury of announcing
their conversions with considerable fanfare while adopting a
tun tigi model of Islamic practice. Rather, in order to mark
their transition to Dyula status, they had to pray regularly,
abstain from alcohol and impure meats, and in general imitate their more orthodox mory neighbors. Indeed, such standards of piety—obligatory hallmarks of Muslim identity in
the new diaspora communities in the south—were gaining
ground among the tun tigi as well.

As mory standards of piety concerning prayer, fasting, alcoholic beverages, and the like continued to gain general currency within Korhogo's Muslim community, the continued
participation of tun tigi, Milaga, and Dieli in lo initiation societies was bound to become a matter of contention. Matters
came to a head in the mid 1940s. Significantly, pressure to
abolish these societies came, not from the scholars, but from
young prospective initiates. There were a variety of reasons,
not all of them religious, why these youths objected to the
initiation societies. Initiates were subjected to physical and

psychological hardships; they were obliged to pay various fees and fines and to work in the fields of initiation-society elders. One purpose of the initiation societies was to reinforce the physical, psychological, and economic subjection of youths to their elders. However, the economic changes that accompanied French rule tended to make such youths more and more economically independent of their elders, as new opportunities opened up to replace declining traditional crafts such as weaving. Young men objected to the initiation societies, not only on ideological grounds, but also because the time, effort, and expense involved distracted them from their new careers, seemingly for no purpose. It is perhaps symptomatic that the ringleader of the resistance to the initiation societies was a Milaga "blacksmith" rather than a Dyula, a young peddler-turned-tailor from Korhogo named Seydou Fofana. Here, in other words, was a young man following an entirely new craft occupation—sewing machines had only just been introduced into Korhogo; moreover, he belonged to a group who had just recently converted to Islam and adopted a new mode of religious behavior, involving regular prayer, fasting, and other such signs of "orthodox" Islam. Seydou and his peers had a vested interest, of course, in abolishing initiation: why should they bind themselves to their elders when the means of independence were increasingly available? It would be unnecessarily cynical, however, to attribute exclusively economic motives to the young rebels. Some—Milaga and Dieli—were recent converts to Islam; others, the *tun tigi,* were nevertheless adopting new rules of religious observance. In either case, it might easily seem that the initiation societies were incompatible with "orthodox" Islam; their *mory* neighbors provided an obvious example. Indeed, the sincerity of Seydou and his followers was quickly put to the test. When they refused to bow to the threats of their own elders, they were summoned before the (now Muslim) chief or Korhogo, Gbon Coulibaly, who took an equally dim view of such rebelliousness, especially as his own authority over his Senufo subjects still rested in large measure on his control over the initiation societies. The youths were severely beaten. When they continued to resist, their elders predicted that those who persisted would all be dead within a year. Such mystical death was commonly threatened as a punishment for those who flaunted the rules of the initiation societies. Under ordinary circumstances, the occasional recalcitrant individual might be poisoned or otherwise done away with in order to maintain the credibility of the threat, but the elimination of an entire cohort was out of the question. The abolition of forced labor in the French colonies in 1946 strengthened the hand of the rebellious youths. Until then, Gbon Coulibaly, as chief of Korhogo, had been able to send off young "troublemakers" or political opponents to the labor camps. One way or the other, the rebels held their ground, refusing to give in to threats or beatings, and demonstrating, by their very survival, their triumph over the mystical powers of the *lo* societies. This example sparked off a movement that led in a decade to the abolition of virtually all the Dyula initiation societies in the region. Henceforth, the religious practices of all Muslims were in principle uniform. The distinction between *mory* and *tun tigi* lost all salience whatsoever. Behavior that had been admissible, and indeed appropriate, for certain categories of Muslims in the past, was now considered distinctly "non-Muslim."

In short, to be Dyula, one had to be Muslim, and to be Muslim, one had to observe what were once only *mory* standards of piety. One could, however, be identified as "Dyula," not only in Korhogo, but also in the new and fast-growing communities in the south of Côte d'Ivoire, where many Dyula from Korhogo had emigrated during the first half of the twentieth century. In the south, all Manding-speaking Muslim immigrants were known as "Dyula," whether they were from Côte d'Ivoire or from neighboring countries such as Guinea, Mali, or Upper Volta. In short, the "Dyula" were a highly heterogeneous community of "outsiders" linked by a common language and a common religion. Originally, of course, the Dyula community of the Korhogo region had constituted itself in the same way, over the centuries incorporating Manding-speaking immigrants from a wide variety of origins. However, by the twentieth century, the Dyula of Korhogo defined themselves as an indigenous, rather than immigrant, community. The assimilation of such groups as the Milaga and the Dieli had, for a while, preserved the division of the socio-religious universe of Korhogo into two categories: Manding-speaking Muslim Dyula and Sienar-speaking "pagan" Senufo. Indeed, the Dyula community of Koko could continue to assimilate outsiders, at least in small numbers, who would attach themselves as "strangers" to one local *kabila* or another.[15] Even the presence of Senufo converts to Islam did not necessarily threaten the equation of religion and ethnicity, provided these converts followed the example of their chief, praying irregularly and continuing to participate in initiation societies. Under such circumstances, Senufo Muslims, behaving as the *tun tigi* used to do, constituted an intermediate category between Dyula Muslims and Senufo "pagans." Religious practice, rather than the profession of Islam as such, constituted a defining criterion of being "Dyula," whether in Korhogo or in the new immigrant communities of southern Côte d'Ivoire.

Until the end of World War II, the fact that Korhogo was the administrative center of northern Côte d'Ivoire seems to have made relatively little difference to most of its residents. All of a sudden, after the war, just as the *lo* societies were being abandoned, the town began to mushroom. The town attracted a growing number of immigrants, Dyula and Senufo alike, from the surrounding countryside, but also from further afield, from other regions and indeed other countries, whose borders, after all, were not far away to the north. Many of these immigrants were Manding-speaking Muslims like the Dyula, and in smaller numbers they would have been assimilated into Korhogo's Dyula community in Koko. But they came in droves and settled, not in Koko, but in new neighborhoods "across the stream." At the same time, the new Senufo immigrants to Korhogo began to convert to Islam, the first step toward a new career in trade, an occupation no longer monopolized by the Dyula of Koko. The neighborhood of Koko, the site of Korhogo's main mosque but also of its largest sacred initiation grove, retained as its nucleus the descendants of Korhogo's various precolonial inhabitants. The Koko Dyula retained their rights over the imamate of the main mosque, but they lost all their monopolies—over trade, over Islam—in Korhogo. No longer were they *the* Muslim minority; they were only one among several.

The consciousness that they were no longer the only yardstick by which Islam was to be measured in Korhogo accentuated the pressures for a uniform standard of Islamic conduct in Koko's Dyula community begun by the abolition of the *tun tigi*, Dieli, and Milaga initiation societies. If it remained true that "being Dyula" also meant "being Muslim," the converse was hardly the case any longer. As a result, the question "What does it mean to be a Muslim?" acquired new salience.

The answer to this question lay, in part, with the Muslim scholars in the community, the *karamogos*. They were the ones with specialized knowledge about what Muslims ought or ought not do. Now that such knowledge was of concern to the entire community, new means of transmitting such information were necessary. In particular, the role of the scholar was broadened from that of teacher to preacher. In the past, this knowledge had been communicated largely on an individual basis, from teacher to pupil or from a scholar to an individual seeking to elucidate a specific problem. Now, public sermons by Muslim scholars began to supplement these older means of transmission as a way of reaching the community as a whole.[16] Sermons were originally introduced as a part of funeral ritual, marking the fortieth day after death. Formerly, this had been the occasion for a particular dance known as *majo*. During the *majo* dancing, young men who were advanced students would deliver brief exhortations to the audience about the principles of proper Muslim behavior. This was now expanded into a full-scale "recitation" (*kalan*), generally consisting of a long, extemporized sermon in Manding. The *majo* dancing, once the climax of the funeral ceremonies, was abandoned, except at the funerals of important elders. Nowadays, even when the dances are held, they are much attenuated and take place separately from the sermons. More important, the sermons are no longer delivered by students but by established scholars, a sign that both the scholars and their audiences treat them more seriously.

Since their introduction, sermons have, in the space of only a few decades, come to replace dancing as the primary means of celebrating Islamic calendar holidays, as well as funerals. This is not, it should be stressed, necessarily a symptom of a wave of Islamic puritanism among the Dyula. Admittedly, the scholars, in a somewhat puritanical vein, disapprove of dancing altogether these days, though their exhortations, in this case, have fallen on deaf ears. More important, though, the sermons are festive occasions, and many people enjoy attending. Both sermons and dances are communal celebrations, and like all such celebrations, they transmit a variety of messages, depending on who organizes them, who attends, on which occasions they are held. In the past, dancing had been an appropriate means of affirming the Islamic identity of the Dyula community; as Muslims, they performed special Muslim dances on special Muslim holidays. Once the Dyula of Koko ceased to be the only, or even the principal, Muslim community of Korhogo, their dances, even if performed on Muslim holidays, were no longer unambiguously identified as Muslim dances; on the contrary, they were Dyula dances. Their performance was not the occasion for all local Muslims to celebrate together, but instead a means of distinguishing Dyula Muslims from other Muslims. Sermons, unlike dances, were a relatively unambiguous symbol of the collective Muslim identity of the Dyula. Such sermons were not peculiar to the Dyula of Korhogo. They were regularly held in the new immigrant Muslim communities of southern Côte d'Ivoire, and became part of a national (indeed an international) Muslim culture in the country. By adopting the sermons, the Dyula of Koko signaled that they were part of the national Muslim community of Côte d'Ivoire, and not simply the local Muslim minority of Korhogo.

If the sermons themselves proclaim the Muslim identity of the Dyula, their content serves to clarify the ramifications of this identity. The sermons stress, above all, the obligations of believers, in other words, what it means, in concrete terms, to be a Muslim.[17] By their form and content, the sermons stress the fact that the Dyula of Koko are part of the universal community of believers of Islam. However, ceremonies have the power to transmit different, and even contradictory, messages at different levels. While the sermon is in progress, the scholar and his message may well be the center of attention, but the organizers and the audience are just as much a part of the proceedings. The sermons are public, and in principle anyone is welcome to come, but they are also one part of an elaborate cycle of funeral rituals; it makes a difference who is or is not invited, who does or does not attend. Funerals, along with weddings—the other major life-crisis ritual among the Dyula—transmit all sorts of messages about social relationships. One such message has to do with the very identity of the Koko Dyula community itself. Each wedding, each funeral, reaffirms—or redefines—the separate identity of the community as such. At crucial moments of the wedding or funeral, representatives of each constituent section of the community must attend. In this manner, the "we" who are holding the ceremony can be extended to include, not only a group of kin and indeed an entire *kabila*, but ultimately the whole community. But, like all blanket principles, the injunction that each segment of the community must be represented is more ambiguous than it might seem. Who is the community? What constitutes a segment? Who, in other words, are "we"?

In 1972, when I first came to Koko, the answers seemed fairly straightforward. The Dyula community consisted of about twenty *kabilas*, grouped into larger units called *makafus*, linking one "host" *kabila* to a number of "strangers." For important ceremonies, each Dyula *kabila* in Koko was expected to send at least one representative. The Dieli and the Milaga were included as obligatory participants, and were thus symbolically incorporated into the Dyula community.[18] Although, by this time, many of Koko's Senufo residents were Muslim, they were for the most part absent from the proceedings, attending, if at all, in individual capacities, as friends, colleagues or affines of the deceased or his close kin. In other words, the ceremonies stressed the separateness of Koko's Dyula community from Koko's Senufo community, as well as from other communities, Manding-speakers or Sienar-speakers, Muslims or unbelievers, across the stream.

By 1985, both the rules and the practice had been modified. It was no longer obligatory for each *kabila* to send a representative; a delegate from each *makafu* was sufficient. More important, Muslim representatives from the various Senufo groups living in Koko (Tiembara, Fodonon, Fono, Kpeem, and Kule) were almost invariably present on such occasions. Their attendance, though it remained optional in principle, was considered absolutely normal. This change was initiated by the Dyula themselves, and not the Senufo: one does not attend such rituals without being invited. The Senufo presence concretizes a growing consciousness of the existence of a multi-ethnic Koko Muslim community as such. The phenomenally rapid growth of the town as a whole—it virtually doubled its size in ten years—has intensified the sense on the part of Koko's residents that they are an "old" community, divided and subdivided into ethnic and clan wards, as opposed to the amorphous settlements "across the stream." Outnumbered by the immigrants, Manding speakers and Sienar speakers alike, residents of Koko are united precisely by their "native" status. Paradoxically, most of Korhogo's residents now consider themselves Muslims. In town, at least, the Dyula of Koko are not a Muslim minority as such, but rather part of a Muslim majority. Their minorityhood is experienced in different terms; they are seen as autochthones as opposed to immigrants. Koko's mosque neatly symbolizes this dual affiliation. On Fridays and other major holidays, it serves the whole town; on ordinary days, it is the local mosque of Koko's residents. The site of the mosque and the fact that the office of imam is reserved for a member of specific *kabilas* of Koko are reminders that this was the first, and once the only, Muslim neighborhood of Korhogo, and that the residents of Koko, as the town's autochthonous Muslims, have certain symbolic prerogatives.

The Dyula of Koko are thus part of variously defined ethnic, neighborhood, and town Muslim communities, as well as, in a very real sense, of a national Muslim community within Côte d'Ivoire as a whole, not to mention the global community of Muslim believers. These communities are not mere analytical abstractions; the sense of community can always be given a symbolic expression, even though the symbols are often polyvalent and ambiguous. Yet this sense of community depends, in each instance, on a sense of its boundaries; in other words, one defines who one is in terms of who one is not. In the past, Islam had served unambiguously to distinguish the Dyula from their "pagan" neighbors as well as identifying them as part of the great West African Muslim trade network. Nowadays, the Dyula can define themselves only in terms of a series of distinctions—Dyula versus Senufo, autochthones versus immigrants, Muslims versus unbelievers—that crosscut one another. Indeed, religion no longer distinguishes the Dyula of Koko from most of their neighbors. Rather, it is because they are part of a national community of Muslims in Côte d'Ivoire that they are still part of a Muslim minority.

The emergence of a nationwide Muslim community has been a very recent phenomenon. During the colonial period, a more uniform Muslim culture had developed in the immigrant communities in the south of Côte d'Ivoire. There was no sense, however, that this culture was in any way national. On the contrary, it transcended national boundaries, involving Malian and Voltaic as well as Ivoirian Muslims. The creation of an Ivoirian Muslim community, conscious of itself as such, was a function of political rather than cultural change. Independence, and the creation of the postcolonial state, marked the turning point. Pluralism has, of necessity, marked the political style of Côte d'Ivoire, a country characterized by extreme ethnic, cultural, and linguistic diversity for its size. Approximately sixty different languages are spoken,[19] but no single group, however constituted, forms a majority. Consequently, the government must avoid appearing to favor any particular group too blatantly; ethnic and regional lobbies are continually clamoring for their fair share. Religions are in a similar situation: neither Catholics, nor Protestants, nor Muslims, nor "animists"—as they are designated in the official statistics—constitute a majority of the population. Religious communities can, like any other community, lobby for government resources. Only the "animists" are excluded from playing at this game and receive no government recognition. This is hardly owing to an anti-"animist" bias on the government's part, but rather to the fact that "animists" are a residual category, rather than a religious community per se. This leaves Muslims in competition with Catholics and Protestants for government resources. They may, for example, seek government funds for the erection of new mosques and churches. The new mosque in Koko is a product of such government largesse, intended as tangible evidence of the government's concern for the Muslims of Korhogo and of the nation at large. Of course, funds for such buildings are not available as a matter of course; religious communities, either at the national or local level, have to lobby for them. The government also allots television air time to different religious groups. Muslims, for example, have an hourly program called "Allahu Akbar" on Thursday evenings, just as the Catholics and Protestants have religious broadcasts on Sundays.

The government, in turn, needs to be wary of the ways in which it awards largesse to any religious community. For example, the construction of a mosque or church in any particular locality may be interpreted as an act of favoritism, not only of one religion over another, but equally of one town or region over others. Consequently, the government has favored the emergence of a national Muslim association, the AEEMCI (Association des élèves et étudiants musulmans de la Côte d'Ivoire, the association of Muslim students of Côte d'Ivoire). By recognizing and sponsoring such an association, by making it the unofficial—or perhaps quasi-official—

voice of the national Muslim community, the government can better channel the lobbying efforts of Muslims. Thus, the AEEMCI produces the weekly Islamic television program. It also holds national conferences for Muslim youths, such as the one held in Korhogo in 1985. Such conferences can only be held with government sponsorship and rely on the government for money, housing, and space. Again, considerable lobbying was necessary on the part of Korhogo's Muslims (including prominent members of the Koko Dyula community, but also, for example, the Lebanese Shiites of Korhogo) both to obtain such funds and to ensure that Korhogo would be chosen as that year's site.

For obvious reasons, government largesse to religious communities takes highly visible forms: television programs, public buildings (the bigger the better), national conferences. In this way, Muslims are made aware of what the government is doing for their religion. They are, by the same token, aware of what is being done for other religious communities. Seen in this light, Catholicism and Protestantism are direct competitors of Islam. A religious community's success in competing for these government resources depends, at least in part, on the size of its membership. Consequently, each religion has a vested political interest in recruitment. So-called "animists" represent a potential pool of converts. The Korhogo region, from this point of view, is particularly promising; though most townsmen claim to be Muslims, the majority of Senufo in the surrounding countryside are not affiliated to any of the three religious groups and remain unregenerate "animists" in the eyes of census takers. There are Catholic and Protestant missions both in town and in the countryside. These missions were established well before independence, and it would be ridiculous to suggest that their current activities are in any sense politically motivated. The Protestant mission of Korhogo is the most conspicuously engaged in a race for converts, but, for the missionaries, this is a race against the Devil for souls, and not a race against other religions for members. Since Vatican II, the Catholic missionaries have abandoned the image of a race in favor of a more ecumenical vision. Catholicism is impressive in terms of the elaborateness of its hierarchy and the strength of its organization. Korhogo, after all, is a diocese in its own right, with its own bishop.

Compared to Catholics and Protestants, the Muslims of Korhogo have no structured missionary organization whatsoever. There are no professional Muslim missionaries, and consequently every Muslim is a potential missionary. It is through the network of contacts between believers and "unbelievers" that new converts are brought into the fold. For this very reason, I suspect that ordinary Muslims are more sharply aware of the competitive aspect of the relationship between religions in Côte d'Ivoire than are ordinary Catholics, and perhaps even Protestants. In Christianity, the responsibility for recruiting converts falls on the clergy; in Islam, it falls on the congregation. It is the responsibility of the Muslim community as a whole to set an example "unbelievers" would choose to emulate. For many of Koko's Muslims, Catholicism and Protestantism now constitute yardsticks, a means by which they can consciously—indeed self-consciously—assess their own performance. Such comparisons are not necessarily fair-minded; for example, the ideal behavior of Muslims may be compared to a stereotyped and caricatural vision of Christian behavior. Even so, such comparisons reveal a fundamental shift in the way Koko's Muslim community conceives of its place in the world. Formerly, the world of Koko was divided into *silama* and *banmana*, into Muslims and "pagan" unbelievers. The "pagans," it should be mentioned, have not disappeared from Koko. The *poro* society grove in the old Tiembara quarter is still active. Yet the Muslims of Koko are increasingly likely to compare their behavior to that of Catholics or Protestants "across the stream" rather than of their "pagan" neighbors next door. This comparison, however biased, is not always reassuring. One evening, at the end of a funeral sermon, a prominent member of Koko's Dyula community, a man who had personally been very active in lobbying both for the construction of Korhogo's mosque and for the AEEMCI conference, began to harangue the audience. He complained about the beggars who clustered in front of the mosque during Friday services, aggressively clamoring for alms. The services at Catholic and Protestant churches on Sundays, he continued, were never the site of such sorry spectacles. "A be silamaya dogoya," he concluded: "This belittles Islam."

To conclude, the way in which the relationships between Muslims and non-Muslims has been conceived in Korhogo has changed radically in the twentieth century. Before the colonial period, Islam, like long-distance trade and weaving, was essentially an ethnic monopoly, part of a broader system of hereditary social categories. These hereditary categories accounted for differences in religious practice among Muslims, and not simply between Muslims and "unbelievers," and condoned behavior among certain categories of Muslims that, from a strictly legalistic stance, fell short of orthodoxy. Moreover, the system as a whole actually discouraged conversion to Islam. The relationship between Muslims and non-Muslims was essentially a complementary one, where each category had its theoretical place within the total system. During the colonial period, particularly after World War II, this system simply became obsolete. Changes in the economy had opened up new opportunities while rendering certain hereditary specializations increasingly unprofitable or open to outside competition. Islam simply ceased to be an ethnic monopoly, and the distinction between Muslims and non-Muslims had to be rephrased in an idiom other than ethnicity. The outcome was an increasingly legalistic conception of Islamic identity, with a specific focus on prayer. In a local context, Muslims were those who prayed, non-Muslims were (for the most part) those who continued to initiate themselves in sacred forests, to drink, and to sacrifice to "fetishes." The relationship was an asymmetrical one; "unbelievers" represented a pool of potential converts to Islam, but not vice versa. At the national level, however, non-Muslims were prototypically Catholics or Protestants, competing with Islam for resources and for converts.

By definition, Muslim minorities do not live in a vacuum. The existence of salient distinctions between Muslims and non-Muslims raises not only the question, Who is to be classed as a "Muslim"? but also, What is the prototype of "non-Muslims"? The way in which each category is defined—and they can only be defined with reference to each other—determines in the first place the nature of their relationship. In Korhogo, we have seen that this has ranged from complementarity to competition. But, at the same time, the relationship bears on the central question, What does it mean to be a Muslim? The very nature of Islam itself as a religion—at least as it is conceived and practiced by particular people in a specific context—depends as much on "non-Muslims" as it does on Muslims themselves.

4

Pedigrees and Paradigms

The Hijaz in particular and the Arabic-speaking Middle East in general have always constituted points of reference for Dyula Muslims. At the most basic level, Arabic is the obligatory language of prayer and the *hajj* an obligation for those who have the means to perform it. Not only the Qur'an but the vast majority of commentaries, legal texts of reference, and personal prayers are written in classical Arabic, an entirely foreign, quintessentially written language, totally unrelated to the Manding language spoken by the Dyula. The ability to read and to write Arabic was a necessary condition for accession to the status of *karamogo*, or "scholar." Travel for the purpose of study was a common means of acquiring knowledge of Arabic as a language, and of written texts.

Indeed, the Dyula have always valued travel positively. For individuals involved in commerce, travel was obviously an integral part of the process of making a living. As for religious learning, it was by no means remarkable for younger scholars to travel outside their home communities to pursue their education with more knowledgeable or prestigious teachers. Likewise, scholars from established centers of learning traveled to smaller or more distant communities where they might outshine potential rivals and establish a firm and profitable local reputation.

It is hazardous, however, to make an a priori assumption that travel and study in the Arabic-speaking Middle East was the most prestigious form of travel for study or for the dissemination of ideas. Just as Dyula traders were anxious to maintain controls, if not a monopoly, over access to trade goods, so Dyula scholars were concerned to maintain controls over access to knowledge, the equivalent of goods in the spiritual and intellectual realms. Knowledge, in this sense, is not simply that which one knows. More crucially, it is the authority with which one speaks or writes. Such authority depends in part on what one has studied and with whom. Claims to superior knowledge, on the grounds that one has studied directly in the Middle East, may constitute a challenge to the authority of local traditions of scholarship. In the last resort, the exercise of intellectual authority is just as much a question of legitimacy as the exercise of political authority. Like political authority, one can attempt to monopolize it, but the success of such attempts depends—even more than in politics—on the attitudes of one's constituency.

The authority of scholars ultimately derives from their expertise in religious matters. The scholar's role in Dyula communities thus hinges first of all on notions of what Islam is and what it means to call oneself a Muslim. Since the nineteenth century, these notions have changed in important ways, and even in the nineteenth century they were subject to debate. Controversies about the legitimacy of locally trained as opposed to foreign-trained scholars, both nowadays and in the past, are also controversies about different conceptions of Islam and of "being Muslim."

THE SUWARIAN TRADITION
AMONG THE DYULA

Until the mid twentieth century, the extent of a person's religious learning and the degree to which he was expected to demonstrate this learning in his own pious behavior corresponded ideally to the circumstances of his birth—as a *mory* or *tun tigi*, a member of a scholarly lineage or not. It was admittedly meritorious, though hardly obligatory, for individual *tun tigi*, particularly old men, to emulate *mory* standards of piety. Scholars were responsible for establishing these standards of piety, both because their command of Arabic gave them access to the written texts that furnished the necessary guidelines of behavior and because they were expected to set personal examples of piety for others to follow. There was a tendency for scholarship to be a hereditary occupation. Whole clan wards, or a section of a large clan ward, might specialize in scholarship in any given community. In this way, each village tended to have a few, usually quite small, specialized scholarly families. Nonetheless, any Muslim man might choose at any time to pursue his studies at an advanced level and accede eventually to the status of *karamogo*.

In any case, accession to the status of scholar involved the conferring of a second pedigree, intellectual rather than hereditary. This *isnad* was very much like a genealogy. The Dyula words for teacher and pupil are *karamogo fa* and *karamogo den*, literally "scholar father" and "scholar child." The authority of a scholar ultimately derives from his possession of such a pedigree, which places him in a line of teachers and pupils. If one examines any such *isnad*, one notices that the line of teachers extends literally all the way to God, the ultimate source of knowledge and moral authority. Beneath God, a number of angels are also listed as teachers and pupils, after which this knowledge is transmitted to humankind in the person of the Prophet. The name of Malik ibn Anas (A.D. 715–95) is also on every such list among the Dyula, as they all belong to the Maliki school of jurisprudence. More important, the Dyula *isnad*s all converge on the name of al-Hajj Salim Suware in the fifteenth century.[1] The line of transmission from Malik to al-Hajj Salim—a bridge of six to eight centuries—is clearly abbreviated, as it contains only six names, including two identifiable ninth century scholars: ʿAbd al-Rahman ibn al-Qasim of Cairo and ʿAbd al-Salam Sahnun of Qayrawan (Wilks 1968). The convergence of *isnad*s on the person of al-Hajj Salim is by no means a peculiarity of the Dyula of northern Côte d'Ivoire; his influence was so decisive in a belt that runs from Guinea (Hunter 1977, Sanneh 1979) to northern Ghana (Wilks 1968) that it is perfectly reasonable to identify a "Suwarian tradition" in West African Islamic scholarship.[2]

This widespread convergence of *isnad*s conveys a symbolic message about the nature of knowledge and the authority derived from its possession. God and the angels are the ultimate source of knowledge and moral authority. However, in terms of this-worldly geography, knowledge stems first and foremost from the Hijaz (from the Prophet to Imam Malik), then derivatively from Arabic-speaking northern Africa (Cairo, Qayrawan), and finally from the person of al-Hajj Salim, before diverging into various lines. In short, if the Arabic-speaking world is the ultimate earthly source of knowledge, access to this knowledge is mediated by a regional tradition of scholarship; it is not acquired directly at, or closer to, its source.

The Haidara scholars of Kadioha and Boron are a case in point. The Haidara are universally acknowledged in the region as sharifs, direct descendants of the Prophet. A putative Middle Eastern origin is not at all unusual among the Dyula. Various clans privately claim descent from one companion or another of the Prophet, admittedly without providing any genealogical evidence, or have oral traditions about the dealings of their "ancestor" with the Prophet, and how in one way or another they were loyal Muslims from the very beginning. Such claims symbolically anchor the clans in space (the Hijaz) and time (the Prophet's lifetime), but they are not socially relevant for regulating interclan relationships. Unlike such stories, the Haidara claim falls into the domain of common knowledge. Even so, the Haidara *isnads* also converge on al-Hajj Salim: although they can effectively claim a direct hereditary link to the Prophet, their intellectual pedigree, like that of everyone else, hails from West Africa and from al-Hajj Salim.

Al-Hajj Salim's scholarly activity was centered on the town of Jagha in the Western Sudan, but his influence was greatest along the southern fringes of the Manding trade network, and corresponds to the period of the disintegration of the old Malian empire. This was a region in which such Manding-speaking Muslims as the Dyula lived as a minority among various groups of "unbelievers." The tradition of scholarship founded by al-Hajj Salim stressed the religious coexistence of these two categories, Muslims and unbelievers, with, as we have seen, the attendant separation of religion and politics. It would be a serious misconception to label this tradition as "pacifist," however. Warfare, whether with Muslims or unbelievers, remained a distinct possibility. Rather, the Suwarian approach was neatly mirrored in the Dyula distinction between the hereditary categories of *tun tigi* and *mory*, those whose business was ideally warfare and politics and those whose business was ideally religious scholarship. Relations between the Dyula and their "pagan" neighbors might range from open hostility to active alliance, but in no case was religion a deciding issue. The Suwarian tradition not only fostered the development of relatively peaceful coexistence between Muslim minorities and their neighbors, but also sanctioned the existence of different hereditary categories within the Muslim community itself, making outward piety an obligation for some Muslims, especially scholars themselves, but only an ideal for others.

THE FIRST CHALLENGE: MILITANT JIHAD

In short, the Suwarian tradition incorporated a number of basic distinctions between politics and religion, hereditary and intellectual pedigrees, the Hijaz as the ultimate source of knowledge and moral authority and a local tradition of scholarship. Beginning in the late eighteenth century, comparable traditions of Islam and Islamic scholarship were subjected to challenges in much of West Africa in the form of militant jihad movements. Several of these movements attempted to draw their legitimacy from direct study in the Hijaz as opposed to local scholarly traditions. Usuman dan Fodio's teacher, Jibril ibn Umar, studied in the Hijaz (Hiskett 1973), as did al-Hajj Umar Tall (Robinson 1985). It would be far too simplistic to explain the jihad movements exclusively in terms of the diffusion of ideas from the Middle East to West Africa. The *hajj* itself, especially combined with study in the Hijaz or elsewhere in the Middle East, constituted a different principle of legitimacy, an alternative source of intellectual and moral authority. Under certain circumstances it could be explicitly opposed to the authority of local scholarly traditions.

The *hajj* has always been a powerful Islamic symbol among the Dyula. Until recently, the journey itself was exceedingly long, hazardous, and difficult. Indeed, I know of no individual at all from the Korhogo region who successfully completed the journey before the twentieth century. On the other hand, I was shown a manuscript list of various illustrious Manding scholars who had accomplished the *hajj*. Twelve scholars are cited in all, hailing from various communities in Mali and particularly in Guinea and western Côte d'Ivoire. Not surprisingly, al-Hajj Salim Suware headed the list. This list hearkens back to a sort of "golden age" of Islamic scholarship in the region, when scholars were in direct contact with the Hijaz and when the Suwarian tradition itself came into being. After this era, the *hajj* became an ideal rather than a reality. For example, the Cisse of Kadioha relate that their ancestor, Mammadu, left his native town of Bakongo in Guinea to undertake the *hajj*. Along the way, he stopped in the village of Kadioha, where he was finally persuaded to abandon his pilgrimage and to settle instead. Whether or not the story is true, the ancestor is remembered for his piety, not because he accomplished the *hajj*, but rather because of his intention to perform the journey. The *hajj*, situated in the distant past or in terms of intentions rather than accomplishment, constituted a symbolic link between the Dyula and the ultimate source of their faith, much as did the claims of various clans to descent from companions of the Prophet. But it did not necessarily represent an alternative source of moral authority.

This is not to say that the *hajj* was never used as a challenge to the authority of the Suwarian tradition. The career of al-Hajj Mahmud Karantaw among the Kantossi of the Volta Basin, to the east of Korhogo, provides a critical example.[3] The Kantossi, like the Dyula, were a Muslim minority of Mande origin living in the midst of "unbelievers." Mahmud studied with local teachers and was trained in the Suwarian tradition before undertaking the pilgrimage. During his journey, he stopped to study in Syria with a Qadiri teacher, Shaykh ʿAbd al-Rahim, who apparently persuaded him to undertake a jihad on his return. This jihad against neighboring "pagans" was launched in the mid nineteenth century. Al-Hajj Mahmud attracted some support, both among his fellow Kantossi and in the nearby town of Wa, a major center of Muslim learning in the region (Wilks 1988). With this army, he was able to conquer some of the surrounding area and to found the polity of Wahabu. However, Muslims in the area were strongly divided over support for the jihad, with the majority opposing Islamic militancy and favoring the maintenance of friendly relations with neighboring "pagans," whether on moral, political, or commercial grounds. Ultimately, the movement was a very limited success, and Wahabu was limited to a small cluster of villages.

Al-Hajj Mahmud's movement demonstrates, first of all, that peoples like the Dyula belonging to the Suwarian tradition were aware of and not always impervious to the jihad movements that swept through much of West Africa. Second, like a number of other jihad leaders, al-Hajj Mahmud sought legitimacy through a direct appeal to study in the Arabic-speaking world, effectively attempting to supersede the mediating role of local scholarly traditions. Finally, this attempt, though not entirely a failure, did not win the support of the vast majority of local Muslims, both scholars and ordinary believers, who continued to affirm their loyalty to the Suwarian tradition. In Korhogo, such loyalty was hardly surprising. Not only were Muslims outnumbered ten to one by their "pagan" neighbors, but they were also more heavily involved in local as opposed to long-distance trade, and they relied on their Senufo neighbors both as customers for their wares and as suppliers of food for purchase in the marketplace. A jihad would have been a dangerous gamble, calling into question their relations of cooperation with their neighbors, which the Suwarian tradition legitimated. However, the Dyula were well aware, not only of jihads, but also of the religious issues involved in either supporting or opposing them. The absence of such movements in the Korhogo region must be taken, not as a sign of inertia, of an unquestioning respect for the force of religious tradition, but rather as a deliberate confirmation of the principle that religious authority, though it might stem ultimately from the Hijaz, was to be mediated by established local lines of scholarship rather than by a direct appeal to contemporary teachings in the Arabic-speaking world.

THE SECOND CHALLENGE:
THE "WAHHABI" MOVEMENT

As we saw in chapter 3, the imposition of French colonial rule was to lay the groundwork for the redefinition of what it meant to be Muslim among the Dyula, and consequently new grounds for calling the Suwarian tradition into question. Formerly, trade, Muslim identity, and membership in the Koko Dyula community all coincided in Korhogo. Now, these three features became dissociated. A Muslim identity remained a precondition for entering the sector of local trade. However, the relationship between trade and Islam changed in a crucial, if not immediately obvious, manner. In the past, Muslims, defined in terms of their Dyula ethnic identity, had monopolized trade. Now, non-Muslims could enter the trade sector by converting to Islam. Indeed, new converts might adopt Islam individually without renouncing their membership in communities that also included unbelievers. Their newfound Muslim identity was most conveniently expressed through the adoption of outward forms of piety—praying, fasting, and so on—once typical of Dyula *mory* but not of *tun tigi*. Such forms of piety were recognizable signs of an Islamic identity anywhere, outside as well as within the region. In any case, with the abandonment of the *lo* societies, the *tun tigi/mory* distinction ceased to be socially salient.

The immediate consequence of this shift was to reinforce the leadership role of scholars in the Dyula community. Their personal behavior was expected to set a standard, not only for the *mory*, but for the entire community. They were re-

sponsible for explaining to the entire community the kinds
of behavior that were proper or improper, forbidden or enjoined. The guidelines they set had to be acceptable, not only
to Dyula Muslims, but to Muslims from other communities as
well. In the short run, this newfound "*shari'a*-mindedness,"
to use Marshall Hodgson's (1974) term, provided Dyula
scholars with more moral authority in the community than
ever before. In the longer run, however, it provided a basis
for challenging, rather than reinforcing, the legitimacy of
scholars trained in the Suwarian tradition. Islam among the
Dyula had formerly been predicated on the notion that different kinds of religious behavior were appropriate for different categories of persons: *tun tigi, mory,* and *karamogos*. By the
1950s, a single standard of piety was held to apply, not only
to all Dyula, but effectively to all Muslims. Once the principle
is established that all Muslims throughout the world ought to
conform to the same norms of piety, perceived discrepancies
appear as problematic. Indeed, if there is a universal standard of piety, the status of a local tradition of scholarship is
effectively altered. Islamic knowledge has universal applica-
tions, and there ceases to be any a priori reason why a local
pedigree, anchored in the Suwarian tradition, is necessarily
preferable to any other.

Discrepancies are only a problem if they are perceived as
such. However, the *pax colonia*, by favoring the freer movement of individuals from place to place, broadened the contact of Dyula with other Muslims (though the Dyula, as traders, were never isolated from such contacts) and increased
the likelihood that individuals might perceive discrepancies
of various kinds. In particular, it became easier to accomplish
the *hajj*, though as long as the pilgrimage remained an overland journey, it was still both long and hazardous. Few individuals from Korhogo actually undertook such a journey. It
involved leaving one's family for years on end and finding
odd jobs from place to place along the way to pay for each leg
of the trip. Those who made the trip are remembered as having accomplished something remarkable, but not for returning with new ideas, new conceptions of Islam, and being

Muslim. Still, the very fact that such journeys were actually made was itself significant. "Al-Hajj" ceased to be a title applied only to names on a list hearkening back to the remote past, but became a contemporary reality. The journey to the Middle East and to the Hijaz, to the ultimate source of religious knowledge and authority, was no longer an ideal, which for all intents and purposes was almost unrealizable, but a real possibility, even if beyond the means of most.

Although the overland *hajj* did not have a direct intellectual impact on Islam among the Dyula of Korhogo in the first half of the twentieth century, it did for other West African Muslim communities with whom they were in touch. Toward the end of World War II, when the Dyula of Korhogo were in the process of abandoning the *lo* societies, a number of Manding-speaking pilgrims returned from the *hajj* with a different set of ideas. Al-Hajj Tiekoro Kamagate returned to Bouake, the second largest town of Côte d'Ivoire, after a prolonged sojourn in the Hijaz and the Arabic-speaking world, and began to preach against various practices associated with the Suwarian tradition. Roughly at the same time, a small cadre of young *hajjis* from Guinea and the Gambia, notably al-Hajj Kabine Kaba and al-Hajj Muhammad Fode, returned from several years of study at al-Azhar in Cairo, where they had chosen to remain as students on their return from the Hijaz. During their stay, they were exposed to the reformist ideas of Muhammad 'Abduh and his disciples. On their return, most members of this group ultimately chose to settle in Bamako, a more central and cosmopolitan location than their home communities. These individuals in Bouake and Bamako were disparagingly labeled "Wahhabis" by the French colonial authorities, who took a dim view of their activities.[4]

In both towns, they directly challenged the authority of established scholars. First of all, they criticized the formalism of the Sunni legal schools and attacked the Sufi orders. Although Sufism is a relatively peripheral feature of Islam among the Dyula, most *karamogos* belong to the Qadiriyya or the Tijaniyya. The *hajjis* denounced all forms of saint worship as illegitimately positing the existence of intermediaries be-

tween God and the ordinary believer. Like Sufism, saint worship is not a central feature of the Suwarian tradition, but the
tombs of certain founders of scholarly lines are considered legitimate objects of veneration. Challenging this notion called
into question the legitimacy of such lines of scholarly authority, and by implication the intellectual pedigrees of Dyula
scholars. They attacked all forms of magic as illegitimate—
for example, the manufacture of written amulets, which constituted a part of the earnings of scholars. Last but not least,
they denounced aspects of life-crisis and calendrical rituals,
particularly the distribution of prestations, labeled *saraka*,
"charitable donations," by Suwarian scholars and their followers. These, the Wahhabis argued, did not constitute charity at all and so conferred no religious merit.

The Wahhabi critique went considerably further than the
challenge of nineteenth-century jihads. Adherents of jihads
had appealed directly to the sources of knowledge in the Hijaz and the Middle East, without necessary recourse to the
scholarly tradition of al-Hajj Salim Suware. The Wahhabis argued that such a direct appeal was not only possible but necessary, that the Suwarian tradition as a whole was corrupted
and characterized by *bidᶜa*, "innovation." It is not hard to understand why the French colonial authorities were openly
hostile to the movement. They had, after long years of suspicion (Triaud 1974, Harrison 1988), come to terms with and accepted the Suwarian tradition. The Suwarian distinction between "religion" and "politics" encouraged Muslim scholars
to come to a modus vivendi with the French, and even, as we
have seen, to proffer active support. Having reached the conclusion that established Muslim scholars were their allies, the
French were alarmed about direct attacks on their legitimacy.
Worst of all, the direct appeal to the Middle East as a source
of knowledge and authority laid open the gates for the spread
of pan-Islamic (and anti-French) nationalism, which, given
the climate of emerging African nationalism at the time, was
the last thing the French wanted to see. Indeed, some scholars have stressed the link between the Wahhabis and the
Rassemblement démocratique africain (RDA), the major

nationalist party in West Africa.[5] However, although most Wahhabis were sympathizers, if not militants, of the RDA, the two movements chose to distance themselves from each other. In Bamako, some of the wealthiest and most prominent Wahhabis chose to support the French (Amselle 1977); on the other hand, RDA support for the Wahhabis would have alienated Muslims loyal to the Suwarian tradition, many of whom also militated for the RDA. Despite French fears, the Wahhabiyya in West Africa was never a proto- or even a pronationalist movement in religious garb. The Wahhabi leadership, taking no official stance against the French, concentrated their attacks on local scholarly traditions.

This Wahhabi attack split Muslim communities throughout Côte d'Ivoire and Mali. There were anti-Wahhabi riots in Bamako in 1957, and scuffles in Sikasso, just across the border from Korhogo. In communities with a large Wahhabi presence, including Bouake in Côte d'Ivoire, control over the main mosque was a major issue, and the secession of the Wahhabis a frequent outcome. In general, the Wahhabis symbolically expressed their separation from the masses, who continued to follow the lead of Suwarian scholars. The Wahhabis made a point of praying with their arms crossed instead of outstretched in the Maliki fashion. They also embarked on a program of educational reform, establishing religious schools of their own. Such schools were partly modeled on Western forms of secular education, with separate classrooms and an emphasis on language instruction as opposed to rote memorization. These schools were intended as an alternative not only to traditional Qur'anic instruction but also to the rapidly expanding state-run secular school system, which Wahhabis—and also many anti-Wahhabi Muslims—accused of undermining Islamic values.

Korhogo avoided the violent clashes between Wahhabis and their opponents that plagued other West African communities. Nonetheless, the town was by no means isolated from the split between Wahhabis and Suwarian loyalists. The Wahhabis succeeded in making a few converts among the Dyula of Koko, notably among those living in Bouake, but also several who remained in Korhogo. In 1972–73, I repeat-

edly heard impassioned anti-Wahhabi arguments. Supporters of the Suwarian tradition of scholarship were on the defensive, eager to castigate their opponents as dangerous and
ignorant innovators. Naturally, local scholars were all militantly anti-Wahhabi, as their own credentials were at stake.
However, anti-Wahhabi sentiments were by no means limited
to scholars; in this matter, they had the firm backing of the
vast majority of Koko's Dyula community.

At stake was the relationship of Islam—of being Muslim—
to community identity. The Suwarian tradition had not only
tolerated but legitimated distinctions of status within the
Dyula Muslim community. In the past, *tun tigi* and *mory* had
been allowed two different standards of religious behavior.
Although this was no longer true, communal "Muslim" rituals gave expression, not only to ethnicity, to membership in
neighborhood or village communities, but also to clan ward
membership, elder or junior status, and even to slave or free
origins. The Wahhabis, on the other hand, denied the religious salience of such distinctions. For them, there were only
"pure" Muslims—themselves—and ignorant Muslims. For
this very reason, others perceived their behavior as a form of
exclusiveness. Implicitly or explicitly, the Wahhabis constituted a new kind of community, distinct from traditional
bases. The Dyula stereotype of typical Wahhabis was of
wealthy merchants, often relatively recent converts to Islam:
Senufo for example, but also groups of traditional "caste" status like the Kooroko (Amselle 1977) or even slaves. It seems
that the Wahhabis were particularly successful in recruiting
converts from among those groups and individuals who during the initial years of the *pax colonia* had moved into such
new towns as Bouake or Bamako, converted to Islam, and
wrested trade monopolies from groups such as the Dyula.
They represented, in effect, the nouveaux riches among
Manding-speaking Muslim traders, but the danger remained
that they might also woo away the loyalties of successful merchants from communities such as Koko, who might be
tempted to throw in their lot with wealthy colleagues of heterogeneous origins rather than to acknowledge their obligations to less prosperous kin and neighbors.

Within the Suwarian tradition, intellectual pedigrees and hereditary statuses, while they were kept distinct, were closely related nonetheless. Access to knowledge was mediated by one's place in a locally anchored line of scholarly transmission; one's identity as a Muslim was mediated by one's hereditary membership of a local Muslim community. The Wahhabis denied the legitimacy of both of these criteria. Knowledge and moral authority came directly from al-Azhar and the Hijaz; indeed, some Wahhabis have recently begun veiling their women, a practice unknown until now in the Korhogo region. True Muslims are to be known, not from their birth, but rather from their behavior, which sets them apart from the mass of ignorant believers.

In 1972–73, although the Wahhabis made few converts in Koko, they attracted a number of sympathizers and seemed to be gaining ground in the community. When I returned some twelve years later, I found to my surprise that the issue had ceased to become controversial. To be sure, individuals were willing, in response to my questions, to list the multifarious errors into which the Wahhabis had fallen, but no one bothered to raise the subject on his own. The Wahhabi presence in the town as a whole was actually more conspicuous than before, if only because one could not help noticing the presence of women (even in small numbers) wearing the veil. However, among the Dyula of Koko, Wahhabi influence was on the decline. The example of one prominent Wahhabi, a prosperous trader living in Bouake, may demonstrate why. By 1984, he had acceded to the headship of a section of a large clan ward, and was now a prominent elder. As such, he was responsible for organizing life-crisis rituals such as weddings and funerals, involving himself in the distribution of *saraka* prestations and inviting scholars to preach sermons— the very kinds of activities the Wahhabis vocally condemned. Though a Wahhabi, he was respected and well liked in Koko; the price he had to pay was public behavior that flagrantly contradicted his Wahhabi ideas. Ultimately, the exclusiveness and dogmatic rigidity of the Wahhabis precluded their winning many converts in Koko. One could not simultaneously behave like a Wahhabi and like a prominent elder. One could privately hold Wahhabi beliefs and publicly behave like everyone else, exposing oneself to mild ridicule. Hard-line Wahhabis, uncompromising in their behavior, were not tolerated in Koko. Such a stance would cut one off from one's kin, and no one I knew from Koko was prepared to go to such lengths. On the other hand, the kind of compromises necessary to remain simultaneously a Wahhabi and an active member of the Koko Dyula community tended in the long run to discourage further conversions.

THE THIRD CHALLENGE:
THE NEW LITERACY

Paradoxically, whereas the Wahhabis themselves continued to be rejected by the Koko Dyula community, many of the ideas central to their conception of Islamic reform have become increasingly attractive. More than anything else, the spread of Western-style secular education has been indirectly responsible. Western education came very late to Koko. Northern Côte d'Ivoire, far removed from the capital and particularly impervious to missionary influence, had always lagged considerably behind the rest of the country. Only after World War II did any children from Koko attend Western-style schools, and only because they were recruited by force. Such force quickly ceased to be necessary, as it became clear that Western-educated youths had access to relatively lucrative salaried employment, but the north continued for a long time to lag far behind Côte d'Ivoire as a whole. As late as 1963, a survey of the Korhogo region indicated that only 17 percent of school-age children were enrolled in primary school (SEDES 1965, 1: 60). As a result, the first generation of educated males in Koko are only now in their fifties. They are old enough to be considered elders, though not senior elders, but a few are quite wealthy, and others relatively well-to-do, giving them a far greater influence than their age would normally merit. Partly as a result of their example and their influence, the number of educated, among women as well as men, has increased steadily, though the employment prospects for the educated have proportionally diminished at an even faster rate.

The spread of Western education has altered Dyula perceptions of Arabic literacy. The Suwarian tradition of scholarship stressed rote learning. Texts, beginning with suras from the Qur'an, were memorized. The written word functioned partly as an aid to memory, as a means of assuring that texts were properly learned and as a corrective to faulty recall. Even among *karamogos*, knowing a text meant in the first place knowing it by heart, as well as understanding the meaning of particular words and passages. I was constantly impressed by the facility with which scholars could reproduce Arabic texts from memory, rather than relying on the books in their libraries.[6] It must not be forgotten that the Suwarian tradition developed at a time when copying was the only means of procuring a text, when paper was a scarce and valuable commodity, and when libraries were highly perishable. Nowadays, when printed books in Arabic are readily available in the marketplace, human memory is not the only means of storing knowledge. Western education furnished another model for acquiring literacy. Of course, Western education also involved considerable amounts of rote learning, but children were from the very beginning introduced to the alphabet, to the meanings of specific words, and to basic principles of grammar. French, moreover, was also a spoken language in Korhogo, and could be used to communicate, not only with French administrators, but with Africans from other parts of Côte d'Ivoire. In the Suwarian tradition, the first use to which reading was put was the recitation of texts; in secular education, reading allowed the literate both to speak French and to understand various kinds of written texts at their disposal.

One of the first actions of the Wahhabis in Bamako had been to establish Arabic schools modeled to some extent on the Western secular school system—not a surprising idea from individuals trained at al-Azhar and fluently literate in Arabic. The idea of a *madrasa*, a school that taught Arabic literacy like French, did not remain a Wahhabi monopoly. Such schools constituted an alternative to a purely secular education.[7] The idea spread late to Korhogo, precisely because of Korhogo's lag in the field of Western education, but in 1971 the first such school, the Ecole Franco-Arabe, was founded in town. The purpose of the school was to educate children, both in the standard primary school curriculum—French, mathematics, history, and so on—and in the Arabic language and Islam. Pupils were prepared for the primary school certificate as a means of entry to modern employment, but in a way that would reinforce religious values rather than conflict with them. However, such schools were not officially recognized by the government, and thus could not furnish an official transcript, required for admission to secondary school. Initially, this discouraged most parents from enrolling their children, but as employment prospects for secondary school leavers became more bleak, the benefits of such a combined system of education seemed more attractive. The Ecole Franco-Arabe has not only survived, but has spawned a host of imitators in Korhogo. In 1973, it was common to pass groups of boys sitting outside, reciting texts from writing boards under the watchful eye of an adolescent with a rod ever ready, poised over their heads, to strike pupils whose memories faltered. By 1984, two scholars from Koko had opened their own *madrasas*, complete with schoolrooms, blackboards, and French- as well as Arabic-language instructors, and the old system of Qur'anic education was virtually defunct in town.

The hope of such students and their parents is that they may pursue their education in the Arabic-speaking world. Various Arab countries offer scholarships to such students from time to time. The head of the Ecole Franco-Arabe keeps in constant touch with various embassies in the capital, hoping each year to extract promises for a few reserved slots. In 1985, for instance, he was offered three scholarships from Egypt, and graduates from that year's class were urged to travel to the capital in order to take a competitive examination to determine who would go. In past years, I was told, Saudi Arabia, Kuwait, various Gulf emirates, and even Syria offered scholarships. (Admittedly, the Syrian case was a fiasco; almost no parents were willing to send their children. This reluctance may have stemmed from the fact that Lebanese traders, who are either Christians or Shiʿi Muslims, used to be known as "Syrians." As a result, African parents may have felt that "Syria" was hardly the place to procure a worthy Sunni Muslim education.) The winners of such scholarships might even obtain a university education in the Arab world, either in religion or in some secular subject. One could never be sure in any particular year which countries, if any, might offer scholarships, but as long as some pupils were chosen from time to time, the hope remained.

I do not know what has happened to individuals from Korhogo who left for study in the Middle East, as this is such a recent development. However, other communities in Côte d'Ivoire, most notably Abidjan and Bouake, as well as in other African countries, began sending students rather earlier. Such students, if they do not return with marketable technical skills, are prime candidates to teach in the new *madrasas*. They have firsthand experience of classroom teaching in Arabic, and they have achieved a considerable degree of fluency in spoken as well as written Arabic. Those who study in Saudi Arabia have a particular advantage, as the Saudi government has apparently been interested in underwriting some of the costs of such *madrasas*. According to the director of the Ecole Franco-Arabe, two Saudi teachers were originally sent to a school in Bouake, but they suffered from severe culture shock and had to be recalled. Since then, the Saudi government has preferred to pay the salaries of African-born teachers, trained in Saudi Arabia, as a form of assistance. One such teacher, a young man from Sierra Leone, was on the staff of the Ecole Franco-Arabe in 1985.

Aside from classroom teaching, individuals trained in the Arab world may choose to become full-fledged Islamic scholars. One such young man passed through Koko in 1985 and delivered a sermon. Local Dyula, particularly those educated in French, were impressed. It was pointed out to me that he could pronounce Arabic in the way that Arabs do (the mass media have familiarized Dyula with "Arab" Arabic pronunciation), and not with the heavy accent of locally trained scholars. He read texts fluently out loud (rather than reciting them from memory) and could comment readily on the meaning of different words, glossing them in Dyula with greater ease, in the opinion of his audience, than local scholars could.

Locally trained and foreign-trained scholars thus possess two distinct styles of Arabic literacy. For Suwarian scholars, knowledge is first and foremost memorized knowledge of a relatively standardized corpus of texts; as one of them commented to me quite explicitly, "It's what's in my head, not in my library, that counts." Foreign-trained scholars have a conception of knowledge that more closely resembles Western notions. Knowledge consists in large measure of the ease with which information can be retrieved from written texts, as well as the fluency with which individuals can write and speak, as well as read and understand, Arabic. Literacy, in short, is a skill rather than mastery of a relatively fixed body of texts. For Western-educated Muslims, study in the Middle East is valued for the new style of Arabic literacy to which it gives direct access.

Fluency in Arabic, however, is not the only quality that attracts the Western-educated to this new generation of Arab-trained scholars. Among students in the secular school system, there is a revival of interest in Islam, associated with the emergence of the Muslim students' association of Côte d'Ivoire, (AEEMCI), which is officially recognized, and indeed partly funded, by the national government. The AEEMCI broadcasts a popular weekly program on state-run television, and organizes study sessions for students, as well as an annual national conference. Indeed, the conference was held in Korhogo in 1985, and was heavily attended by local residents, as well as by delegates from around the country. Significantly, the association has links with the Arabic-speaking world and with Africans trained there. For example, the director of the Ecole Franco-Arabe in Korhogo is active in the local chapter, and the guest speakers chosen for its television show are frequently young scholars trained in the Middle East. Like the Wahhabiyya, the association and its

Arab-trained scholars represent a "reformist" style of Islam. It preaches above all an Islamic morality—against drugs, alcohol, delinquency, prostitution, and premarital sex, stressing the importance of prayer, fasting, and the *hajj*. In itself, such moralizing does not conflict with the Suwarian tradition of scholarship; local scholars preach on much the same issues. The difference lies in what the AEEMCI and the Arab-trained scholars choose to ignore and in subtle ways to devalorize—those rituals, typical of local Islamic traditions, associated with life crises and Muslim calendar holidays.

This devalorization—one television show, for example, warned against overly ostentatious funerals—is consistent with the attitudes of a younger generation of Western-educated Dyula Muslims. Unlike the first generation of school graduates, they are not assured of lucrative employment. Many of them can hope for a reasonably cozy living, but hardly for senior appointments in the foreseeable future. They are neither old enough nor wealthy enough to have much voice in local community affairs, but many of them are (or can aspire to be) prosperous enough to attract demands from their kin, particularly on such occasions as funerals and weddings. Their attitude to such rituals can be summed up by a comment made privately to me by a young military technician during his grandmother's funeral: "Ça pue le fric" ("It stinks of cash"). These young educated Muslims feel attached in important ways to their home communities, but in other respects wish to distance themselves, and feel unconcerned by many local goings-on. The Suwarian tradition, stressing so heavily the importance and obligations (monetary and otherwise) of community membership, is associated in their minds with the heavy demands that the home community makes on them. The kind of Muslim identity advocated by the AEEMCI still permits them to express their solidarity with their home communities—Islam is, after all, a minority religion in Côte d'Ivoire—without making the same kind of demands on their resources.

Like the Wahhabiyya, the AEEMCI and the younger Arab-trained scholars thus constitute an ideological alternative to the local scholarly tradition. However, unlike the Wahhabis, the AEEMCI rigorously avoids confrontation. On the contrary, individuals active in the AEEMCI make every attempt to maintain cordial relations with locally trained scholars, inviting them, for example, to the graduation ceremonies at the Ecole Franco-Arabe. This policy is dictated in the first instance by the national government, which underwrites some of the association's expenses, and without whose cooperation a weekly television show would be unthinkable. Indeed, the government is quite willing to foster the association's cooperation with conservative Muslim countries such as Saudi Arabia and Egypt, and in this way counteract the possible appeal of the "radical" ideology of states such as Libya or Iran. However, the association's conciliatory stance toward local scholars is not simply dictated by the state. Unlike the Wahhabiyya, the association neither rejects Maliki "formalism" nor seeks to distinguish itself doctrinally from the Suwarian scholars. The differences are primarily those of style and emphasis. This allows the association to seek the support of local scholars for some of its goals, and gives scholars no legitimate grounds for denouncing its activities. Ordinary Muslims are thus not faced with choosing definitively between local scholars trained in the Suwarian tradition and Arab-trained scholars associated with the AEEMCI.

Individual preferences for one or the other group are not the subject of controversy and consequently do not split the Muslim community. Paradoxically, this peaceful coexistence of two scholarly styles is the greatest threat yet to the survival of the Suwarian tradition. More and more Muslims now own television sets; a novelty in Koko in 1973, they are now a common sight, even in relatively poor households, and villages in the north are beginning to receive electricity, which will permit villagers to own their own sets. The younger Arab-trained scholars' access to television is a considerable boost to their prestige. Their new style of literacy in Arabic is intuitively perceived as superior, not only by Muslims with Western secular education, but also by those educated in the *madrasas*. The fact that the Arab-trained scholars distance

themselves morally from the practice of ostentatious prestations during life-crisis rituals without denouncing such practices vocally attracts younger Muslims, particularly educated
Muslims living away from their home communities, who privately resent the demands on their resources that such practices entail but do not wish to make a public stand against
them that might alienate their older kinsmen.

In short, the spread of new forms of education, both in
French and in Arabic, have led to a certain disenchantment
with the Suwarian tradition and its scholars. An *isnad* tracing
one's intellectual pedigree directly back to al-Hajj Salim Suware is no longer a sine qua non for being acknowledged a
Muslim scholar; training in the Middle East now constitutes
a universally accepted alternative. This is not to say that
the Suwarian tradition is defunct. *Karamogos* are still being
trained in the Suwarian tradition, though these are usually
older men, villagers, or scions of locally established scholarly
families. However, as more and more generations of educated Dyula Muslims accede to edlerhood, it seems likely that
the Suwarian tradition, once the only legitimate scholarly tradition in the region, will become more marginal.

CONCLUSIONS

The Hijaz, and, more generally, the Arabic-speaking world
have always constituted a source of origins for the Dyula, origins conceived both in terms of heredity (when different
clans trace their origins to the Hijaz during the Prophet's lifetime) and in terms of the transmission of knowledge and
moral authority (as expressed in *isnads*). Until the twentieth
century, these origins were largely situated far away in space
and time. Appeal to these origins was mediated by the presence of local scholarly lines of transmission of knowledge.
This principle of mediation, and the legitimacy it conferred
on local scholars, was always subject to possible challenge, to
the notion that it was possible to acquire knowledge directly
from its geographical source and thus to short-circuit the Suwarian pedigrees. Such challenges have occurred in three

sets of circumstances: in the mid nineteenth century, with the rise of militant jihad movements; after World War II, with the emergence of the Wahhabi movement; and in the past decade, in the form of an Islamic revival among educated Muslim youth. These instances were not accidental. Individuals did not simply happen to study in the Middle East and then attempt to bring back new ideas to their home communities. The trip itself was until relatively recently a formidable one, and even now is by no means easy. Study in the Middle East represented a quest for an alternative and superior source of knowledge, and consequently an implicit, if not explicit, calling into question of the local scholarly tradition.

These challenges all revolve around the issue of legitimacy, of the respective moral authority of a direct as opposed to a mediated appeal to the original sources of knowledge. The question of whether direct study in the Middle East does or does not supersede the authority of local lines of transmission is ultimately decided in the home community, by individuals who for the most part are not themselves scholars. The fact that such issues have repeatedly split local communities, often violently, suggests that a great deal more is at stake than the reputations of individual scholars trained in one tradition or another. For this very reason, such challenges are not made lightly, and the circumstances in which they occur are highly significant. In each case, the underlying issue was the nature of the Muslim community itself. The jihads called into question the status of Muslim communities as minorities living in the midst of unbelievers. The Suwarian tradition held that different hereditary categories of persons might legitimately observe different religious practices. While it might be meritorious for anyone to emulate "*shariʿa*-minded" standards of behavior, only certain hereditary categories of individuals were under an obligation to do so. Unbelievers, provided they were not apostates and did not interfere with the religious practices of Muslims, were not necessarily to be fought, much less converted. In this way, Suwarian scholars legitimated patterns of relations between Muslim minorities and their "pagan" neighbors; proponents of jihad, on the other hand, dictated that such relationships be jeopardized. Such movements advocated the creation of a new political and economic as well as religious order. In communities such as Koko, where most individuals stood to benefit from the status quo, such ideas were not received with a great deal of enthusiasm.

By the end of World War II, the nature of the Muslim community in Korhogo had changed substantially. For reasons largely outside the control of the Koko Dyula community, "Muslims" had ceased to be a hereditary category. Korhogo was full of new converts, both from within and outside the region. However, the Koko Dyula community continued to exist as such, and membership in it or in its constituent parts was continually expressed through rituals presided over by local scholars, who thereby implicitly asserted its legitimate existence in Muslim terms. Wahhabi leaders, invoking both their experience of the *hajj* and their training at al-Azhar, denied the legitimacy, not only of the Suwarian tradition, but more crucially of traditionally constituted communities within the larger community of Islam. They denied the salience of ethnic, local, slave, or caste origins in favor of the distinction between a truly Islamic community and the mass of believers who remained in ignorance and mingled, in their eyes, Islamic and extra-Islamic practices. Dyula were effectively asked to choose between loyalty to their home community or to the new community of Wahhabi believers. Confronted with such a radical choice, the vast majority were unwilling to renounce their membership in their local communities, and Wahhabi influence was limited.

The growth of Western secular education was again to alter the nature of the community and to provide the basis for yet another challenge to the authority of traditional religious leadership. A new social category is in the process of emerging, consisting of young educated men (and increasingly women), often living outside their home communities, who are relatively well-to-do but hardly wealthy. These individuals are subjected to demands from their kin, often in the context of life-crisis rituals that express both community membership and the status of individuals within it. These demands are often resented, but such persons are not financially or socially well enough off to wish to sever themselves from their relations. Their situation differs from that of the Wahhabis in one crucial respect. Wahhabis are mainly merchants, involved in a sector largely dominated by Muslims, and so they can reasonably aspire to the constitution of a new, largely mercantile, Muslim community. The Western-educated, on the other hand, find themselves in a category dominated by non-Muslims from other parts of Côte d'Ivoire, and so cannot express their social identity, their class position if one prefers, in religious terms. They can, however, look to younger Arab-trained scholars, individuals of their own age-category, for religious leadership.

These scholars and their followers are careful not to contest the authority of older local scholars or of the community rituals over which they preside, but they emphasize those aspects of Islam that stress the universal nature of the community of believers as opposed to those that implicitly validate traditional social categories. In this way, recourse to the Middle East as a direct source of knowledge and moral authority does not constitute a radical challenge to the Suwarian tradition of mediated knowledge, but rather poses itself as an alternative. However, for these very reasons, Suwarian scholars are left with no grounds for objection; nor can members of their home communities accuse their younger educated kinsmen of wishing unequivocally to renege on their obligations.

Underlying these three sets of challenges to the Suwarian tradition of scholarship is a single issue: does Islam recognize, and by implication legitimate, hereditary social distinctions of any kind? The Suwarian tradition has always acknowledged the salience of hereditary categories, initially in the form of differences in religious practice, more recently in the modified recognition that it accords to community rituals. Within this tradition, *isnads*, while they are never assimilated to genealogies, perform an analogous function: scholars are attached to a local line of transmission of knowledge in the same way that ordinary believers are attached to local ethnic, political, and kin units. The appeal to direct, unmediated contact with the Hijaz or, more generally, with the Arabic-speaking world provides a model for a different kind of Muslim community that in principle ignores all hereditary distinctions and focuses exclusively on religious practice as the criterion for inclusion in the Muslim community. Study in the Middle East frees the aspirant scholar from dependence on the local religious elite in the same way that newly constituted Muslim communities liberate their adherents from dependence on hereditary chiefs and clan elders. As long as the Dyula in the Korhogo region constituted the sole Muslim community, enjoying various economic, political, and social monopolies, the Suwarian stress on the principle of heredity was attractive to the vast majority. With the erosion of these monopolies, as avenues to social, economic, and political success lay increasingly outside the community's control, this stress on hereditary principles appealed less and less to those individuals who were relatively successful, but whose age or social origins relegated them to a subordinate position in traditional terms. Those who found new sources of wealth, power, or prestige were also attracted to sources of knowledge and moral authority that, in a sense, were also new (in that they lay outside the local community). Yet, as they were geographically located at the wellsprings of religious knowledge, these new sources of authority simultaneously enjoyed the aura of venerability, of a return to tradition rather than a departure from it.

In short, the spread of influence from the Middle East to West African Muslims like the Dyula has not simply been a question of diffusion, of a radiating outward from a "center," but rather has been part of a quest by groups and individuals for a set of religious principles that might call into question the salience of locally anchored hereditary social distinctions and ultimately reevaluate the relationship between the local Muslim community and the global community of Muslims.

Such quests have led individuals to seek knowledge outside their home communities, specifically in the Arabic-speaking world; equally important, others in their communities have, for the same reasons, looked to these foreign-trained scholars for leadership.

5

The Ritual Arena

In 1972, when I first came to Korhogo, the controversy between the Wahhabis and their opponents was raging. The issue most hotly discussed was, ought one pray with arms crossed or with arms outstretched? My initial reaction, I must confess, was one of puzzlement. Why should this particular detail matter so very much? Obviously, the manner of praying is a symbol of other differences; however, as academics, we must be especially wary of the temptation to conclude that it is only a symbol of deeper differences. Controversies, after all, are familiar enough to academics, as long as they are controversies about ideas. Had Wahhabis and anti-Wahhabis contended about doctrine, I doubt that I would have found their arguments very perplexing. Of course, there really are differences between the ideas of the Wahhabis and the ideas of their opponents, differences that parties to either side of the debate are quite capable of articulating. One might conclude that each manner of praying symbolizes a set of ideas about Islam and about the world. The problem with such a conclusion is that the ideas were discussed much more dispassionately than the issue of prayer; the symbols aroused deeper emotions than the entities they seemed to symbolize.

Symbols pose a special problem for "intellectualists" like Robin Horton (1971, 1975a, 1975b), who rather self-consciously avoids confronting the problem of symbols and of the rituals in which such symbols are regularly embodied. There are, it must be said, sound reasons for such reticence; the exegesis of ritual symbols—a fortiori those of another culture—is a perilous exercise at best. Provided that, in one way or another, the symbols "express" the cosmology, they do not present an entirely intractable puzzle. But what if the symbols have no relation to cosmological ideas? In what way, for example, does praying one way rather than another explain, predict, or control anything at all?

In fact, religious controversies among the Dyula, at least in the past fifty years or so, have been in one way or another about ritual, much more explicitly than about cosmology. The *lo* societies were abolished on the grounds that it was improper for Muslims to offer blood sacrifices to local spirits and to participate in initiation rituals. Few, if any, questioned the existence, the nature, perhaps even the power of the spirits. "Fetishism," for modern-day Dyula, consists, not in believing in spirits, but rather in worshiping them. Religious debate is concerned, not with what Muslims should believe, but with how Muslims should behave. The issues are essentially moral, not cosmological.

Like morality, and unlike cosmology, ritual is concerned with the actions of individuals, with what people should or should not, must or must not do under specific circumstances. Moreover, ritual obligations are in and of themselves moral obligations, whereas it is quite unclear exactly what one is morally obliged to believe as a Muslim, aside from the fact that there is no God but God and that Muhammad is his messenger. Debates about ritual are thus both literally and metaphorically debates about morality; deliberately praying the "wrong" way is immoral, both in and of itself, and because of what such "wrong" prayer expresses. It is precisely for this reason that ritual issues are the ones that incite most passion. The ideas of one's opponents are simply ignorant or silly; their behavior, on the other hand, is objectionable, if not frankly evil.

Of course, there is nothing new about the idea that ritual "expresses" moral notions; since Durkheim and Robertson Smith, such a statement has been a commonplace in anthropology. The problem with the Durkheimian formulation and with most of its successors is that it sees ritual as the expression of the relationship between "society" and the individual; ritual symbols are simply the "collective representations" of this relationship, taken as given. "Society" is taken for granted, as if it were always clear to which society any given individual or group belongs. Conflict, in the religious domain, thus appears to be anomalous, a symptom, for Durkheim, of "anomie." However, there is nothing at all anomalous about conflict and disagreement, at least in the history of Islam—or, for that matter, Christianity. It would be extremely rash to dismiss differences of opinion about ritual among the Dyula as evidence of "anomie."

The question remains, how do such differences of opinion express different moralities? What, in other words, is at stake besides ritual itself? The answer, I would suggest, is that rituals express, among other things, the existence and nature of moral communities.[1] Moral communities, however, are by no means identical with "society." "Society," as such, is an abstraction of sociologists and anthropologists; no one is conscious of belonging to a "society" per se, but individuals are quite aware of their allegiance to specific, named moral communities. As we shall see, there are different kinds of moral communities, and individuals and groups may simultaneously belong to moral communities of different orders.

It is important to bear in mind that differences of opinion among the Dyula are not about ritual per se, but about the relationship of ritual to Islam. People are specifically concerned with the question of what *Muslim* ritual is. In other words, what kinds of ritual are associated with, appropriate to, or required of Muslims, and what kinds of rituals are not? The question is, of course, highly ambiguous. For example, is a ritual "Muslim" if only Muslims perform it, even if it is not required on religious grounds? Such questions, however ambiguous, remain fundamental precisely because Islam provides legitimacy to the existence of the community whose very nature is expressed by ritual; it is Islam, in other words, that makes a community a *moral* community.

Broadly speaking, Muslims belong to two contrasting kinds of moral community: on one hand, global and universalistic; on the other hand, local and particularistic. In the first instance, there is the *umma*, the global community of

Muslims, a community that transcends regional, national, political, ethnic, and linguistic boundaries. Within this community, all believers are in fundamental ways morally equivalent. In principle, a single standard of conduct applies to all individuals, a single set of rules by which believers may find favor with God, or else call down His ire. Admittedly, this moral uniformity is not absolute, and Islam gives explicit recognition to certain distinctions, notably between males and females and between adults and children. Even these differences are relativized in the moral domain; ideally, the piety of women is not supposed to differ radically from the piety of men.

There is only one *umma*, one global community of Muslims, but, of course, there are many Muslim communities. The morality of the *umma* is of necessity impersonal; only an abstract code of conduct can govern relationships between Muslims throughout the entire world. The local community, on the contrary, is a highly personal realm, governed by regular face-to-face interaction. Within such communities, the differences between members, rather than their equality before God, are of paramount importance. Those distinctions that, if recognized, are at least relativized at the global level— between male and female, adult and child, slave and free[2]— are of primary importance within the local community. To these, each local community may add a host of distinctions that the global community of Islam in principle ignores entirely: ethnicity, kin-group affiliation, types of occupations, generation, order of birth, and the like. In a fundamental sense, the global community postulates the essential equality of all humans, the local community their essential difference.

Ritual provides a ready-made medium for the expression of such principles of moral equivalence or difference. The moral axioms of ritual action are, as it were, childishly simple: equivalent categories of persons perform identical actions; distinct categories of persons perform different actions. In ritual, even more than in everyday life, there is a fundamental interrelationship between the theatrical and the sociological notion of "role." It follows that the two kinds of moral communities, global and local, are associated with two different kinds of ritual. In ritual that expresses the importance of the *umma* as a moral community, all participants should act identically; on the other hand, ritual associated with local communities as moral communities will involve different categories of persons in explicitly different capacities. These two kinds of ritual can justifiably be contrasted as "universalistic" as opposed to "particularistic."

It is tempting to conceptualize particularism and universalism as opposing poles of a single continuum. The implications of such a continuum would be that a community's emphasis on universalistic ritual is in inverse proportion to its emphasis on particularistic ritual. Such a conceptualization is ultimately teleological: as societies evolve from small-scale microcosms to large-scale macrocosms, religions evolve from polytheistic particularism to monotheistic universalism. In the long run, the nature and direction of change should be predictable. The crucial assumption on which such a unidimensional model is built is that microcosm and macrocosm, particularism and universalism, are *polar* opposites. There is, of course, another possibility, which is that they might constitute separate dimensions. It is not necessarily a contradiction to assert that all Muslims are alike, and that they are different. It is precisely as Muslims that they are alike, and in terms of other social identities that they may be different.

It is through ritual that groups and individuals express the kinds of social identities they hold to be salient and morally acceptable, if not enjoined. In a fundamental way, attitudes toward ritual have as much to do with religious sensibilities as with doctrine; rituals may seem meaningless or empty as well as morally objectionable. Over the years, religious sensibilities in Koko have clearly changed, though not always in obvious and easily predictable ways; moreover, it is certainly not now, if it has ever been, the case that such sensibilities are uniform. The differences are differences of emphasis, of universalism as opposed to particularism—of what kind of universalism, what kind of particularism, and of their inter-relationship.

ISLAMIC PARTICULARISM

Until the middle of the twentieth century, particularistic rit-ual of one kind or another pervaded religious practice among Dyula Muslims. It served, in other words, to express and ul-timately to legitimate social distinctions between categories of groups and persons within the local community. This is not to say that universalistic ritual was absent, or even unim-portant. Islam is, of course, a universalistic religion. The local Muslim community must, of necessity, be part of the *umma*, of the global community of Muslims. If not, what sense does it make to call oneself Muslim? Of course, if being Muslim is to have more than a purely local meaning, it must have some tangible, universally recognizable, signs; these are, quite ob-viously, prayer, fasting, abstention from alcohol and ritually unclean meats—in short, the various ritual prescriptions of the *sunna*. All Muslims—whether or not they perform these actions punctiliously—recognize them as quintessentially "Muslim." All of these signs, all of these ways of behaving, were familiar to the Dyula in and around Korhogo. As mem-bers of a Muslim trading diaspora, they were, in any case, in-volved in a supra-local economic as well as religious system. Yet even those very actions that, in a supra-local context, ex-pressed a "universalistic" content served, in a purely local context, to distinguish between social categories of Muslims, and not only to differentiate Muslims from unbelievers. As we have seen, only the *mory*, the "scholars," were bound to observe this ritual code scrupulously. The *tun tigi*, the "war-riors," might observe the code only sporadically.

The *lo* societies into which all male *tun tigi* were initiated were even more expressly particularistic. The term *lo* re-ferred, not only to the initiation society as a whole, but to specific named spirits, as well as to the particular masks rep-resenting them. Each spirit, each mask, was ultimately the property of a specific clan ward, rather than of the initiation society as a whole. As a result, each local society (and there might be more than one in a large village or quarter) took the form of a fortuitous constellation of the spirits and masks owned by its constituents units. The particularism that characterized the *lo* societies, as well as the *poro* societies of their Senufo neighbors, was expressed in the idiom of ownership. This idiom operated at a plurality of levels. Within a single *lo* society, a mask was the property of a single ward. Within the village as a whole, it was the property of one particular *lo* society; within the region, it was the property of a specific village. Ultimately, masks were ethnic properties, Dyula masks as opposed to Dieli or Senufo masks.[3] Some masks were unique; others were commonly found in many Dyula communities. Some masks were harmless, and acted the buffoon in public to amuse the crowds; others, the sight of which might even be forbidden to all non-initiates, had the power to kill. Not surprisingly, the most powerful masks tended to be the unique ones, as rights over their exclusive ownership were more jealously guarded. Ownership of such powerful masks was a matter of considerable local pride, a pride the *mory* could share with their *tun tigi* neighbors even though they did not participate directly in the initiation ritual.

The ritual practices of the *mory* and of the *tun tigi* were, in a sense, complementary. The ritual observances of the *mory* provided a link between the local Dyula community and the Islamic world in general; the initiation societies of the *tun tigi* furnished visible signs, in the form of masks, of the differences between one community and another, indeed between one clan ward and another. Each segment of society, *mory* and *tun tigi*, participated to some extent in the symbolism of the other. After all, *tun tigi* were Muslims, who could and sometimes did pray; *mory*, as members of specific villages or quarters, also, if only indirectly, "owned" masks. Even so, the local community, as a Muslim community, was characterized by two very distinct patterns of ritual. Adherence to the *sunna*, while it might be a *global* sign of Muslim identity, was associated locally with a specifically *mory* identity. Only some third category of ritual could adequately signify a Muslim identity in a local context, a category of ritual in which *mory* and *tun tigi* participated on an equal footing. This category consisted, in the first place, in the celebration of Muslim calendar holidays: *sun kalo*, "the month of fasting"—that is, Ramadan; *tabaski*, the annual slaughter of sheep during the season of pilgrimage to Mecca; *donba*, commemorating the birth of the Prophet. Along with this celebration of the Muslim year was the celebration of a Muslim life, the rituals of birth (*den sereli*), marriage (*furu*), and death (*su ko*). In the broadest sense, a Muslim was one who celebrated the annual Muslim holidays and who was named, married, and buried in a Muslim fashion. Participation in these rituals distinguished *silama* from *banmana*, Muslim from unbeliever, far more effectively than adherence to the *sunna*.

These celebrations of the communal Muslim identity of the Dyula were, by and large, festive occasions,[4] characterized by drumming and dancing of all sorts. *Lo* society masks were by no means excluded from these Muslim holidays, but would emerge in particular to celebrate the end of Ramadan.[5] Characteristically, the name the Dyula use for the Prophet's birthday, *donba*, literally means "the big dance." These occasions were marked by decidedly particularistic manifestations, emphasizing social distinctions within the Muslim community at the same time as they celebrated its overall Muslim identity.

The *donba* celebrations in the village of Kadioha, which I witnessed in 1985, are a good example of "particularistic" Muslim ritual. Unlike *donba* celebrations in neighboring Dyula communities, those of Kadioha have a particularly militaristic flavor. Kadioha was the seat of one of the few Dyula-ruled chiefdoms in the Korhogo region,[6] a fact its peculiar *donba* celebration seems to flaunt. However, the atypicality of Kadioha's celebrations is, in a larger sense, quite typical. Each village—in some cases, each clan ward—takes pride in its own particular way of celebrating calendar holidays, marriages, and so forth. The differences are in some cases minute, but they are symbolic markers of an *esprit de minaret*,

a means of asserting the village's or ward's distinct identity—
its distinctiveness, as it were. To return to *donba* in Kadioha,
the festivities begin after midday prayer, when bands of adolescent boys, grouped clan ward by clan ward, roam dancing throughout the village, girdled with a cloth, their faces
daubed white, sporting bows and arrows (mostly the rubber-
tipped variety in 1985), with which they gesture menacingly.
This was the only instance in which I witnessed mock warfare in Dyula ritual of any sort or in any place; even in Kadioha, it is strikingly unusual, restricted to this one day each
year. At the same time, adolescent girls, again grouped ward
by ward, also dance throughout the village, separately from
the boys. After the evening prayer, the military glory of the
chiefdom is once again celebrated. One by one, young men
representing each ward dance, brandishing a spear, before an
assembly of elders. Each, in turn, commemorates the military
exploits of his ancestors. After every ward has had its turn,
there is a procession to the hilltop that overlooks the village,
which houses jinns. These particular jinns, it should be
noted, are Muslims, and they are credited with repulsing a
"pagan" Senufo attack on the village; so it is not, after all, inappropriate to honor them as part of the festivities of a Muslim holiday. After the procession returns, elder men and Koranic students adjourn to different places in the village to
chant liturgical texts in Arabic. They gather, in fact, at the ceremonial meeting places of the various *makafus;* in other
words, one's kin-group membership determines where one
will adjourn. The chanting, which continues until daybreak,
if not even later, partakes of the festive tone of the entire occasion. Groups of Koranic students and younger men may jo-
vially compete with one another to see who can chant the
loudest or most melodically. The chanting is punctuated by
the periodic distribution of refreshments, as lavish as possible, such as grilled meats or sweet drinks. Like the chanting, there is a competitive edge to the catering, with prosperous families and individuals vying to provide the most expensive and elaborate food in sufficient quantity so that
everyone may be served.

Clearly, these festivities serve to mark the existence and importance of a variety of social identities and distinctions situated at different levels: Muslims—the village as a whole, but also its nearby jinns, its protective spirits—in contrast to their "pagan" Senufo neighbors; the village, as opposed to other nearby Dyula villages, in terms of its glorious (or at least glorified) military past, as the seat of a chiefdom; the various clan wards of the village, who dance separately, and who compete with one another in providing the most lavish refreshments during the sessions of chanting. Within the village as well as within each ward, gender and generational differences are also given ritual expression. Adolescent males and females dance in separate groups. Juniors dance, elders are danced to. Younger men are, at least symbolically, warriors, while elders preside over, if they do not participate in, liturgical chanting. (In this, as in other contexts, young men relatively advanced in Qur'anic studies are partly assimilated to elders; they, too, have special knowledge that gives them privileged access to God.) Thus the festivities as a whole recapitulate many of the major divisions of the social universe: Dyula Muslims versus Senufo "pagans"; village and clan ward affiliation; males versus females; elders versus juniors; even the relatively wealthy versus the relatively poor, in terms of who provides refreshments for whom.

NEOTRADITIONALISM

As long as the local Dyula community and the local Muslim community were one and the same, celebrations of Muslim calendar holidays such as the *donba* festivities in Kadioha could bear a plural symbolic weight, simultaneously expressing the allegiance of the entire community to Islam and the internal division of this community into its salient components: male and female, elder and junior, slave and free, members of one kin group or another. By the early 1950s, this was certainly no longer the case in Korhogo, which attracted a sizable community of Muslim immigrants, many from outside Côte d'Ivoire, and where a growing number of Senufo were converting to Islam. Of course, such Muslims observed the same Muslim calendar holidays, but they did not, by and large, participate in the festivities that marked these occasions for the Dyula. As a result, such celebrations could no longer symbolize a Muslim identity per se. Rather, they were typical of the Dyula, but "Dyula" and "Muslim" were no longer synonymous in a local context. In a real sense, the festivities ceased to be religious and became part of the local folklore, like Mardi Gras in certain Catholic communities.

There is, indeed, a decided ambivalence concerning this whole domain of ritual. In an ethnically plural Muslim community, these celebrations seem to distinguish Dyula Muslims from other Muslims, rather than, as in the past, Dyula Muslims from Senufo unbelievers. As folklore, as the self-conscious expression of custom, of tradition, of one's own "roots" as opposed to the roots of one's neighbors, they are more frankly and flagrantly particularistic than ever. The question is no longer whether they are part of Islam, but whether it is proper for Muslims to participate in them. These were the very grounds for abolishing the *lo* societies among the Dyula *tun tigi*, as well as, somewhat later, excision ceremonies for adolescent girls; such practices, it was argued, were "pagan" and not Muslim. While there were, of course, additional extra-religious motives for abolishing initiation and excision ceremonies, the principle that they were religiously improper was upheld and vindicated. Singing, drumming, and dancing, particularly on occasions such as *donba* or during the month of Ramadan, have been called into question for similar reasons. The scholars of Koko are quasi-unanimous in voicing their disapproval. Muslim holidays, they argue, are serious occasions, and such frivolities only distract participants from true religious concerns. Such objections are, for the most part, unchallenged and ignored. The scholars, while they have failed to persuade many people to cease the festivities, have indeed convinced them that the singing and dancing have nothing to do with religion.

Perhaps the most paradoxical outcome of this process of the "folklorization" of formerly religious ritual has been the resurgence in recent years of *lo* masquerading. When I was first in the field, in 1973, I concluded that such masquerading had almost completely ceased. Exceptions were negligible, as when Dyula youths in Kadioha borrowed the costumes of their Senufo neighbors to run around the village at the end of Ramadan, playing the role of bogeymen to smaller children and clowns for adults. In 1984, on my return to the field, I began hearing reports of much more elaborate masquerading activity. At first, I assumed—much to my chagrin as an ethnographer—that such activity had escaped my attention a decade before. The truth turned out to be more surprising. During the preceding decade, there had been a revival of *lo* masquerading in certain Dyula communities. This revival involved a collaboration between two generations, the old men and the adolescent youths. The old men were the last generation to have been initiated, and, as such, some were nostalgic about the *lo* societies. The middle-aged men, the generation that followed, consisted precisely of those who had revolted against initiation, and who were responsible for the demise of the *lo* societies. The fascination of adolescents seems, at first sight, to be evidence of a pendulum swing of opinion, generation by generation. Yet the reality is more complex. *Lo* masquerading represents something entirely different for adolescents and for their elders. The adolescents have never really experienced the *lo* societies in operation, even at a distance. On the other hand, the masquerades of the *poro* societies of their Senufo neighbors are quite spectacular. Such masquerading, rather than the whole process of initiation, fascinates the adolescents. The *lo* masks have been revived, but not the *lo* societies. In many respects, *lo* masquerading, like the dancing during Ramadan and *donba*, has lost its religious content and become "folklore." What was, for a whole generation in revolt against initiation, a symbol of unacceptable "paganism" has become, for a new generation, a symbol rather of "tradition," of local pride. Not surprisingly, attitudes toward this kind of masquerading are highly ambivalent. There is no question, for example, of reviving masks in Koko; those communities where masquerading has resumed are all villages or small towns. Dyula in Koko sometimes comment superciliously that their cousins in the bush are somewhat backward in religious instruction, and that if they only knew better, they would abandon masquerading. Clearly, such behavior, even more than dancing during Ramadan, is not quite proper for good Muslims. On the other hand, Dyula in Koko are not only in constant contact with groups and individuals involved in *lo* masquerading, but they regularly attend events where such masquerading takes place. Not even the scholars publicly condemn the masquerading.

One way or the other, neither the Muslim holiday festivities nor *lo* masquerading symbolize the religious identity of participants any longer. No one is obliged to participate; they are largely, if not purely, for enjoyment. They are neither Muslim nor pagan, but rather Dyula, and often typical of a specific local community or even a single clan ward. They remain ritual expressions of particularism, but they have been desacralized. Such expressions are no longer legitimated by the religious idiom; on the contrary, from a religious point of view, their propriety can be called into question, particularly as they distinguish the Dyula from their Muslim, rather than from their "pagan," neighbors.

It follows that the primary ritual symbols of religious identity must now be symbols the Dyula share with these new Muslim, non-Dyula neighbors. These are, of course, the ritual expressions of Muslim universalism, of the *umma*, the global Muslim community, the symbols that once, locally at least, typified the *mory* rather than all Muslims per se. The most compelling symbol of this universal Muslim identity is prayer (*seri*), the regular performance of the five daily prayers. The symbolic equivalence of prayer and Islam is embodied in ordinary conversation. One does not generally ask about a stranger, "Is he a Muslim?" ("Silama lo wa?"), but rather, simply, "Does he pray?" ("A be seri ke wa?"). Prayer is by no means the only such symbol: abstaining from alcoholic beverages and from the worship of "fetishes" (*jo*) through blood sacrifices, as well as fasting during the month of Ramadan, have a similar function. Still, of all these symbols, prayer is far and away the dominant one. This is because prayer is a positive and public action, which can readily be observed. One can observe someone drinking alcohol; one cannot literally observe someone abstaining. The importance of visible signs of compliance explains why Dyula spit so frequently in public during the daytime at Ramadan. The rationale is that a person who swallows his own saliva is breaking the fast, and while one cannot observe someone fasting, one can observe him spitting. Spittle is in this way turned into a tangible (sometimes all too tangible) sign of the refusal to eat or drink during the daytime.

Prayer, then, is the visible sign of the proper observance of the code of the *sunna*, and thus of true inclusion in the *umma*, the abstract community of believers. But the *sunna* itself is a complex code, embodied in texts written in Arabic, a foreign language, accessible only to scholars, whose interpretation is indeed subject to scholarly dispute over legal subtleties. Unfortunately, it holds true in Islam that ignorance of the law is no excuse. For the ordinary believer, partly if at all literate in Arabic, this possibility of ignorance can lead to a sort of existential dilemma. In principle, good faith is not enough; one must constantly strive to know as precisely as possible the details of the code one is morally bound to follow, details that are not accessible firsthand but only through the medium of scholars (*karamogos*) who can translate them into the vernacular. This anxiety extends to the very domain of prayer itself. Prayers are not all equal. Particular prayers may be more or less efficacious, depending in the first instance on the time and circumstances in which they are performed. More important, prayers may be valid or invalid; a lapse, even involuntary, in ritual detail may "spoil" a prayer. These preoccupations are reflected in the sermons that have relatively recently become an integral part of Dyula funeral ritual. Scholars frequently stress the importance of prayer in general, but equally the necessity of praying correctly: the correct pronunciation of prayers in Arabic, the correct techniques for performing ablutions, indeed what may or may not render the water used for ablutions (*seri ji*) ritually impure. Nor may one conclude that these details reflect the concerns of scholars as opposed to their (often captive) audiences. Bilingual manuals in Arabic and French, replete with illustrations, explaining the details of prayer and ablutions and transcribing Arabic prayers more or less phonetically into French, are readily available in the marketplace and are eagerly studied by those pious Dyula whose literacy in French surpasses their knowledge of Arabic.

At first glance, it might seem that the Dyula have neatly compartmentalized ritual into two mutually exclusive domains: "religion," characterized by a preoccupation with universalistic ritual, notably prayer; and "tradition" (or, as the Dyula would call it, *lantan*, "custom"), the exuberant celebration of particularism through singing and dancing on calendar holidays. However, this compartmentalization breaks down during the life-crisis rituals associated with birth, marriage, and death, where it is not always so easy to separate "custom" from "religion." Of course, life crises are marked, not by isolated rituals, but by whole sequences of ritual events, some of which are unambiguously "customary," others unambiguously "religious." Thus the singing and dancing that accompany births and weddings, but also the funerals of elders, are clearly in the "customary" domain. On the other hand, Islamic law prescribes quite specific burial procedures for Muslims, and their public observance obviously falls within the religious domain. Still, aside from such obviously "customary" or "religious" ritual manifestations, all life crises involve the elaborate public distribution of prestations of various kinds, often on more than one occasion. The gatherings where these prestations are distributed are inevitably formal, and their sobriety contrasts with the exuberance of the singing and dancing, which are often going on at the same time. More important, one essential category of prestations involved on these occasions—indeed the central category involved in funeral ceremonies—is labeled *saraka*, derived from the Arabic term *sadaqa*. For example, as part of the fortieth-day ceremonies at a funeral, *saraka* is distributed to the close kin of the deceased, particularly those not directly involved in the distribution of prestations (e.g., widows); the members of the senior generation of the deceased's *kabila*, in strict order of seniority; Islamic scholars present during the ceremony, in order that they may afterward recite blessings (*duau*) for the deceased; representatives of all the other *kabilas* in the officiating *makafu*; representatives of all the other *makafus* (if not *kabilas*) in the village or Dyula quarter; representatives of all other villages or quarters present at the ceremony. The number of groups represented is often surprisingly large, if only because persons invited in their individual capacities as friends, kinsmen, or affines of the deceased or of members of the deceased's entourage are nevertheless treated as "representatives" of one social group or another for the purposes of the ceremony. In addition, various categories of joking partners of the deceased will snatch the portions destined to them, in ritualized mock theft: *senanku*, members of patronymic groups who joke with one another; "grandchildren," classificatory and real; and (in the case of a *horon*, a free individual) *worossos*, slaves "born in the compound," as opposed to purchased or captured slaves.

It is significant that all segments of the village or Dyula quarter must be represented. In this way, the very identity of the local community as a whole, in terms of its component parts—*makafus* and *kabilas*—is not only given symbolic expression but is in a fuller sense legitimated. Paradoxically, the moral unity of the community is expressed precisely in terms of the distinctions between different categories of members: members of different *kabilas*, of different generations, of free or slave descent. At the same time, the ritual concretely acknowledges the individual network of ties—of kinship and affinity, but also of friendship, clientship, and so on—linking the deceased and members of his immediate entourage to other individuals in the same *kabila*, to members of other *kabilas* in the same village or quarter, and finally to members of other local communities. A rigorous protocol governs the order in which prestations are publicly presented, as well as the relative amount distributed. In most instances, these are token prestations: small change, a plate of cooked food, or (in town, where time and fuel are increasingly valuable) a handful of grain; however, given the large number of groups and individuals entitled to a share, the total amount distributed is never negligible. These prestations, while they are not, strictly speaking, a religious obligation, are nevertheless construed as a religious act, a gift of charity. Not only does the giver thus accumulate merit, but the ostensible purpose of the whole ritual is to obtain the blessings of the entire community, so that God may grant a long and happy life to a newborn infant, harmony and children to a marriage, or that He take mercy on the soul of the deceased in the afterlife. For these reasons, the ostentatious distribution of prestations constitutes an essential part of what is perceived locally as a "Muslim" wedding or funeral.

These distributions of *saraka* during life crises, like the festivities during calendar holidays, define individual participants in terms of their salient attributes: gender, generation, age, free or slave status, membership of specific kin groups and villages. Formerly, both kinds of ritual were unambiguously perceived as "Muslim" and served to mark a Muslim identity locally. Now, however, their "Muslimness" is perceived somewhat differently. Singing and dancing on calendar holidays are "Muslim" only because of the time when they take place. The occasion is intrinsically Muslim, the activities are not. By way of contrast, the occasions on which *saraka* is publicly distributed—births, weddings, and deaths—are not intrinsically Muslim. Rather, it is because certain of the prestations are defined as *saraka* that the ritual assumes a specifically Muslim character. To give *saraka* is a religious act, an act of piety, but, equally crucially, it is not an obligatory act, from a strictly religious point of view. Only Muslims give *saraka* (at least during life-crisis rituals),[7] but one can, in principle, be Muslim without being obliged to give *saraka* on any particular occasion.

In short, the attitude toward ritual to which the majority of Dyula in Koko subscribe, an attitude that might be labeled "neotraditionalist," admits of two tiers of religious ritual. The first, universalistic tier is typified by prayer. It is prayer, along with the observance of the *sunna*, which prayer expresses, that distinguishes Muslims from unbelievers, both locally and globally. The Dyula are Muslims because they are part of the *umma*, and not simply, as in the past, because they are Dyula. However, a second, particularistic tier, exemplified during life-crisis rituals, legitimates the identities of individual Dyula as members of local communities, and, as such, of *kabilas*, of generations, and so on, in religious terms. Islam still legitimates the local community, both as a whole and in terms of its salient internal distinctions. But the local community is now conceived as only a part, rather than as a microcosm, of the *umma*, the global community of believers.

REFORM

In a sense, neotraditionalism seeks to have its cake and eat it too, to function at the most particular and most abstract level, by positing the coexistence of two conceptually distinct moral communities: the community of believers and the local community, the ritual practices of the one emphasizing the intrinsic sameness of all Muslims; those of the other, their difference. The possible logical contradictions implicit in such a stance are not necessarily felt as such; in different contexts, one or the other register takes precedence. However, it is also possible to attempt to point out and to refuse to tolerate perceived contradictions, by asserting that only one of these registers—the universalistic—is "truly" Islamic, that Islam recognizes the local community only as part of the *umma* as a whole and not in and of itself. Such a critique excludes all particularistic ritual from the realm of Islam. As we have seen, such a process has already taken place with respect to many particularistic rituals, which have been relegated to the status of "custom," *lantan*. In its weaker variant, the reformist critique simply carries the process to its logical conclusion, banishing all ritual manifestations of particularism to the limbo of "local tradition," where Islam is, in the last analysis, irrelevant. In its stronger variant, however, such rituals are labeled anti-Islamic, a breach of both the spirit and the letter of the law.

The reformist stance has typified the various challenges to the Suwarian tradition of scholarship, a tradition that at present is solidly "neotraditionalist." Indeed, it was in its most radical form, exemplified by the Wahhabi movement, that reformism first made its appearance in Korhogo. The Wahhabis inveighed against all forms of particularistic ritual: the distribution of *saraka* during life-crisis rituals; Sufi orders; saint worship. Their opposition to such forms of ritual was perfectly consistent with their stance that hereditary distinctions between believers, in terms of ethnic origin, "caste," and free or slave status, had no place in Islam. Not surprisingly, the Wahhabis attracted converts among groups who were, in one way or another, hereditarily stigmatized by other Muslims as slaves, "casted" individuals, or "pagans."[8] On the other hand, Wahhabism was also associated with well-to-do merchants. The combination is not really surprising. The *pax colonia*, by undermining many precolonial monopolies, opened up new avenues of opportunity, which such stigmatized groups were often quick to seize upon. Particularistic ritual, by emphasizing the salience of hereditary identities, condemns such groups and individuals to second-class status as Muslims in spite of their prosperity. The Wahhabi ideology lends legitimacy to this newfound wealth, while at the same time strongly condemning ostentation, not only in the form of conspicuous ceremonial largesse but also, for example, in clothing. This refusal of ostentation is only apparently paradoxical, for ostentation legitimates rather than creates one's social position—in order to maintain one's standing, one may be obliged to spend more than one can afford—while it also sanctions a certain ethic of reciprocity, where prestige lies in giving rather than in possessing. To the Wahhabis, particularistic ritual is wasteful and vain, a sacrilegious exercise in self-aggrandizement. To their opponents, the Wahhabis seem stingy, while their conspicuous austerity—white flowing robes for men and, increasingly, veils for women—seems simply a transparently disguised form of "reverse" ostentation.

Wahhabi ritual focuses exclusively on the universalism of the *sunna*, and consequently prayer is the focal symbol for defining the global community of believers. Yet if both Wahhabis and neotraditionalists stress the all-importance of prayer, what is to distinguish them, save that the Wahhabis abstain from particularistic ritual? The solution they have chosen is to pray differently. Neotraditionalists, following the Maliki rite overwhelmingly predominant in West Africa, pray with arms outstretched. Consequently, the Wahhabis pray with their arms crossed, in the fashion of the other three Sunni schools. Not surprisingly, neotraditionalists have focused their vehement disapproval of the Wahhabis on this manner of prayer, for it is in this way that the Wahhabis implicitly define themselves as belonging to a community of believers that excludes the neotraditionalists.[9] Thus, their critics maintain that the universalistic ideology of the Wahhabis translates itself in practice into a form of (thinly) disguised exclusivism. Whereas they reject the claims of the majority of Muslims to belong to the true community of believers, their opponents characterize—or rather caricature—them as wealthy parvenus jealous to preserve their newfound prerogatives. If Wahhabis reject those religious rituals that legitimate the local community as it is "traditionally" constituted, it is—so their detractors claim—in order to form another sort of community where newfound wealth erases any stigma associated with one's origins.

Although the Wahhabis have successfully established a foothold in Korhogo, they have made few inroads among the Dyula of Koko. Nevertheless, a growing number of Muslims among the Dyula have come, if not to reject outright, at least to disparage particularistic ritual in Islam. This is especially true of younger individuals with Western-style schooling past the primary level, the individuals attracted, as we have seen, to the AEEMCI. The semi-official status of the organization ensures that it avoids the kind of controversy that the

Wahhabis openly seek. Rather than condemning particularistic ritual, it ignores it, stressing exclusively the practice of the
sunna. This is a stance local scholars do not—indeed cannot—find objectionable, particularly as the association has
been very diplomatic about recruiting their support. Younger
members of the Western-trained elite, stationed for the most
part away from Korhogo, still retain close ties with their families. Yet their social position, their place in a hierarchy of
privilege—modest as it may often be—depends on a bureau-
cracy, on a system of values totally separate from and out of
the control of the local community per se. This is not to say
that their community of origin is of no importance to them.
Strong affective bonds link them to kinsmen and friends.
Moreover, there are individuals in or from Korhogo, indeed
from Koko, with varying degrees of political connections and
influence in the world beyond the local community, and who
can, under certain circumstances, give a boost to their careers. For these young men, Koko is the hub of a network of
friends, of kin, of useful connections. It is not, on the other
hand, primarily a mosaic of *kabilas*, of elders and juniors,
slaves and freemen. In terms of such traditional criteria of
identity, they remain very junior, and as such their voices
carry little weight in the affairs of the local community. They
have appreciably more wealth and access to politically influential individuals than most members of their home communities, but not enough of either to merit treatment as
quasielders. In any case, they are largely unconcerned by the
very system of values that particularistic ritual seeks to underscore and dramatize. Neither their careers nor their daily
lives depend very much on the prestige or influence they enjoy in Koko. For such individuals a more purely universalistic
Islam suits their needs, particularly in a country where Muslims are a minority; the bonds of prayer constitute in and of
themselves a link with their home communities that sets
them apart from many of their fellow citizens from other regions. Yet their place in life is determined in the national, not
the strictly local, arena. The sums that they find themselves
obliged to spend for the marriages and funerals of kin are

both necessary—they are still a precondition for effective membership in one's "home" community—and onerous, if not wasteful, in that they serve to articulate the position of groups and individuals within a system of values to which they no longer subscribe without reservations.

SECULARISM

So far we have been able to distinguish between various attitudes toward ritual in terms of their relative emphases on universalistic ritual, stressing the membership of participants in the global community of believers, and on particularistic ritual, stressing the place of individuals within local, face-to-face communities. In fact, for the majority of Koko's Muslims—those I have labeled "neotraditionalists,"—both kinds of ritual are crucial. But is it possible, conversely, to identify a set of attitudes which de-emphasizes both kinds of ritual? For example, if one can be a "practicing Muslim," one can, by implication, be a "nonpracticing Muslim": one who drinks alcoholic beverages, who does not pray regularly or observe the fast of Ramadan, and so forth. Superficially, the behavior of a modern-day "nonpracticing" Muslim would seem very much like that of the *tun tigi* in the past. The resemblance, however, is only superficial. In the first place, the *tun tigi* were members of a hereditary category of Muslims; in the second place, ritual—calendar holiday festivities and life-crisis rituals, if not the prescriptions of the *sunna*—defined the individual as a member of the community of Islam.

"Nonpracticing Muslim," however, is not an entirely adequate characterization, placing, as it does, primary emphasis on behavior, rather than focusing on the significance of behavior within an overall system of values. An individual who fails to pray regularly may simply be a lax Muslim who accepts without question that prayer is a fundamental expression of "being Muslim." On the other hand, one can consider prayer as, at best, an act of personal faith; at worst, a social obligation; not, at any rate, as the core of Muslim identity. From this perspective, a Muslim is anyone who identifies as such; whether and how this identification is translated into ritual terms is one's personal business. In this sense, the category "Muslim" functions much like an ethnic label: just as forms of speech, dress, and so forth, may symbolize ethnic identity but are not equivalent to it, so Islamic ritual may symbolize Muslim identity without defining it. Whether Islam is conceived as a faith in the full sense of the word—a question of interior commitment—or as an identity label, it is either more than or less than—in any case other than—a moral community.

This attitude bears close resemblance to a Westernized secularist mentality and one would expect to find it, if at all, among Western-trained members of the Dyula community. Public expression of such an attitude in Koko is still inconceivable. Public declarations of sympathy for the Wahhabis are unpopular, but they are not unknown. However, Wahhabism is at its very root a public commitment; secularism, to the extent that it conceives of Islam as a private faith and a public identity, is perfectly consistent with a pattern of behavior that might uncharitably be characterized as hypocritical. But, if no one flaunts such an attitude in Koko, the fact remains that certain categories of individuals are commonly suspected of practicing Islam only in public contexts—that is to say, of not praying when they can get away with it unnoticed. Suspicion falls first of all on the young—not all of them, by any means, for some have a reputation for being serious and others of being frivolous, if not good for nothing. In and of itself, the laxity of the young does not call into question the Islamic values of the majority. On the contrary, particularistic ritual emphasizes the difference between the young and elders (even incipient elders). The young are expected to behave differently until they begin to be socialized as elders, until their voice has at least minimal weight, at the moment they enter the lowest rung of the hierarchy of eldership by marrying and having children. The young may be sermonized ad nauseam about their immoral behavior, but to a certain extent such behavior is tolerated and even expected, provided they grow out of it.

But another category of individuals represents a far greater
threat: those with high-paying employment outside the region. The better off they are, the more likely they are to fall
under suspicion. These are the individuals who have not
only received a Western education but have reaped its full
benefits. They live in expensive villas and own modern appli-
ances and fancy cars. More important, their very success is
measured by their belonging to a social milieu comprised, in
Côte d'Ivoire, mostly of non-Muslims, and one that aggressively sports a Western lifestyle. This success is admired in
Koko, and its outward signs—villas, cars, refrigerators, video-
cassette recorders, and so forth—are exhibited whenever
possible by individuals who, by the neotraditionalist standards of the majority, rate as unambiguously pious. But this
very admiration is, in a sense, only a passive acknowledge-
ment of success in an arena outside the local community's
control. Success is not measured in terms of the values of the
local community, as expressed in particularistic ritual. On the
contrary, the values of the local community must adjust to
forms of success outside its ability to define, in and of itself.
These individuals are members of an elite—economic, bu-
reaucratic, and political—as far removed from the abstract
community of Muslim believers as from the local community.
Religion, ethnicity, and local community of origin are by no
means irrelevant; recruitment may depend on locally anchored networks of patronage, or alternatively may reflect attempts to achieve some sort of representative balance at the
national level. Nevertheless, the elite is constituted according
to a system of values that is both national (if not international) and secular. This is not to say, by any means, that
members of this elite who happen to be Dyula necessarily reject a universalistic standard of Islamic values in favor of a
purely secular one. However, more than anyone else, they
are in a position to do so if they please.

Paradoxically, certain members of this elite participate
quite actively in particularistic ritual, as systematically as
(and perhaps more enthusiastically than) in prayer. Such participation is essential for anyone with political aspirations.

Establishing one's local identity in this way is a precondition for developing a base of support in one's home community. Active displays of generosity on such occasions translate success in the national arena into local terms. This double accumulation of prestige is a luxury the wealthiest and most powerful can easily afford. However, this is not the case for those who, in national terms, are simply well off but not really rich. Such individuals are faced with three conflicting sets of demands on their resources: maintaining a lifestyle, in terms of consumer goods, appropriate to their station; aiding close relations (friends, kin, affines) in their networks, particularly in their home communities; and distributing gifts and money generously on appropriate occasions in local particularistic ritual. It is far harder for the moderately prosperous, unlike the very wealthy, to have their cake and eat it too by satisfying all three sets of demands simultaneously. Yet, even if they participate actively and enthusiastically at marriages and funerals, wealthy bureaucrats are in a very different situation from ordinary members of the local community. Their situation is defined by values and standards independent of the local community; they have the freedom to choose whether or not to translate this prestige into local terms. Local standards of values remain in any case secondary, and their prestige in local terms depends on their position in the national arena. Their participation in local particularistic ritual is instrumental, a demonstration that they can impinge upon, rather than that they are subjected to, the local hierarchy of prestige.

CONCLUSIONS

As we have seen, each type of ritual stresses an individual's commitment to a specific kind of moral community, and consequently to a specific set of values. At stake are three different ways of defining the individual: as a member of a specific kin group within a specific village or quarter, as male or female, elder or junior, free or slave; as a "Muslim," more or less pious depending on the rigor with which he or she observes the ritual and moral code of the *sunna;* and, finally, in terms of type of occupation, amount of wealth, degree of Western education, and political clout—in other words, for want of a better word, "class."

The first system of definition, in terms of village and kin-group affiliation, generation, gender, and so on, only retains its salience within the "microcosm," the close-knit community where everyone knows everyone else, where any given individual's position in the local hierarchy depends on a combination of ascribed characteristics and "reputation" together determining the weight his or her voice will carry in local affairs. The third system, in terms of the attributes of "class," transects not only the local but also the global "Muslim" community. An individual's position is expressed in terms of signs that have no place in religious ritual, either particularistic or universalistic; such signs include the amount and nature of goods they own and consume, the way they speak French, and ultimately the various means by which other individuals with established positions in the hierarchy mark them as peers, superiors, or inferiors. In other words, both the close-knit local community and the national system of "class" are essentially hierarchical. Grosso modo, to the extent that individuals are in a position to choose the system of values by which they wish to evaluate themselves and be evaluated by others, their stake in either system depends in large measure on the rank they can plausibly claim or, at least, reasonably aspire to. These two systems cannot, however, be placed on an equal footing. As we have seen, a high position in the national arena can be translated and transferred into a local idiom. The reverse is obviously not the case.

This leaves the second system of definition, in terms of a global "Muslim" identity. To the extent that one can meaningfully speak of a principle of hierarchy here, it is a hierarchy of piety, apparently divorced from such criteria as birth or class. The great in this world will not necessarily find favor in the eyes of God in the next. But this is not to say that the last shall be first—the Sermon on the Mount is not part of

Islam's debt to Christianity—or even that the global moral community of Islam is in some deep sense egalitarian. The moral hierarchy of piety may supersede one's rank in this world, however reckoned; it does not deny it. It is significant that the categories of individuals most readily attracted to varieties of reformism occupy positions that are, in certain respects, anomalous in terms of the local hierarchy of influence and the national hierarchy of class: those whose wealth or Western education places them "above" their station in the local hierarchy without justifying their inclusion in the upper echelons in the national hierarchy. This applies to the Wahhabi merchants, who may be wealthy but lack Western education, and who are often (but not inevitably) members of low-ranking hereditary categories in the "traditional" local scheme of values. But it applies equally well to younger secondary school and university students and graduates, who are educated but whose current prospects of achieving considerable wealth or political influence are severely limited, and whose very youth, in the absence of real wealth or clout, places them for the time being toward the bottom of the local hierarchy of respect and influence. By observing the *sunna*, as they interpret it, more rigorously than anyone else, they assert their moral superiority both over traditional elders, guilty in their eyes of mingling Islam with particularistic ritual, and the Westernized elite, suspected of a tepid commitment to Islamic strictures. In this respect, reformists do not so much deny as relativize the modern national values of "class." Wealth or education are not denigrated as such, but must be combined with the "proper" observance of Islam in order to determine the individual's ultimate worth.

Among neotraditionalists, the relationship between standards of piety and the locally defined hierarchy are expressed in somewhat different terms. Elders are expected to be more pious than juniors; men more pious than women; scholars more pious than ordinary believers. The universalistic values of Islam thus, in a way, legitimate the position of individuals in the local hierarchy of influence, while at the same time serving as a bridge between the purely local realm and the wider community of Islam with which individuals are at any rate involved on a day-to-day basis.

In short, the notion of a global moral community of Islam defines a social arena in Côte d'Ivoire that lies in some respects between and in other respects apart from the close-knit local community, where an individual's position is determined in terms of age, gender, generation, free or slave status, and so on, as well as personal reputation; and the national arena, where wealth, education, and political influence reign supreme, and where symbols of identity are universally recognized. Each kind of identity—local, Muslim, and "class"—has its own quasi-autonomous system of symbolic articulation. At another level, these systems can be combined in various ways to give rise to different varieties of Islamic ideology, expressed in ritual terms. From this point of view, religious change cannot simply be reduced to shifts along a continuum from particularism to universalism. Instead, we are faced with a multiplicity of schemas, each purporting to define the identity of individuals but also the nature of the larger social entity within which this identity is situated, expressed in symbols embodied not only in religious ritual but also in everyday life. By the values they place on these different kinds of symbols, individuals indicate the terms in which they choose or refuse to identify themselves, to evaluate and be evaluated by others around them.

6

The Birth and Demise of a Ritual

During my first visit to the field in Korhogo in 1972 and 1973, I twice witnessed the performance of a certain wedding ceremony. I was present at numbers of other marriages, for none of which this ceremony was performed. In effect, the ceremony was the recent invention of a particular Muslim scholar. Some attempts were being made to diffuse it, but with only limited success. The ceremony itself was not the center of any controversy, though its inventor is a somewhat controversial personality. The very existence of such a ceremony poses certain interesting questions. Why should anyone go to the trouble of inventing a ritual? And why should others go to the trouble of performing it?

It is hardly an accident that ritual innovation is often associated with a break with tradition. Established religions tend to deplore the principle of innovation in ritual practice. Prophets, and in certain cases founders of new sects or cults, may justify their actions in terms of divine inspiration; but claims concerning the legitimacy of various ritual practices are most often expressed in terms of the past. The "religions of the Book"—Judaism, Christianity, and Islam—are particularly averse to the principle of innovation, for a number of reasons. First of all, they all make exclusive claims to the allegiance of adherents. Second, precisely because these religions are practiced by communities widely dispersed over the face of the globe, there is added pressure for religious practices to remain standardized from one group of believers to another; the religious community must effectively transcend the boundaries of local society. But written texts are also a more reliable safeguard of "tradition" than oral memory: existing practices can always be checked against a written text. These religions also have "orthodox" written traditions of interpretation of sacred texts, which place even further limits on innovation.

This is decidedly the case in Sunni Islam. The most powerful symbolic expression of such principles is the notion that the "Gates of Interpretation" were closed in the tenth century A.D., and that since then scholars have no longer legitimately been able to engage in "interpretation" (*ijtihad*) but only in "imitation" (*taqlid*).[1] Modern scholarship has cast serious doubts on the validity of this doctrine.[2] In the first place, it is quite certain that this "shutting of the gates" did not make a great deal of noise at the time; the event seems to have gone unnoticed in the tenth century when it was allegedly taking place. The doctrine was only fully elaborated much later, in the fifteenth century, in order to fix the number of "orthodox" schools of Islamic law (*fiqh*) at four: Maliki, Hanafi, Hanbali, and Shafi'i (Hodgson 1974, 2: 448). Even so, such a principle of fixity can be combined with a great deal of real flexibility. What matters is not so much how a particular judgment is made as how it is construed. Still, the doctrine of *taqlid* has been hotly contested by modern advocates of Islamic reform, who blame it for the sclerosis of Islamic thought in the modern world (Piscatori 1986: 3–10).

Not all Muslims in Koko have been impervious to such reformist views, but the vast majority of Dyula Muslims, including locally trained scholars, are not so much self-consciously "conservative" as unconcerned about such issues. Since they are all Malikis, differences of interpretation between different legal schools are of no theoretical interest to them. In judging different scholars, or for that matter different "lay" Muslims, they do not ask, "Whose interpretation is correct?" but rather "Who knows more than whom?" The principle that Islam is a fixed and immutable body of knowledge is not so much unchallenged as unquestioned. Any deviations constitute *bid'a*, a term usually glossed as "innovation," but that covers not only the introduction of "new" elements to Islam but also the illegitimate retention of any "old" pre-Islamic elements.

The scholar who apparently invented and attempted to introduce this new wedding ceremony in Korhogo is not in any way associated with Islamic "reform." On the contrary, he has been one of the most outspoken opponents of the "Wahhabis," not only in Korhogo, but (since he is actually based in Bouake, the most active "Wahhabi" center in Côte d'Ivoire) in the country as a whole. He would describe himself neither as an "interpreter" nor as an "innovator." At first sight, it seems quite surprising that such an individual would "invent" (to Western eyes) a new ritual. In fact, much of the problem lies in the realm of discourse rather than of action, in the meanings and values attached to the notions of "tradition" and "innovation," and more broadly to novelty and to antiquity. "Innovation" and "tradition" correspond, not to statements of fact, but to principles used to uphold or contest the legitimacy of specific ideas and practices. Within such a context, one can identify two possible frameworks for debate. In the first place, one can disagree about the acceptability or the preferability of novelty as opposed to antiquity, in other words about the principles on which legitimacy should be based. On the other hand, assuming agreement on such principles, one can still debate which of several competing viewpoints is *really* "traditional" or "innovative" as the case may be.

The academic discourse of the modern West constitutes an ideal field of comparison to the Islamic scholarship of the Dyula. The very same viewpoints, among Western academics, may be alternatively categorized as "pathbreaking" or "trendy"; as "outdated" or "sound." On balance, however, academia places a premium on novelty. At the very least, scholars are supposed to be engaged in "original" research, and plagiarism is certainly to be counted among the Deadly Sins. Even so, adjectives like "trendy" or "fashionable" remind us that novelty ought not, in principle, to be pursued for its own sake. On the other hand, the premium set on "originality" provides its own set of temptations, so that scholars can often be accused (not always without justification) of forever seeking to put old wine in new bottles.

By way of contrast, in the scholarly world of Dyula Muslims, "old is beautiful." More properly speaking, knowledge is a straight and narrow path, a venerable one, to be sure, but antiquity is not to be valued in and of itself, any more than novelty in Western academia. Ideas that are, in a real sense, experienced as new are only legitimate if they are "*re*discoveries" as opposed to "discoveries." In this context, one might well compare the Dyula experience of "invention" to the "invention" of relics in the Middle Ages—for example, the relics of Saint James at Compostella; that is to say, to the uncovering of something that was always there but had gone unnoticed for long stretches of time. This new wedding ceremony was thus, in the eyes of its propagator, not really "new" at all, but rather a practice that ought already to have been observed. Its absence could be construed as a "lapse," rather than its introduction as an "addition."

Such considerations may explain how attempts to disseminate such a ceremony might be (and were) justified, but not why any scholar would feel that such a ceremony was necessary, much less why anyone else would be tempted to put it into practice, given that other local scholars, let alone "Wahhabis" and other reformists, were unconvinced of its necessity, even if they did not challenge its "orthodoxy." The attempts to introduce the ceremony need thus to be seen in terms of the circumstances of the time. Islam as practiced by the majority of Dyula in Koko was being subjected to challenges on two separate fronts. While the "Wahhabis" were militantly questioning the orthodoxy of "traditional" Islamic practices in the community, Western education was suspected of disseminating an ideology of "secularism," of undermining the commitment of the young to religious values. Both challenges menaced Koko's religious community— and ultimately the community pure and simple—with crucial defections from the ranks: prosperous merchants might be tempted noisily to throw in their lot with the Wahhabis, while prosperous members of the educated elite might be

tempted, in a quieter if not more hypocritical fashion, to with-
draw their primary allegiance to their home community in favor of membership in a more cosmopolitan social universe.

These challenges thrust scholars into an increasingly visible leadership role, incidentally promoting rivalry between
local scholars for leadership of Koko's religious community.
The expression of this rivalry is most often muted, for a variety of reasons. First of all, it is impious for one scholar explicitly to disparage the learning of another, although this
does not, of course, preclude innuendo, which can in some
cases be an even more effective weapon. Secondly, rival
scholars may have strong links to the same individuals in the
Koko community. An explicit rift would force such individuals to choose sides, placing the scholar held responsible for
the rift at a distinct moral disadvantage. Finally, "Wahhabism" and "secularism" constitute common enemies to all
of these scholars, against which they have an interest of pre-
senting a united front. Nevertheless, such rivalries, while
they may usually remain tacit, are very real, and scholars
have a decided interest in finding new ways to outshine
their rivals.

One possible strategy is to find new occasions for delivering sermons. Muslim calendar holidays and funerals are already used to such ends, but other life-crisis rituals, those associated with birth and with marriage, do not normally
include sermons as part of the ceremonial. As it turns out,
rituals associated with birth (*den sereli*) are not very promising candidates. There are separate ceremonies on such occasions, one performed by females and one by males. The female ceremony remains elaborate, but the male ceremony
has tended to lapse, and the male kin of newborns frequently
neglect its performance altogether. Now that the ritual associated with birth is increasingly associated with women,
scholars, as males, express little interest. Moreover, as exclusively female affairs, such rituals attract relatively fewer people of either sex, whereas both weddings and funerals normally involve large numbers of guests and widespread
participation. Indeed, weddings involve the most elaborate

ceremonial of all Dyula life crises, rivaled only by the funerals of important elders.[3] Different kinds of ritual activity, involving different sets of people, go on at the same time: the *furu* is largely a concern of male elders, while the *konyo mina* centers on the bride(s) and involves the active participation of women of all ages and adolescent males. In crucial respects, first weddings mark the passages of both brides and grooms from adolescence to adulthood. However, by this very fact, the groom himself is debarred from active participation in the festivities of the *konyo mina*, while he is still too junior to be involved in the negotiations of the *furu*. Because of their scale and expense, weddings are generally performed several at a time. Indeed, in some villages, almost all weddings are performed on the same occasion once a year. One way or the other, weddings are far and away the most important ritual occasion where scholars *qua* scholars are conspicuous by their absence, and where they could immediately enjoy a large, readily constituted audience. It is thus easy to see why a scholar might find it attractive to institute the practice of giving wedding sermons.

While it would be naive to deny that wedding sermons are an ideal vehicle for attracting attention to the scholar who delivers them, and even more so to the one who inaugurates the practice, it would be cynical to suggest that the idea was simply self-serving and devoid of any broader legitimate motivation. The form of the ceremony, as I witnessed it, was significantly different, not only from ordinary wedding ritual, but also from ordinary sermons. Certainly the most striking feature of the ceremony was that it focused attention, not only on the officiating scholar, but on the married couple (or, more technically, couples, as it was performed for several couples at the same time on each occasion.) In the *furu*, the senior kin of the bride and groom as well as their respective "networks" are the central participants, whereas the brides occupy the spotlight in the *konyo mina*. Both the groom individually and the couple as a unit stay in the background. In these new wedding ceremonies, bride and groom were made to stand together in front of the audience, each placing one foot on a loaf of (French) bread while holding another loaf of bread in their hands and then placing it together to their lips. It is probably unnecessary to point out that this symbolism, much less the ideological emphasis placed on the couple *qua* couple, is quite alien to "traditional" Dyula cultural practice. Indeed, on the second occasion I witnessed, perhaps because of the newness and unfamiliarity of the ritual, one of the couples involved were distinctly ill at ease, unsure of what they were expected to do, and had to be coached repeatedly at each step. As they nervously lifted the bread to their lips, one *worosso*, a second-generation slave entitled to joke at the expense of freemen, called out from the back of the audience, "Don't eat it, don't eat it!" to the couple's added discomfiture and to the audience's general delight. As each couple moves to center stage, the officiating scholar recites a short speech in Arabic to the effect that the groom, son of so-and-so and of so-and-so, is being duly married to the bride, similarly identified, adding a blessing to their union. When all the couples have finished, he then begins his sermon, focusing on the nature of the conjugal duties of husband and wife, stressing, for example, that a polygynous husband must not favor one wife over another.

This apparently quaint ritual can only be understood as a combination of a Muslim sermon with a loose pastiche of a civil wedding ceremony. This implicit reference to civil marriages was by no means fortuitous. In 1964, Côte d'Ivoire promulgated a new Civil Code,[4] whose explicit aims were to foster the development of the independent conjugal family, then considered an indispensable motor to economic growth. In principle, it outlawed future polygynous marriages, and stipulated rules of inheritance as contrary as possible to "traditional" patterns. However, the Code applied only to legally registered civil marriages, and consequently its applicability was rather limited. The vast majority of individuals did not, of their free will, register their marriages. In the first few years, local administrators forcibly recruited registrants, particularly among the Dyula, whose elaborate wedding ceremonies involving numerous couples at a time made them a convenient target. Nevertheless, some individuals did in fact have an interest in registering their marriages. This included couples who decided to elope against the wishes of the woman's family, but with the collusion of the man's; since the civil ceremony was legally binding, it effectively forced the hand of the bride's kin. Perhaps more important at the time, salaried wage earners were also eager to register their marriages. Family allowances were given by the government to provide for the wives and children of duly registered marriages of salaried employees. In fact, government employees accounted for the vast majority of salaried wage earners. Such individuals were typically Western educated to one degree or another and already relatively well-off, sometimes frankly quite prosperous. In other words, these were the individuals most likely to succumb to the temptations of a "secularist" ideology of one sort or another. Thus civil marriages, civil servants, and "secularism" tended to go hand in hand, though of course there were numerous exceptions. The new wedding ceremony was clearly intended as an ideological alternative, particularly as the Civil Code itself quite explicitly represented a Westernizing, secularizing ideology. "Muslim" ceremonies were enacted as a counterpart to civil ceremonies, just as Islam was an alternative to rampant "secularism."

The new ritual thus addressed an issue—the spread of "secularism"—of widespread concern to the local Muslim community, and was not simply a self-serving vehicle for its propagator. Even so, it could not be taken for granted that people would choose to perform it. Such ceremonies cost money. The officiating scholar must be rewarded for his services, and refreshments must be distributed to everyone in attendance. During the ceremonies I attended, such refreshments included coffee liberally laced with sweetened condensed milk (a staple refreshment at sermons), but also, more lavishly and unconventionally, sandwiches of grilled lamb.[5] These costs, in themselves, might not seem prohibitive, but weddings are already extremely expensive affairs (by Western and not only by Dyula standards!) and a financial drain on the budgets of all but the very rich. Any added

expenses, such as wedding sermons, are likely to be unwel-
come, all else being equal. It is one thing to affirm that such
ceremonies are a worthy idea in principle, and quite another
to commit oneself to meeting the expenses necessary to perform one on any particular occasion.

In 1972 and 1973, I was particularly concerned with studying patterns of marriages among the Dyula, and so I had the
occasion to witness numerous weddings, both in Korhogo
and in nearby villages. In the vast majority of cases, the new
ceremony was not performed. I witnessed it twice, and knew
of one other instance when it was performed in my absence.
It is consequently instructive to examine those cases where
the ritual was in fact undertaken. As the chart illustrating
marriage readings in 1972–73 shows clearly, all the individuals for whom it was performed are part of a single kinship
network. The scholar who was trying to introduce the ritual,
Mammadou-Labi Saganogo, is in fact neither a native nor a
resident of Korhogo or its immediate hinterland. A scion of
one of the most prestigious of all the Dyula scholarly families, he hails from Kong and is based in Bouake, the second
largest town in Côte d'Ivoire. Unlike any of Koko's local
scholars, he enjoys a national following; tapes of his sermons, and even tapes of his son's sermons, can be purchased
in local marketplaces. Not surprisingly, he has a following in
and around Korhogo, but, more important, he also has close
ties with specific individuals and families, based on the value
placed on the teacher/pupil bond.[6] In particular, he is or was
the teacher of two individuals identified in the chart: the first
is Mustafa Kone, a young scholar born in the nearby village
of Dyendana, recently appointed imam of one of Korhogo's
neighborhood mosques; the second is the late Bakari Toure,
father of a prominent group of brothers, including a local politician, Abou Toure.[7] To the extent that the teacher/pupil relationship is assimilated in many respects to the father/son
relationship, the ties between an individual and his father's
teacher are still morally binding. In any case, as the genealogy shows, Abou Toure and his brothers are cross-cousins of
Mustafa Kone. The relationship is emotively stronger and

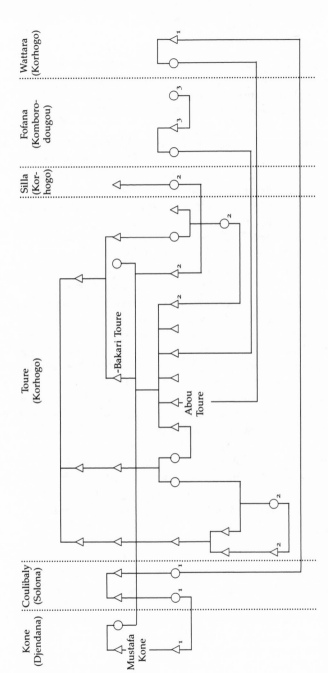

Marriage Readings, 1972 to 1973

1 = performed July 3, 1972 (Mammadou Labi Saganogo presiding): 2 = performed December 2, 1972 (Mustafa Kone presiding); 3 = performed June 1973 (Mustafa Kone presiding).

closer than the cross-cousin tie necessarily dictates. The brothers are personally very fond of Mustafa and of his family in general, and proud of his scholarly abilities; they have shown a close interest both in his personal affairs and in his career.

The genealogical information provided underscores the crucial role of the Toure brothers in promoting performances of the ritual. In fact, to one extent or another, they underwrote the expenses of all the weddings involved, and particularly those of performance of the wedding sermon. Indeed, the brothers themselves account for two out of the six marriages involved, both performed on December 2, 1972. The third couple for whom the ceremony was performed on the same day were more distant agnates in the same section of their *kabila*. Ordinarily, they might well not have arranged for the performance of the ceremony, but since they were married on the same day as the two brothers, they were included as a matter of course. Similarly, Mustafa's own marriage, which the Toure helped to arrange and finance, naturally involved performance of the ceremony; again, the other couple, a cousin of Mustafa's bride and one of the brothers' wife's brothers, were included because they were being married in the same place at the same time. The third case involved not only a wife's brother but also an apprentice of another of the brothers; the relationship was thus considerably closer than the genealogy itself would indicate. In short, a relatively restricted core of individuals were systematically committed to performing the ceremony, but they were able on these various occasions to recruit the participation of other members of their kin network.

Perhaps the most striking feature that emerges from this consideration of the instances on which the ceremony was performed is the association between a local politician and his brothers on the one hand and a Muslim scholar and his local disciple on the other. Indeed, politicians and ambitious scholars in Koko have much in common; they are both seeking positions of leadership over the community as a whole, in both cases encroaching to some degree on the authority of elders who hold traditional office (the imam in the case of scholars, clan elders in the case of politicians), even though they scrupulously avoid openly challenging this authority. Since scholars and politicians are not seeking the same type of leadership, they are natural allies. Each has his personal following; if they associate, these followings may be pooled together, each leader providing followers for his ally. Moreover, in a Muslim community, association with a scholar cannot help but give a politician a certain extra legitimacy.

For the scholar, innovation, perceived in Western rather than in Muslim terms—that is to say, the introduction of practices not previously prevalent in a given community—is a political move, a bid for leadership of the community. If his innovation is adopted, his claim to leadership is reinforced, and he is likely to augment his following. The consequences for him if the innovation fails to win general acceptance depend on the extent to which he has committed himself to its promulgation. In Mammadou-Labi's case, he devoted most of his energy in Koko to denouncing the Wahhabi movement. Neither he nor his disciples made a very systematic attempt to push acceptance of the new wedding ceremony very hard. As a result, his credibility was not seriously in jeopardy even if the ritual failed to catch widespread attention. For a politician associated with a scholar, the scholar's innovation may also work to his advantage. Should the scholar's bid for religious leadership be successful, the politician can capitalize on his support of the scholar. Thus the politician has a certain incentive to use his influence to spread an innovation, especially at the outset, in the hope that it will gain a momentum of its own. However, a politician is even more unlikely than a scholar to commit himself too deeply to such an innovation, lest its failure damage his credibility too seriously.

Seen in these terms, both scholars and politicians stand to gain an increased following from innovation, and stand to lose credibility should the attempts to introduce something new fall flat. The situation, however, is more complex than such a simplistic "cost-benefit" model might suggest. Both scholars and politicians have rivals, and factions may coalesce around and against both religious and political leaders. To put it another way, scholars and politicians not only have followings, but also an opposition. This may be more obviously and inevitably the case with politicians, but is also a very real possibility among scholars. The dilemma is most acute if the followings of scholars and politicians do not already coincide to a large degree, if the following of each includes backers of the rivals of the other. In such cases, if the association between a scholar and a politician is too close, one or both may not only fail to win followers from among the other's supporters, but may actually be faced with defections.

Indeed, Koko was characterized by overt and latent factional cleavages, both in the political and scholarly domain, in 1972 and 1973. Abou's political fortunes had ebbed and flowed since independence in 1960. An early militant in the RDA—he was caught, severely beaten, and imprisoned by the French—he was rewarded after independence with a prominent position in the local party hierarchy. When it was announced in 1963 that there had been a plot to overthrow the president, however, Abou was one of many politicians who fell from grace, although he was luckier than some others and was not imprisoned. In 1971, it was announced that there had never, in fact, been an attempted coup, and the victims of the earlier accusations were rehabilitated. By 1972, Abou was again officially a member of the local party hierarchy. He was perhaps the leading Dyula politician in the region, but local political allegiances do not run entirely along ethnic lines, and his political rivals have also been able to recruit supporters from within Koko's Dyula community. However, his fortunes were on the rise at the time, making him a more effective and attractive ally.

Within Koko, there was a pronounced tendency for factional allegiances to run along lines of clan-ward affiliation. In fact, the Toure clan ward, being very much larger than most other wards, would, if united, constitute a powerful

bloc in Koko in and of itself. Broadly speaking, Koko was politically divided into pro- and anti-Toure factions. Scholars
tended to be associated with one or the other faction, and effectively formed two separate "pools," each clan ward select-
ing a scholar from its own "pool" to deliver a funeral sermon,
for example. Matters came to a head during the celebrations
of *donba*, the Prophet's birthday, in 1972. In principle, one
scholar should have delivered a sermon for the entire community. In fact, the senior scholar in each pool was determined to deliver the sermon. No attempt was made by either
side to conceal the overtly political nature of the confrontation. Both sides competed for the privilege of giving their
sermon in the precincts of the mosque. Both attempted to
provide the most lavish refreshments possible. Finally, mi-
crophones and amplifiers were used to drown out the other
side's sermon.

In such a highly charged atmosphere, it might seem that
there was no conflict between allegiance to particular scholars and to particular politicians. However, this was not absolutely true. The political loyalties of individuals are not
overtly public. They tend to be public knowledge, and sometimes arouse public attention, but do not invariably call for
public declarations of support or opposition. On the other
hand, when it becomes necessary or desirable to invite a particular scholar to deliver a sermon, this is in effect a public
statement of confidence, whatever one's private opinions
may be. Politicians can thus try to lure away individuals from
the opposite camp, though conversely they face individual
defections from the ranks of their supporters. Public loyalty
to a "pool" of scholars, if not to individual members of
the pool, is a collective affair, affirmed by specific invitations
to deliver particular sermons. At one level, this would involve the public defection of an entire clan ward from one
"pool" to the other, a possible but relatively unlikely occurrence. On the other hand, this leaves different scholars relatively free to compete with one another for loyalty within,
rather than across, each "pool." In 1972, while the rivalry between "pools" was publicly flaunted, rivalry within "pools"

was much more muted. Even so, any very close association between a politician and one scholar in his "pool" as opposed to others was likely to alienate the other scholars and their most loyal followers, inviting political defections from the ranks.

Given these various considerations and constraints, it is easy to understand why Abou Toure, as a politician, might both be attracted to the new wedding ceremony and unwilling to commit himself too unambiguously to its diffusion. He and his close kin were the first to arrange for the ceremony's performance in and around Korhogo, introducing it to the public at large not only in town but in nearby villages, and involving more distant kin in its performance without obliging them to underwrite the expenses. Were the ceremony to "catch on," he could share the credit with the scholars involved. On the other hand, as long as the orthodoxy of the ceremony was not at issue—and it was not—his participation could be construed as an act of personal piety, perhaps above and beyond the strict call of his religious duties, but certainly not reprehensible. By choosing to set an example, but without pursuing the matter further, he could avoid controversy, particularly within the ranks of his own followers.

When I left the field in 1973, it was my guess that the ceremony would not, in the long run, be generally adopted in Koko. Neither the politician nor the scholars involved had a real interest in pushing the matter too hard, in the reasonable apprehension that such efforts might well prove counterproductive. The performances I witnessed provided occasions to test the waters, to judge the extent to which the ceremony drew a response from audiences—a response that, all told, had to be favorable enough to induce numbers of individuals to incur additional expenses at weddings. When I returned to the field some twelve years later, my guess turned out to be correct. I neither witnessed nor heard about a single performance of the ceremony. Had I not been present in 1972, I would never have been aware that such a ceremony had ever existed.

In the intervening period, a number of factors further militated against the likelihood of the ceremony's adoption. First of all, scholarly rivalries were increasingly divorced from factional party politics. A compromise had been reached concerning *donba* sermons: in alternate years, they were to be delivered by the senior scholar of each pool. In 1972, scholars could be overheard making disparaging remarks about the learning of their colleagues, particularly in the rival pool. In 1984, scholars again and again stressed how impious it was to set oneself up above one's peers. Any public show of disunity was out of the question. Perhaps more important, the issue of "secularism," if not moot, was fading from public attention and the attention of scholars. It was increasingly and painfully clear to a younger generation that Western education was no longer a quasi-automatic passport to wealth, power, and prestige. For such individuals, secularizing ideologies of one variety or another lost much of their appeal. Even civil weddings faded into relative insignificance. The family allowances to which they entitled salaried wage-earners were a drain on the country's already strained budget. It was not even necessary to abolish them, at least in the short run, a move that might be politically unpopular. The government simply neglected to increase the allowances to keep pace with inflation, letting them grow more negligible in real terms from year to year. They ceased to make any appreciable difference in people's earnings, and, consequently, the incentive to register marriages disappeared. In general, the economic prosperity and optimism of the early 1970s had given way to a certain degree of pessimism and belt-tightening by the 1980s, even if the economic outlook was not yet alarming. There seemed little point in incurring added expenses to perform a ceremony to exorcise the specter of a "secularism" that was steadily losing ground all by itself.

This story of a ceremony that never quite "made it" is nonetheless instructive. Discussions of change tend, by and large, to privilege "success stories" of one sort or another. We tend, of necessity, to think of change retrospectively, to compare time A to time B and to record those features that have indeed changed in one way or another, by accretion or deletion. This is often, of course, quite a sensible way of examining change, and frequently the only possible way. Nevertheless, it can sometimes obscure certain facets involved in the process of change, a process I suspect is often one of trial and error. If one considers only those changes that have successfully been adopted, "history" tends to take on an aura of inevitability, with "past" and "present" as two points on a vector leading in a certain direction. Such a teleological view can obscure the obvious fact that changes are often the outcomes of conscious decisions by specific individuals. Such decisions, however, always carry the risk of failure. The circumstances in which individuals fail to institute certain changes tell us as much, in the long run, as the circumstances in which they succeed. The fact that a scholar and a local politician attempted to introduce a new wedding ceremony is perhaps far less remarkable than the fact that, owing to the accidents of circumstance, its brief moment of glory did not escape notice.

7

One Who Knows

One afternoon in Korhogo, while I was visiting a young scholar and friend of mine, I decided to ask him about his colleagues in town. I began by asking him who the other *karamogos* were in the community. I had thought this would be a straightforward question. I would normally translate the Dyula term *karamogo* as "scholar." In my conversations in Dyula until then, this is precisely how I had heard and used the word, without any difficulty in understanding or making myself understood. To my surprise, rather than supplying individual names, my friend began listing entire clan wards in town and in neighboring villages. "Surely," I interrupted, "these people don't all read, write and teach Arabic." "No," answered my friend, "most of them are quite ignorant. A *karamogo* is someone who prays five times a day, abstains from alcohol, fasts during Ramadan, etc. A person who teaches Arabic is called a *lon-ni-baga*." Although this was the first time I had heard the expression, it way easy enough to understand. *Lon* is a transitive verb meaning "to know (something)"; *ni* is a suffix that transforms a verb into a noun; and a *baga* is an individual who typically performs an action or occupation. A *lon-ni-baga* is thus literally a "knowing-person," a "professional knower"; the expression is an apt Dyula translation of the Arabic word *ʿalim*.

The confusion was not simply a question of which specific word or phrase is the appropriate Dyula translation of "scholar" or *ʿalim*. At issue, rather, is the relationship between two different facets of the Dyula notion of scholarship: on one hand, the proper observance of Sunni strictures; on the other, the knowledge and ultimately the ability to teach

the reading and writing of Arabic. Indeed, the proper observance of the *sunna* already implies the possession of a considerable body of knowledge: of prayers in Arabic, of techniques
for ablution, of forbidden and obligatory categories of action.
Beyond this, many Dyula men, both now and in the past, had
and have some knowledge of written Arabic, though the
number of those with the acknowledged capacity to teach has
always been relatively restricted. In one sense, all such individuals are knowledgeable, some more so than others.
Though religious knowledge is obviously on a continuum,
there has always been one means or another in Dyula for expressing the difference between those who pray correctly and
those who also teach. Until relatively recently, it was broadly
true that those who prayed were called *mory*, those who
taught *karamogo*.[1] While *mory* boys typically received some
instruction in Arabic, teachers tended to come from only a
few *mory* clan wards specialized in Arabic learning, the
Diane of Koko quarter in Korhogo or the Haidara of Kadioha,
for example. Although the term *karamogo* was applied most
particularly to individuals who taught at an advanced level, it
could also be used more loosely; for example, it is often said
of members of clan wards specialized in study and teaching
that "they are all *karamogos*," although it is by no means literally the case that they are all teachers, even on a part-time
basis.

The distinction my friend made between the terms *karamogo* and *lon-ni-baga* was thus quite comparable to the older
distinction between *mory* and *karamogo*. Plausibly, as the term
karamogo came to be used more and more loosely, a more specific term for "scholar" was required to take its place. Still,
there are some important differences between this new contrast between *karamogo* and *lon-ni-baga* and the older contrast
between *mory* and *karamogo*. *Mory* status was, it must be remembered, hereditary. A *tun tigi* who prayed five times a
day, fasted during the entire month of Ramadan, abstained
from alcohol, and otherwise observed the canons of piety
with reasonable diligence, was still a *tun tigi*. When, after
World War II, Dyula initiation societies were abandoned and

uniform standards of piety applied throughout the Dyula community, the *mory / tun tigi* distinction ceased to be socially salient. It is probably no accident that the scholar to whom I was talking is in fact of *tun tigi* descent. He cannot claim that he and his entire clan ward are *mory*, but, by calling them all *karamogo*, he can stress that they observe the old *mory* standards of piety. There are even more subtle differences between the older use of the term *karamogo* and the new expression *lon-ni-baga*. Although scholarship was never a hereditary monopoly, it was formerly the hereditary specialization of a restricted number of *mory* families within any community. The formal title of *karamogo*, conferring on its holder the right to teach advanced students, was bestowed by a special ritual of enturbanment (cf. Wilks 1968: 169). However, an individual's learning was only one of the factors taken into account in deciding whether and when he should be enturbaned. His age, and whether or not he was a member of a kin group with a hereditary specialization in scholarship, were also critically important. Senior men were, and still are, more readily enturbaned than younger men (who might well be more learned), particularly if the latter were not from families with a special reputation for scholarship. This was indeed the case of my friend who, at the age of about forty, was awarded the imamship of one of Korhogo's daily mosques, but who was still considered too young for enturbanment. Not surprisingly, by identifying himself as a *lon-ni-baga*, he was proposing a view of "scholarship" that stressed knowledge alone, without reference to age or social origins.

It would be misleading, of course, to assume on the basis of one conversation that seniority and social origins are no longer relevant to contemporary Dyula notions of "scholarship." Specialized clan wards still continue to produce scholars, though scholars from such wards do not necessarily enjoy an enhanced reputation as compared with their colleagues from nonscholarly families. Seniority is even more important for governing protocol among scholars, at least in certain contexts. Nevertheless, when I raised the issue of scholarship, either with scholars or with ordinary individuals, the conversation almost inevitably turned to the question of "knowledge." Ultimately, a scholar should be judged in terms of what he knows. One lauds a scholar by saying that "he really knows things"; one disparages his reputation by insinuating that "he really doesn't know very much." For certain specific purposes, the seniority and social origins of scholars largely determine to which specific scholar Dyula will turn for services. These criteria are paramount in contexts where scholars are needed to perform a public role. In private contexts, however, such considerations are secondary, and individuals will seek out and follow the counsels of those scholars whom they believe "know" most.

The principle that one scholar "knows" more or less than another might seem relatively straightforward. In fact, any attempt to apply such a principle raises two fundamental and difficult questions: first, what exactly is meant by "knowledge"; and second, how is the "knowledge" of particular individuals assessed?

The kind of knowledge scholars possess falls into two distinct categories: *bayani karamogoya* and *siru* or *siri karamogoya*. Previously, I have glossed these domains as "theology" and "magic" respectively (Launay 1982: 39); with hindsight, I feel this is a crude and somewhat misleading translation. The knowledge of *bayani karamogoya* belongs essentially to the public domain; *siru karamogoya* is private and generally secret.[2] *Bayani karamogoya* is connected with "education," both in a broad and a narrow sense, and specifically with the idea of *kalan*. Like all key words, *kalan* has a variety of distinct, if closely associated, meanings. It is almost certainly derived from the Arabic verb *qar'a*, "to recite," the root from which the name of the Qur'an is derived. The Manding word *karamogo* is thus a slight deformation of *kalan mogo*, a "*kalan* person, one who does *kalan*." *Kalan* means, in the first instance, "to read" or "to recite aloud from a written text." The notion of oral recitation and indeed of psalmody—Arabic texts all have associated melodies—was intimately connected with the very idea of "reading" until very recently, when a very different paradigm of reading was introduced with Western schooling. Young boys were taught to recite texts aloud with accuracy well before—if ever—they learned their meaning. During certain ceremonies—the recitation of "*salatu*" at funerals, the recitation of the sura Ya Sin before moving into a new house—pages of a text will be distributed to all members of the audience capable of reciting, who will do so simultaneously. In this way, the entire book of *salatu* is "read" in a few minutes. Not surprisingly, *kalan* also means "to study," specifically by means of books; Western schooling is unambiguously classed as a form of *kalan*. A teacher, either of Arabic or in Western schools, is a *kalan fa* or *karamogo fa*, literally a "*kalan* father" or "*karamogo* father"; a pupil is, logically enough (and quite regardless of age), a *kalan den*, a "*kalan* child." Finally, *kalan* includes the extemporized sermons or homilies in the vernacular that are part of funerals and of calendar holidays, even though these "recitations" are only indirectly derived from books.

Bayani karamogoya is, in large measure, the practice of *kalan* in one form or another. It includes study in the Arabic language and in religious doctrine from the most elementary to the most advanced levels. Beyond the transmission of knowledge from teacher to pupil, *bayani karamogoya* involves its dissemination to the community at large, both in the form of sermons and as advice to individuals who seek clarification of specific issues. Undoubtedly the most important, although not the only, part of *bayani karamogoya* is knowledge of the proper performance of one's religious duties: what must or should one do, what mustn't or shouldn't one do, as a devout Muslim? It is a scholar's duty to convey this knowledge to all who seek it (and from time to time to some who don't). Such knowledge may be sought privately by individuals who want to know their religious obligations in specific circumstances—for example, to determine how much *zakat* they should distribute. Even so, such knowledge exists and is used for everyone's welfare. *Siru karamogoya*, on the other hand, is knowledge applied to the pursuit of essentially private and this-worldly ends: health, wealth, power, success. *Bayani karamogoya* is essentially moral knowledge, *siru karamogoya* amoral; its test is whether or not it is ultimately efficacious. The ends it seeks to achieve may be legitimate or they may be reprehensible. Of course, a morally worthy scholar must refrain from ever using such knowledge for evil purposes, but it is generally recognized that unspecified individuals willingly use this knowledge to harm rather than to help. *Siru karamogoya* encompasses a variety of techniques: the manufacture of written amulets (*sebe*); preparation of a mixture of ink and water (*nasi ji*) from formulae washed off writing boards, which is subsequently ingested; determination of lucky and unlucky days for specific undertakings.

These two forms of knowledge also differ in the rules governing their transmission and in the ways in which scholars are rewarded for their services. The acquisition of *bayani karamogoya* is invariably tied to the context of the teacher / pupil (*karamkoko fa / karamogo den*) relationship. At any one time, a student has one and only one acknowledged teacher, whose pupil he remains until he has completed his course of study, however long this may take. This is true for elementary study, until the pupil has successfully "put down the Qur'an" (*kurana jigi*), a process generally repeated several times if he wishes to pursue his studies; and with advanced study, ultimately leading to enturbanment. Students may seek a new teacher for advanced study, but otherwise the teacher/pupil relationship is an enduring—indeed lifelong— bond. The relationship is ultimately embodied in the *isnad*, the chain of learning, which the student receives upon his enturbanment, linking him to his teacher and his teacher's teacher, all the way back to the Prophet and then up the hierarchy of angels to God, the ultimate source of knowledge. In this way, *bayani karamogoya* is effectively conceptualized as a unitary body of knowledge. Individual scholars differ, not so much in the specifics of "what" they know, but in how well they have mastered it. By contrast, *siru karamogoya* is piecemeal knowledge. There are no acknowledged teachers of such information. Individuals acquire bits of knowledge from whomever is willing to impart it, eclectically and unsystematically. Teachers of *bayani karamogoya* can and do transmit some of their knowledge of *siru karamogoya* to their pupils, although they are under no obligation to do so. It is a moral obligation to transmit knowledge of *bayani karamogoya* to all who seek it; knowledge of *siru karamogoya* can legitimately be withheld at one's discretion. Teachers and advanced students of *bayani karamogoya* are presumed to know a good deal of *siru karamogoya*. However, such knowledge is available to anyone with a reasonable mastery of written Arabic, and so individuals with mediocre teaching credentials or indeed none at all may have a reputation for being highly versed in *siru karamogoya*.

Ideally, and to a large extent in practice, *bayani karamogoya* does not involve fees for services. In Korhogo, it is increasingly the case that elementary Arabic language and religious instruction is dispensed in schools modeled after the formal state school system, with grade levels, classrooms, tuition fees, and (in principle) salaried instructors. This, it should be noted, is a very recent innovation, and does not apply at all to advanced study. Scholars also received a modest, but by no means negligible, fee for delivering funeral sermons. However, the income scholars derive from *bayani karamogoya* is largely in the form of gifts: from students and their families, from members of the audience at a sermon, from individuals who have benefited from their counsel, and in general from those who seek religious merit through pious donations. In other words, it is a religious obligation of scholars to impart such knowledge as a free gift to all who seek it, and an act of piety to reward this most valuable of gifts as best one can. *Siru karamogoya*, on the other hand, is involved in outright commercial transactions. One pays, not only for the services of the expert practitioner, but also for any specific bit of knowledge that one seeks to acquire. Such knowledge can also, of course, be transmitted as a free gift—from teacher to pupil, in particular—but such gifts are specific favors rather than a general moral obligation.

Bayani karamogoya and *siru karamogoya* thus have two distinct, if largely overlapping, sets of practitioners, as well as two distinct (though also overlapping) clienteles. Most obviously, *bayani karamogoya* is of interest to Muslims only (if one discounts anthropologists and their ilk); *siru karamogoya* is of service to anyone, Muslim or not, willing to pay for it. Precisely because *siru karamogoya* is essentially a private affair, the clientele of any particular practitioner is likely to be eclectic. Indeed, people may well prefer to consult practitioners with whom they have no other social ties. Thus one scholar, who practices *bayani karamogoya* for the most part in Korhogo, would from time to time tour southern Côte d'Ivoire selling amulets and remedies when he was short of cash. All in all, virtually anyone is a potential client, and it is both easier and more lucrative to develop a reputation outside rather than inside the local community. One's reputation in *bayani karamogoya*, on the other hand, is established first and foremost at home. For most purposes—delivering a funeral sermon, giving advice on religious matters, teaching one's children the rudiments of Arabic—any reasonably reputable scholar in the neighborhood is up to the task. Ultimately, scholars may develop a reputation in *bayani karamogoya* that goes beyond their own community. These are the scholars under whom advanced students seek to study. They may from time to time visit Korhogo, where they will be treated with more deference than most local scholars, and individuals may take advantage of the opportunity to solicit advice or to attend any sermons such a scholar may deliver. Such sermons are now available on cassette tapes, readily purchased in the local marketplace. Moreover, scholars from other communities who are not well known by name may also pass through Korhogo, delivering a sermon or two, which local residents may happen to attend. In short, because *bayani karamogoya* is a public affair, individual Dyula in Koko can easily compare their local scholars, not only one with another, but also with scholars from outside the community, both well known and unknown. By consulting scholars on religious matters and listening to their sermons, anyone in Koko has at least some basis for assessing their knowledge of *bayani karamogoya* as compared to their colleagues'. Because of the very nature of *siru karamogoya*, this kind of comparison is impossible; individuals' reputations in this domain are effectively a matter of hearsay.

For both *siru* and *bayani karamogoya*, it can be said that one scholar "knows" more than another. However, the implications of such a statement are quite different for each domain in determining how scholars are perceived in their own community. Dyula from Koko will readily seek the services of a practitioner of *siru karamogoya* outside the community, but practitioners within the community will just as readily attract clients from elsewhere. For *bayani karamogoya*, people generally seek the services of a scholar from within their community. Consequently, a relatively limited number of local scholars are constantly being compared one with another.

It stands to reason that scholars themselves are the best qualified and most likely to make such comparisons. Collectively, they "know" more than ordinary individuals and are in a position to judge who amongst them "knows" more than whom. Indeed, this is an issue with which they must concern themselves, since a scholar's professional reputation rests on the perception that he "knows" more than his colleagues. One might well expect scholars to claim outright that they do "know" more than certain other colleagues, but this is not the case. On the contrary, scholars are particularly loath to rank themselves with respect to their peers, or even to compare other scholars one to another. This aversion to ranking is by no means a sign of a sense of corporate solidarity among scholars, but rather a function of proper norms of Muslim behavior, which the scholars themselves proclaim to their audiences. Both in sermons and in conversations, scholars constantly warn against *yere fo* and *yere bonya* (literally "to speak oneself" and "to aggrandize oneself"), the sins of pride and boasting. It is the essence of *yere bonya* to consider oneself better than one's neighbor, and the essence of *yere fo* to say so. Scholars are expected to set an example for the community, to practice what they preach. Boasting about how much they "know" compared to others would thus endanger rather than enhance their reputations. For example, my friend who identified himself as a *lon-ni-baga* was quite unwilling to state outright that he "knew" more than any of his colleagues in Korhogo. He readily admitted that certain particular scholars had nothing to teach him—in other words, that they were not his superiors and implicitly his equals at best. In this way, he could insinuate that he had a limited respect for their scholarship, but this was as far as he would go in ranking them. Of course, his professionally imposed modesty did not prevent him from naming individuals whose scholarship was superior to his own. He named his own teacher, of course, a scholar well known in Korhogo but from outside the community and based in another town; within Korhogo, he specifically cited the imam, as well as the Diane clan ward, traditionally specialized in Islamic learning, as a whole. Even this list of intellectual superiors cannot be taken at face value. The reputation of the Diane as scholars in Koko was far more brilliant in the past than it is nowadays. Indeed, when I mentioned my friend's remarks to several Diane elders, they chuckled. With the professional modesty appropriate to scholars, they explained that my friend had learned the Qur'an from the Diane. Although he pursued his studies with a more illustrious scholar, the Diane remained his "teachers" for life. As their pupil, it was his duty to acknowledge them as his intellectual superiors. Plausibly, the imam was also named out of deference to his position rather than out of respect for his "knowledge." The imamship of Korhogo's Friday mosque is the property of one clan ward in Koko, shared with one of its "stranger" wards. Succession to the office of Friday imam is determined in much the same manner as succession to chieftainships or to headships of clan wards, in strict order of seniority. Women and *worossos* (individuals of slave status descended on both sides from slaves) are excluded. Among men of free status, seniority depends on one's generation and one's relative age within that generation. Of course, the imamship, unlike other offices, entails certain qualifications—namely, one must be an enturbaned *karamogo*. The imam is always the senior recognized scholar in the two wards. Thus in 1984, the imam of Korhogo had first, second, and third assistants—the next three individuals in order of succession to the office. This system not only very efficiently precludes any factional strife over succession to the office, but also allows individuals with relatively modest reputations as scholars to accede. Indeed, the imam's reputation for "knowledge," voiced deferentially by my scholarly friend, was by no means universally echoed throughout the Dyula community of Koko. In short, scholars in Koko are precluded from disparaging their colleagues and enjoined to express deference to current and former teachers and to certain established senior scholars. In either case, while they can (and do) cast oblique aspersions on one another's competence, they cannot openly rank one another in terms of their "knowledge."

In a similar vein, scholars avoid openly confronting one another, and indeed engaging in polemics of almost any kind. This avoidance extends to written polemics. Koko's scholars do not attempt to justify their ideas, one way or another, in writing. Conceivably, this aversion to polemics is characteristic of the Suwarian tradition, which emphasizes the oral transmission of learning from teacher to pupil, the personalized bond whose ultimate expression is the *isnad*. Until the relatively recent introduction of public sermonizing—and indeed in large measure even now—the knowledge of scholars was transmitted privately and directly to those individuals who expressly sought it out, either as students on a regular basis, or occasionally in order to clarify a particular issue of concern. Discussion of religious issues, not only between scholars and laymen but even between scholars themselves, was inevitably tinged with a hierarchical component; one individual was always seeking clarification from another who, even if not one's teacher, was acknowledged to "know more."

These rules of discourse had a number of important consequences. First of all, the nature and perhaps even the content of religious discourse was highly context ridden; the kind of explanation or justification given would depend on who was speaking to whom. "The Qur'an says this" or "According to *hadith* . . . ," laymen would often be told, referring them, in general terms, to the authority of a text or body of texts. One scholar, speaking to a junior scholar or an advanced student, might be more specific, citing—literally *reciting*—a specific passage in Arabic (these texts, it should be noted, were committed to memory). In neither case was it possible to divorce the authority of the text from the authority of the scholar. Discourse was doubly authoritative, as it were. One could not challenge the authority of the statement without directly challenging the authority of the scholar, not only on this particular issue but in a general way. One could, of course, if one were unconvinced, consult some other scholar in private. However, this elaborate protocol served— and in many respects continues to serve—to keep certain religious issues outside the arena of public debate, not only spoken but written.

Even the practice of delivering public sermons has not fundamentally altered these rules. Whatever else the audience may expect from sermons, as we shall see later in this chapter, they are definitely not supposed to be "controversial." Only the Wahhabis, by directly challenging the authority of the scholars, have managed to force them into a polemical stance. This challenge ultimately played into the hands of the scholars, furnishing them with an argument against the Wahhabis. By refusing to accept the scholars' authority, the Wahhabis were effectively claiming to "know more" than *karamogos* past and present; by rejecting the Maliki mode of prayer, the Wahhabis implicitly dismissed, not only the Suwarian, but virtually all West African traditions of Islamic learning. Yet, individually, the Wahhabis were not necessarily very learned in Arabic. The Wahhabis might claim to possess a better understanding of the faith, but not a fuller knowledge of the texts. As we have seen, a younger generation of scholars trained in the Middle East can now make such a claim, but for the most part these scholars have astutely avoided openly challenging their Suwarian seniors. In spite of the real divergences of religious sensibilities, if not

points of view, which we have seen in chapters 4 and 5, virtually everyone in Koko appears—at least in public—to acknowledge the principles of seniority governing social interactions within the quarter, which maintain at least the
apparent authority of the Suwarian scholars.

Of course, it is not because scholars avoid disputing one
another in public, or even ranking one another in private,
that laymen have no grounds for forming opinions about
them.[3] Indeed, laymen are free to express their opinions
about the relative merits of particular scholars without exposing themselves to the criticism that they are guilty of *yere fo* or
yere bonya, boasting or pride. The result is something of a par-
adox: while scholars are professionally qualified to judge
who "knows" more then whom, only laymen will freely express opinions on the issue. Privately, laymen in Koko
tended to judge local scholars rather harshly. No scholar from
Koko, and indeed none from Korhogo town as a whole, enjoyed a reputation for *bayani karamogoya* that extended very
far beyond the bounds of Korhogo and surrounding villages.
They were compared unfavorably with scholars who had
managed to establish a national reputation. Most such scholars were based in Abidjan or in prosperous towns to the
south, such as Bouake, Daloa, or Gagnoa, but there were also
a few who continued to practice in their home communities, small towns or even villages of northern or central Côte
d'Ivoire. Compared to such scholars, local *karamogos*, I was
told, did not really "know" very much. Even so, it was clear
to virtually everyone that some local scholars knew more
than others. No clear pattern emerged from individual
statements of preference. Some scholars—the imam, for example—were rarely if ever cited by laymen as comparatively
learned. Ties of kinship, clanship, and personal friendship
on one hand, and factional rivalries within the community on
the other, tended to predispose individuals for or against particular scholars, but though choices might be biased, they
were hardly predetermined. Laymen were often quite critical
of scholars to whom they were socially "close" and sometimes (more rarely) grudgingly admired scholars with whom
they or their kin did not get along very well. But if laymen

readily venture opinions about how much or little any particular scholar really "knows," it is far more difficult to elicit the
specific criteria by which they reach such conclusions. A layman's statement about how much a specific scholar "knows"
is simply another way of saying how highly he respects him
professionally.

Even if the criteria for making such judgments are hope-
lessly vague, one cannot conclude that such opinions are entirely arbitrary and capricious. Since a scholar's reputation
for *bayani karamogoya* is a matter of concern in the public domain, individual laymen are aware of one another's opinions
and take these into account. Even in the absence of clear consensus, a scholar's overall reputation can by no means be reduced to a series of isolated individual opinions. Indeed, the
tendency of laymen in Koko to disparage local scholars is
largely a reflection of scholars' national reputations, or at
least their reputations outside their home communities. Implicitly, such reputations do take into account the judgments
of other scholars as well as of laymen. The teacher/pupil relationship, specifically at the level of advanced study, serves
as a rough index of such judgments. It is a striking fact that
the teachers of scholars, not only in Koko but in Korhogo as
a whole, virtually all come from and practice in other communities, particularly the towns in the south of Côte d'Ivoire.
Scholars in Korhogo, however, do not generally attract such
students, even from villages in northern Côte d'Ivoire.[4] In
other words, aspiring scholars will seek out the most learned
scholars to whom to apprentice themselves, and it is no secret that they will not come to Korhogo for this purpose.
Scholars who succeed in attracting advanced pupils are thus
implicitly more learned than those who, like the local scholars of Koko, do not. There are, however, other ways in which
the names and reputations of scholars from elsewhere come
to the attention of laymen in Koko. Given the numbers of
Dyula from Koko who have emigrated permanently or temporarily to other communities (Launay 1982: 97–101), such
reputations spread easily by word of mouth. In any case,
Dyula in Koko have always been aware of the reputations of

scholars in other communities, if on a rather more limited scale. At the other extreme, mass media and especially television have very recently become influential. There is a weekly program on national television that discusses Muslim religious issues, and the appearance of a scholar on the program immediately brings him to the attention of a national audience. Finally, tapes of scholars' sermons are readily available in marketplaces throughout Côte d'Ivoire, along with pirated tapes of popular music and tapes of local traditional music. Such tapes are of commercial value only if the scholar has a wide extra-local reputation. The commercial availability of a particular scholar's taped sermons is thus both an index of his national reputation and a means of expanding it. While tapes of sermons by scholars from Koko circulate privately in Korhogo, there is no market for them—proof, if it were needed, that they have no national reputation.

Nationally known scholars thus constitute one yardstick for measuring how much local scholars do or do not "know." Some of these nationally known scholars are personally familiar to various individuals in or from Korhogo, and indeed they visit Korhogo from time to time. It confers considerable prestige on a family to invite such a scholar to deliver a funeral sermon, but such prestige is an expensive luxury. This is not to say that such a scholar necessarily charges highly for his services, in the literal sense of the word; scholars are not supposed to "charge" for *bayani karamogoya* at all. However, to invite such a scholar without receiving him lavishly would expose one to ridicule and would be utterly self-defeating. Only the wealthiest and most politically ambitious members of the community are willing to go to such lengths, and even so, they hardly stand to lose face when, as is usually the case, they resort to the services of a local scholar.

Funeral sermons are nowadays the most public way in which individuals use the services of scholars. A sermon is virtually obligatory at the funeral of any reasonably senior member of the community, man or woman. There is no hard and fast rule for determining exactly how old a person must be to merit a sermon. Anyone with grown children or who has reached about age fifty qualifies, though younger individuals with kinsmen who can afford the expense are often thus commemorated. Generally, these sermons are delivered on the fortieth day after the burial.[5] Additional sermons may also be given on the first, third, or seventh days after burial, or one year afterward. Alternatively, two or more different scholars may give sermons on successive nights. Again, there is no hard and fast rule, but the more senior and prominent the deceased, the more elaborate the commemoration tends to be. Wealthy members of the community may vie for prestige either by arranging sermons for deceased close junior kinsmen or by underwriting elaborate ceremonies for prestigious elders with whom they have had close ties, but who were more distantly related.

At one level, then, funeral sermons, as part of funeral ceremonies in general, serve to express both the status of the deceased and of those, be they close kin, distant kin, or "patrons," responsible for financing the arrangements. For scholars, on the other hand, sermons represent the primary occasion where they can both convey and display their specialized knowledge to the public at large. Of course, it would be both unnecessarily cynical and patently unfair to suggest that scholars are exclusively concerned on such occasions with projecting an image of knowledgeability. A scholar's life is by no means an easy or indeed an assured path to financial success, and those who choose it do so from deeply religious motives and not for venial reasons. A scholar's first concern in his sermons is indeed to convey proper ideals of Muslim conduct to his audience. However, a scholar can only convey such a message if he finds people to listen, and if he is taken seriously. Consequently, he must compete for this respect in an arena occupied first and foremost by his local colleagues. Thus sermons provide the means, not only for scholars to inform the lay public about Islam, but also for laymen to judge the performance, and by implication the "knowledge," of different scholars.

The task is made somewhat easier in that for the lay public, sermons represent a form of entertainment as well as of instruction. They are major social gatherings, events that break the routine of everyday life. Refreshments, in certain cases lavish ones, are distributed to the audience. Most of all, the sermon itself is a performance, a deliberately staged occurrence, with its own definite aesthetics. Although attendance is sometimes a social obligation, many laymen enjoy listening to sermons, not only when they are delivered but also on cassette recordings. It is not unusual at all to find as many as six or seven cassette recorders taping any particular sermon in Koko. As mentioned above, taped sermons by local scholars are not sold in the marketplace, but they are stored in numerous personal libraries and freely lent out to interested listeners. It is impossible unambiguously to distinguish the value of such tapes as entertainment from their value as a means of religious instruction for pious laymen. For example, one friend of mine would regularly purchase such a tape to play in his car as he was driving to the capital, much, he commented, as his son would purchase a tape of current "pop" music. The tape constituted a welcome distraction from the tedium of a long drive, with the added bonus that it was morally edifying. This is not to say that the medium had effectively replaced the message. Rather, for pious Muslims, sermons are the most worthwhile form of entertainment because of the valuable "knowledge" they contain.

Most scholars are consequently eager to deliver sermons, not only at funerals but on any other occasion. This includes certain dates in the Muslim annual calendar, notably *donba* (Arabic *mawlud*), *kurubi den* (Arabic *laylat-al-saghir*) and *kurubi ba* (Arabic *laylat-al-kabir*). As we have seen, there was even an attempt to introduce sermons as a part of wedding ceremonies. Of course, scholars are free to deliver sermons whenever they please, or on no particular occasion at all. However, there are good reasons why most local scholars avoid doing so. Since no one is obliged to attend, they have no assurance of a large audience, and would stand to lose face if turnout were small. A scholar invited to deliver a sermon not only receives some sort of fee but also attracts pious donations of *saraka* from members of the audience; such donations may be far from negligible if different groups and individuals attempt to outdo one another in public displays of generosity and piety. If, however, the sermon is delivered on no special occasion, there is no recognized incentive for ostentation on the part of the audience, and the scholar risks leaving empty-handed for his pains. Consequently, uninvited sermons tend to be delivered by scholars from outside the community. An unknown scholar passing through risks nothing but his time, since he has no prior local reputation to maintain or enhance. A nationally known scholar on a visit to Korhogo may also deliver an uninvited sermon, but this is an "event" of some note, and he can count on a heavy turnout and consequently a more generous audience. There was only one partial exception to this rule. This was a Hausa scholar, born in Burkina Faso and with close family ties to a Hausa family established in Koko since the early twentieth century. This man would regularly spend much of the year in Koko, when he would often deliver uninvited sermons in the evening outside the main mosque. The turnout tended to be modest, though large enough to attract notice and avoid ridicule. However, the audience consisted mostly of young men and women, unmarried or recently married, who tended to be considered more pious and in general more "serious" than their age mates. Elders, who are supposed to have more serious business, rarely attended. Members of the audience were seldom in a financial position to be generous. Even if they were, they were too young to engage appropriately in ostentatious displays of generosity, the behavior one expects from "elders" rather than from "children." In short, this scholar had one foot—but only one—in the Koko community; for example, he was never to my knowledge invited to deliver funeral sermons in Koko. His sermons at the mosque were thus a means, though not a directly remunerative one, of maintaining an active presence in the community, though this presence was still largely that of an outsider.

Since local scholars rely essentially on invitations to deliver sermons, the question of how scholars are ultimately chosen for specific occasions is critical. Technically, the individuals responsible for the funeral arrangements are free to choose any scholar they please. However, while no individual scholar is certain of being automatically selected on any particular occasion, choices tend to be quite constrained, and the outcome is rarely a surprise. As mentioned in chapter 6, there are two pools of scholars in Koko, each with its separate constituency. These constituencies consist of entire clan wards; each clan ward usually resorts to the services of scholars in one or the other pool. Within each pool, a number of other factors enter into the consideration. On one hand, scholars never deliver sermons at the funerals of their close kin. On the other hand, there is a preference for scholars with more distant ties of kinship to the deceased, particularly but not exclusively a member of the deceased's own clan ward. Not atypically among the Dyula, questions of seniority are even more important than the nature of the scholar's kinship to the deceased. Paradoxically, norms of seniority as they are applied to sermonizing are ambivalent. On one hand, seniors should take precedence over juniors. On the other hand, senior elders ought ideally to avoid engaging in strenuous activities that their juniors should perform on their behalf. Delivering sermons is strenuous, so that in principle the oldest and most senior scholars should refrain from giving them, although middle-aged scholars ought to be preferred over younger ones and "free" scholars (*horon*) over *worossos* of slave status. It should be remembered, however, that funeral sermons are a relatively recent phenomenon among the Dyula of Koko. The eldest generation of scholars, people like the current imam, were never very actively involved in sermonizing, while scholars who are now middle-aged were the first to take the initiative and have always been active in this domain. In a sense, it is very convenient for senior scholars who were never very good at sermons to argue that they are too old now for that sort of thing. The problem is rather that middle-aged scholars seem quite reluctant to renounce their prerogatives of seniority now that they are approaching fuller elderhood, particularly as these are precisely the individuals most in demand and for whom sermons are consequently the most financially rewarding. For the time being, senior scholars in each pool expect to be offered the first opportunity, passing on the request to their juniors only if they cannot for one reason or another preside. If, for example, two sermons are held the same evening, they are likely to accept the one that can be expected to attract a larger audience and leave the other to their junior.

This protocol, while it constrains choice, is not a hard and fast rule. In any case, the funerals of important elders—which are precisely those with the largest audiences, and where scholars receive the most lavish prestations—frequently involve the delivery of two or even more sermons on different nights. In such cases, it is perfectly possible to invite the senior scholar in one's habitual pool on one occasion and a more junior scholar whom one prefers personally and/or whom one considers actually more "knowledgeable," or even a scholar from outside the pool entirely, on another. The protocol is fairly consistently respected in this way, but outright lapses do occur, and they inevitably incur resentment. For example, on the occasion of the fortieth-day ceremonies held for the mother of one scholar, his colleague, the senior scholar in his pool, cut short a visit to southern Côte d'Ivoire in order to return to Korhogo to deliver the sermon. To his chagrin, he found that yet a third scholar had been invited in his stead. This third scholar, a native of a nearby Dyula village, was established elsewhere in Korhogo. Since the Dyula of Koko maintain close ties with Dyula in all the villages of the region, he was personally quite well known in Koko. However, his regular clientele hailed from outside Koko quarter, where he rarely preached. Dyula of Koko were admittedly familiar with his sermons, not to mention his overall reputation as a scholar, since they are frequently invited to funerals in other parts of town or in neighboring villages, where he more usually preaches. For a while, the incident caused considerable bitterness, and the scholar who had been passed over complained quite openly about what he felt to be a public and unprovoked rebuff. He was able to save face to some extent because he had also been invited to deliver a sermon that same night in another part of town, though this was a much smaller (and certainly less lucrative) affair. He had originally intended to pass on this second commission to a junior scholar in his pool, but in the end the junior scholar was left without any sermon to deliver.

Given this protocol, the frequency with which individuals are invited to deliver sermons in Koko is not a reliable indication of their overall reputation for "knowledge." This is not to say that the personal preferences and opinions of groups and individuals responsible for specific invitations are absolutely irrelevant. If they have strong feelings, they may attempt to bend the rules or manipulate the situation in such a way that they can invite the scholar they really want. However, unless they are deliberately seeking to express their displeasure with a particular scholar, they must proceed with tact or else run the risk of inadvertently giving offense. Funeral sermons are in any case a frequent event, and though scholars from outside are rarely invited to deliver them in Koko, it is not unusual for scholars from Koko to be invited to other parts of town where social networks are more fluid and where protocol is less an issue, as well as to villages nearby, where the reputations of scholars from town may eclipse those of their village colleagues much as the reputations of nationally known scholars eclipse those of Koko's scholars. Similarly, the social networks of laymen in Koko, particularly of elders whose opinion in such matters counts most, extend well beyond the confines of the quarter, so that they are frequently invited to funerals elsewhere. In this way, quite apart from their knowledge of sermons on tape, laymen from Koko have ample opportunity to attend and to judge sermons by all local scholars, even those more junior scholars who are less frequently invited to deliver them in Koko, and to compare them to sermons delivered by village scholars, as well as scholars based elsewhere in town.

Scholars are well aware that their sermons are compared with those of their colleagues, and that laymen's reactions affect not only their overall reputations but more directly the likelihood that they will receive subsequent invitations, either from other neighborhoods in town or even, despite protocol, from Koko itself. After all, one may decline to invite a scholar both because he is too junior or because he is too senior. Ultimately, rules of protocol apply only in choosing between scholars with reputations as "regulars"—those who are routinely associated with delivering sermons in Koko. I knew many individual scholars who, it was widely acknowledged, were qualified to deliver sermons, but who were rarely, if ever, invited to do so. One, for example, had the unenviable reputation of putting any audience to sleep.

Crucial as the sermons are in determining a scholar's reputation, the task of delivering a successful one is difficult indeed. This is precisely because of the dual nature of sermons, as a form of entertainment and as a means of edification. A scholar thus needs to accomplish two quite different, and sometimes conflicting, goals: to hold his audience's attention, and to convey an image of "knowledgeability." (The sermons, it should be noted, although falling under the rubric of *kalan*—which includes the activities of "reading," "recitation," and "study"—are always freely extemporized.) This is in sharp contrast to the *khutba* the imam recites in Arabic from a book of collected homilies as part of the midday Friday prayers. No one, to my knowledge, ever pays much, if any, attention to *khutba*.[6] Sermons do not necessarily, or even usually, have a single set subject. Not surprisingly, funeral sermons often dwell on the afterlife and specifically on the subject of *kiyama lon*, the day of judgment. This generally entails a discussion of various things Muslims must or must not do in order to avoid a prolonged or, worse, permanent sojourn in the fires of hell (*jahanama*). In any case, since virtually all human actions will fall under divine scrutiny, this gives scholars wide latitude to dwell on whatever they please, and either to touch on a few subjects in detail or to embark on a grand tour of human failings. Although catalogues of do's and don'ts of various kinds, ranging from lists of mortal sins to those of impurities that render water ritually unfit for ablutions, are included in virtually every sermon, scholars are free to touch on any topic having to do with Islam in one way or another. The sermons are subjected to constant interruptions. This is far less the case now than in the past, when they sometimes lasted all night. Nowadays, members of the audience are anxious that they end before midnight, partly out of increased concern over bands of armed thugs (and overzealous policemen out looking for armed thugs), partly because more and more individuals hold salaried jobs and must report to work the next morning. Even so, at any moment, either the scholar himself or any member of the audience with sufficient learning may break out into chanting pious songs in Arabic or, occasionally, in Dyula. The scholar himself is likely to choose to chant when he has exhausted a particular train of thought, thus allowing himself the time to decide what he will discuss next. On the other hand, chanting by members of the audience generally interrupts the flow of the sermon. After any such interruption, the scholar may either pick up the discussion where he left off, or embark on a new subject. I suspect that scholars frequently embark upon the second course because, taken by surprise, they have lost track themselves. As a result of such interruptions, scholars frequently begin to discuss one subject and suddenly go off on a tangent, returning to the original subject if and when they remember what it is and where they left off. The scholar must always appear in total command of the situation, ready to continue with a steady flow of discourse until the next interruption. At times, to keep up appearances, scholars will repeat themselves or alternatively seem to lose the entire logical thread of their own argument until they can pick up some—any—other such thread and keep the sermon flowing. In short, they must be prepared from time to time to sacrifice coherence for eloquence and, above all, poise.

Needless to say, sermons cannot simultaneously be incoherent, entertaining, and edifying. Given the mode of presentation, the various parts of a sermon rarely if ever fit together as a unified whole. However, even the most patient and sympathetic of audiences will lose interest if they cannot follow what the scholar is talking about at any given time, and neither are they likely to be impressed in such cases with a scholar's "knowledge." One way in which scholars frequently deal with this problem is to introduce narratives into their sermons. On one hand, a story constitutes a ready-made guide for the scholar. Once the story is begun, the plot line determines what comes next. The scholar does not have to make the choice for himself, much less remember his own prior decision in the face of constant interruptions. As long as he can remember where he left off after any given interruption, he can easily continue without much reflection. Moreover, a good story, well told, immediately enhances the sermon as entertainment. A scholar who happens to be a good storyteller possesses a quasi-infallible device for maintaining the attention of his audience. Indeed, because of the interruptions, he can always conveniently launch into a story at almost any point in the sermon, either because he feels he is in danger of losing his audience or simply because he is not quite sure what he wants to say next.

Stories give coherence and entertainment value to sermons, but it is not always equally clear that they are very edifying. Parables are an obvious solution to this dilemma. They simultaneously contain a clear moral lesson and permit the scholar to display his skills as a storyteller. The problem with parables is that, like jokes, the best ones tend to be short and to the point. They provide scholars with only a brief respite from their problems of deciding what comes next and of how to keep their audience awake and alert. Longer stories not only solve such problems more effectively, they also hold the audience's attention over a longer period of time. Indeed, one scholar makes a regular practice of telling stories about patriarchs and prophets: Nuhu (Noah), Ibrahim (Abraham), Sulaiman (Solomon), Isa (Jesus), and so on. Such stories can turn into virtual theatrical performances, as the scholar impersonates one character after another. In some cases, clear moral messages are embodied in these incidents from the lives of the prophets, as, for example, in Ibrahim's destruction of the idols. However, I also heard sermons that told of incidents where the behavior of the central character was far from above reproach: Ya'qub's (Jacob's) theft of his brother's blessing through trickery; Dauda's (David's) adulterous relationship with Bathsheba. In each case, the scholar still proceeded to draw a moral at the end of the story. Ya'qub's story was interpreted as a demonstration of the importance of being a dutiful child in order to obtain the powerful blessings of one's family elders; Sulaiman, Bathsheba's son, was God's favorite among all of Dauda's children, showing that one cannot predict which of a man's wives will bear the most worthy children. Unlike parables, these morals hardly followed very obviously from the story itself. In fact, such morals seem to function as a pretext, an additional justification for the story's inclusion in the sermon.

Narratives are not the only means of making a sermon as entertaining as possible. Scholars often include deliberate humor in their sermons. This can be combined with storytelling when a scholar impersonates one character or another. Characters, even prophets, can be turned into temporary laughingstocks, as, for example, when an old and blind Ishaq (Isaac) slowly comes to the realization that he has been tricked into bestowing his best blessing on the wrong son. It is also possible for a scholar to use similar impersonations outside the context of a narrative. One scholar would lapse into pidgin French for comic effect in order to imitate the sinful ways of urban sophisticates: a prospective client trying to attract the attentions of a prostitute, or a thief caught red-handed with stolen goods. The most unlikely subjects in sermons may serve as the subjects of jokes. One scholar, after a very long list of substances that do or do not render water impure for ritual purposes, concluded by admonishing the audience with mock seriousness that they should never leave it lying around unattended; what if dogs or little children were to piss in it? (I should add, lest I be accused of reading humor into sermons where it is not intended, that the entire audience broke out in laughter.)[7]

However, the use of such rhetorical devices as humor or dramatic narrative in sermons is not without its dangers for the scholars. Dyula scholars face very much the same kind of

predicament as university lecturers. On one hand, if they remain completely serious, they run the risk of boring their audience and losing its attention. On the other hand, if they try
to hold everyone's attention by entertaining them in one way
or another, they can be accused of pandering to their audience. Speaking of one scholar's apparent popularity as a ser-
monizer, a layman commented to me, "A kuma ka di" ("His
speech is pleasing"). In context, the comment was hardly intended as a compliment, but rather meant to suggest that this
scholar was eloquent but superficial; it might be entertaining
to listen to him speak, but one didn't really learn much of
value from his sermons. Sermons are ultimately supposed to
edify their audience, to remind Muslims of their duties. As
one layman explained it to me, these duties are extremely
complex, and scholars are presumably better aware of their
precise nature than laymen. It is the layman's duty to seek
out as complete a knowledge of these obligations as he can.
Attending sermons for this specific purpose is consequently
morally praiseworthy, quite like voluntary and disinterested
charitable donations. It is indeed (and scholars often make
this point specifically at the outset or close of a sermon) an
action God will reward in the next world, and conceivably in
this world as well. However, it should be the scholar's task to
convey, in one sense or another, something the layman does
not already "know." Strictly speaking, such knowledge is not
the specific subject of the sermon, since sermons tend not to
have specific subjects as such. Rather, sermons should first of
all convey the sense that the scholar does "know" more than
his lay audience, and second that some of his knowledge is
effectively being transmitted in one way or another during
the sermon. It is easier for a scholar to convey such an impression if he is speaking in a serious tone than if he is making jokes or telling stories, however entertaining. On the contrary, the more entertaining the sermon, the more it may cast
doubts about the overall seriousness of the scholar himself.
The most obvious way scholars can display their specialized
"knowledge" is by lacing their sermons with words or
phrases in Arabic, which can then be glossed in Dyula. It is,

after all, the scholar's superior knowledge of the Arabic language and of texts in Arabic that constitutes the basis of his superior "knowledge" of religious matters in general. All scholars must employ this serious tone during much of their sermons. It is rather the extent to which they also employ such devices as humor and narrative, temporarily leaving this serious tone aside, that varies. Some scholars tend to avoid humor and narrative in their sermons altogether, while others switch back and forth fairly consistently between tones of discourse in order to hold their audiences. But it must not be imagined that a serious tone alone automatically conveys the impression of superior "knowledge." An individual can just as easily be categorized as a pedant and a bore. Laymen are not averse to commenting that some scholars are rarely invited to give sermons because they consistently put their audiences to sleep. If a scholar's reliance on humor and narrative exposes him to the criticism that his sermons are "merely" entertaining, a scholar who maintains a consistently serious tone may simply be labeled pretentious, someone who tries to convey the impression that he "knows" more than he really does and only succeeds in spoiling the audience's evening.

Under the circumstances, it is hardly surprising that local scholars are rarely if ever entirely successful in keeping their audiences both entertained and impressed with their "knowledge." However, it would be far too hasty to conclude that local scholars are ultimately failures at their task. Their problems stem in large measure from their situation, which is not unlike the situation of Koko quarter as a whole. On one hand, Koko is a tightly knit community, structured largely along "traditional" lines, where everyone knows everyone else and where questions of seniority govern rules of protocol. On the other hand, Koko is part and parcel of a modern town, the largest in northern Côte d'Ivoire, with many of its members currently resident in the capital or in other large towns in all walks of life, from menial positions to the upper echelons in the civil service. Individuals live simultaneously in two very distinct social universes: the quarter itself, on one hand, and the town and indeed the nation as a whole on the other. Each universe has its own rules of behavior, its own criteria of "success," but while individuals may participate more actively in one or the other, they all belong to both. This dual universe affects the relationship of local scholars to their clienteles in important ways. On one hand, within Koko, the position of individual scholars depends partly on seniority, partly on the number and strength of the social ties of various kinds that they succeed in developing or maintaining. Within, and sometimes in spite of, the constraints imposed by rules of protocol, these ties can be mobilized to procure invitations to deliver sermons, provided that the individual scholar is recognized as reasonably competent at the task. However, though sermons can be fairly lucrative, they do not of themselves constitute a sufficient living for any scholar. For more purely personal questions, individuals are free to consult any scholar they choose. Indeed, the most prosperous individuals from Koko are likely to be living in other parts of the country, if not in the capital, where they can readily and conveniently consult other scholars. It is only for occasions such as funerals, when they are in any case obliged to return to Koko, that they will necessarily resort to the services of local scholars. On the other hand, precisely because Koko is part of a larger town, individuals in other neighborhoods may use the services of scholars from Koko, either for sermons or for personal business. However, as far as personal consultations are concerned, scholars in Koko compete with scholars based elsewhere in town, not only for clients in the town at large, but even for clients from Koko itself.

Until well into the twentieth century, Koko was, to cite one colonial scholar, "le veritable centre islamique" of Korhogo (Marty 1922: 172). This is hardly to say that Koko was ever an Islamic isolate. It is quite possible to identify the names of scholars from elsewhere who settled in Korhogo in the late nineteenth and early twentieth centuries; more important, both scholars and laymen in Koko were aware of the reputations of scholars living and teaching in other communities. Still, the scholars of Koko enjoyed a quasi-monopoly, not only over scholarship in the quarter, but in the town as a whole. Under such conditions, one's seniority, one's family origins, one's personal network of ties of kinship, friendship, and clientship, were all at least as important as one's reputation for learning. Like all of Koko's other monopolies, this is now a thing of the past. Moreover, new modes of communication have elevated certain scholars to the level of "stars," either on television or on cassette tapes for sale in the marketplace, while modern transportation makes it easy for such "stars" to visit towns like Korhogo, or alternatively for lay individuals from Korhogo to seek out such scholars in search of help and advice. On one hand, local scholars are individuals of a given age, generation, clan affiliation, free or slave status, with personal ties to different individuals in Koko; on the other hand, they also aspire to prominent reputations in the town and region as a whole, and ultimately—if not very successfully—to national "star" status. In the first instance, their success depends partly on accidents of birth, but their skill in handling face-to-face interactions within a small community is more important; in the second instance, success depends on conveying an image of "knowledgeability" to both laymen and scholars, while at the same time maintaining a presence that attracts and maintains the attention of relative strangers as well as of kinsmen and neighbors. In the first instance, the arena of competition is restricted, and success, while by no means easy or assured, is well within the reach of a number of individual scholars from Koko; in the second instance, the field of competition is wide open, with proportionately very few aspirants ever attaining anything approaching "star" status. By managing personal relationships within the community, a local scholar can at least assure himself a modest living, but even in Koko his reputation ultimately depends in part on the extent to which his performance measures up to that of a "star."

The predicament of scholars in Koko is in no sense unique. Modern advances in communications and transportation, the flow of migrants back and forth between different communities, affect individuals all throughout Côte d'Ivoire, though not always to the same degree. Local communities everywhere are drawn in myriad ways into the national and international orbit, without necessarily losing all sense of local identity and cohesiveness. Face-to-face multi-stranded relationships remain the principal way in which most scholars interact with their current and prospective clienteles, while at the same time the national reputations of a few scholars is ever more widely diffused as a different and ever more important standard for judging scholars' performances. Yet precisely because Koko is simultaneously a "traditional" community and a part of town, the tension between these two standards is felt particularly acutely by local scholars and their audiences. For this reason, however much their audiences credit them with "knowing," they never seem to "know" quite enough.

8

Sufism Degree Zero

Studies of Islam in West Africa have repeatedly drawn attention to the importance of Sufi brotherhoods or orders (Arabic *tariqa*, pl. *turuq*).[1] The Qadiriyya was the first of the orders to make its appearance in West Africa, during the eighteenth century; the Tijaniyya arrived somewhat later on the scene in the early nineteenth century. Although there is evidence that Sufi ideas had already been circulating in West Africa for centuries,[2] the appearance of the orders clearly represented an institutional, if not ideological, breakthrough. The eighteenth and nineteenth centuries have long been identified as a period of Islamic "recrudescence" in West Africa;[3] the emergence of the Sufi orders at the very same time was hardly a coincidence. Indeed, it has been argued that the Sufi orders played a crucial role in this process of Islamic recrudescence. For instance, Mervyn Hiskett (1984: 259) identifies the following processes as consequences of "the rise of the Sufi *turuq* in the West and central Sudan":

1. The crystallization of "local patriotism" around the persons of the leaders of Sufi movements and eventually around their tombs as pilgrimage centers[4]

2. The fostering of Islamic universalism through the encouragement of pilgrimage to the Hijaz

3. The formulation of the ideological bases of West African jihad movements[5]

4. Accelerated rates of conversion to Islam, for which, according to Hiskett, the *turuq* were "the main agents"

5. The promotion of Arabic literacy

Sufi orders have even been credited with influencing the course of West African economic development; in particular, extension of the cultivation of peanuts as a cash crop, not to mention their commercialization, has been attributed to the growth of the Mouride order in Senegal (O'Brien 1971, 1975).

Any attempt to explain why the Sufi orders should have exerted—and indeed continue to exert—such a powerful influence on Islam in West Africa must necessarily take into account the general features of the orders themselves. Specifically, three main features are commonly associated with Sufism in West Africa. The first is a clearly hierarchical structure of authority, based on the *shaykh/murid* ("leader"/"disciple") relationship. One cannot simply join an order on one's own. One must first be initiated by a formally recognized *shaykh* empowered to teach his disciples the specific obligations of membership. Ideally, this initiation creates an enduring—indeed virtually indissoluble—relationship of authority; each *shaykh* thus wields authority over the various disciples whom he has initiated throughout his career. This hierarchical link can be extended into a whole chain of command. In other words, the *shaykh* in turn has his own *shaykh* who initiated him or who has succeeded to the authority of his original *shaykh*. At the summit of this hierarchy, there is in principle the founder of the entire order or his successor; in practice, this may mean the founder or successor of a particular branch of the order, rather than the order as a whole, or else a designated *khalifa* who is the head of the order in a particular area (which may be as large as West Africa as a whole). The extent to which the hierarchical principle embodied in the *shaykh/murid* relationship is in fact translated into a centralized system of authority is clearly quite variable; some orders, or at least some branches, appear to be highly centralized, others much more weakly so. The point is that the hierarchical ideology of the order permits, if it does not automatically entail, a certain degree of centralization. The more highly centralized an order or branch happens to be, the more it can coordinate action on a large scale of any sort, whether this be missionary activity, political mobilization, or even the cultivation and marketing of peanuts.

If relationships within any one order are characterized by hierarchy, relationships between orders, and in some cases between different branches of the same order, are characterized by rivalry. To the extent that membership in any order is exclusive,[6] it follows logically that different orders or branches should be in competition for the allegiance of potential disciples. Of course, different *shaykhs* of the same order may also compete for disciples, but as long as they all owe more than token allegiance to the same head, such competition is subject to arbitration at a higher level. At the higher level, there may be factional strife within an order concerning succession to positions of leadership. However, such strife is either resolved or ultimately leads to the formation of separate and essentially independent branches. Finally, the very political effectiveness of the orders or branches promotes rivalry in another way; to the extent that any order uses its authority to mobilize support for any political movement, opponents of that movement are likely to seek support from rival orders. In other words, while the orders may serve to mediate factional cleavages within the ranks of their memberships, they may also accentuate cleavages along lines of membership in different orders.

One final feature commonly associated with the Sufi orders is the development of a corporate sense of identity among members. Such an identity is fostered by the practice of *dhikr*, or "remembrances," ritual recitation of prayers particular to each order and often to each branch. In the first place, these very ritual particularities serve as symbolic markers of a distinctive identity for fellow members of the same order. Moreover, *dhikr* are often recited collectively, reinforcing the sense that each member is part of a larger collectivity. In some cases, Sufi orders have been associated with the rise of new forms of "ethnic" consciousness in modern multi-ethnic towns and indeed in whole nations.[7] In short, the influence and effectiveness of the Sufi orders can be seen as the outcome of the elaboration of distinctive forms of collective ritual combined with clear hierarchical principles of authority. These factors operate to develop a sense of collective identity among members on one hand, and to mobilize this collectivity in concrete ways on the other.

This is the image of the "typical" Sufi brotherhoods as it emerges from the scholarly literature. The image has become so pervasive that in a recent article on Sufism in Burkina Faso, the author expresses his considerable surprise at failing to find these features: "The *turuq* . . . did not, and do not even now, constitute structures through which Muslims could have created, or could create, a counter-movement around an uncontested *shaikh* invested with *baraka*. . . . No Burkinabe refers to himself as Qadiri or Tijani *in the manner of the Mourides of Senegal*" (Otayek 1988: 101 [emphasis mine]). He even qualifies this "phenomenon" as "unique in West African Islam" (ibid.), as if it were a matter of course that Sufism should take the institutional forms described above, and that their absence requires explanation, if not justification. In fact, those Sufi orders or branches that have attracted the most attention from Western scholars are, not surprisingly, those whose influence, not only within but outside the domain of Islam, narrowly defined, has been the most spectacular. However, it is a mistake to consider cases where Sufi brotherhoods are much more loosely institutionalized as in any sense radically atypical. Sufism, in and of itself, cannot account for change. Rather, we must ask ourselves under what conditions Sufi orders develop in specific ways, and under what conditions they fail to so develop.

As it happens, the Sufi orders among the Dyula of Koko, quite like those among their neighbors to the north in Burkina Faso, are conspicuously deficient in all those characteristics ostensibly "typical" of Sufism in West Africa.[8] While both the Tijaniyya and the Qadiriyya are present among the Dyula, there is a total absence of rivalry between the two orders. Informants, whether or not they were members of either order or unaffiliated, almost invariably responded that it was a good idea to belong to an order, but that it did not matter which one. I tried on various occasions to elicit from members of one order or the other the reasons for their choice, and ultimately why they felt their own order was preferable. In every instance, respondents insisted that their order was in no way superior to the other, a particularly surprising answer for Tijanis, who, it is claimed, "believed that their litanies were more efficacious than all other Sufi litanies" (Abun Nasr 1965: 56). One Tijani explained to me that, since it ultimately made no difference, one chose the order whose litanies one found most attractive ("A ka di i ye"). The choice of the adjective *di* is revealing. One can say that something is "good" in one sense or another by saying, "A ka di" or "A ka nyi," but the adjectives *di* and *nyi* have very different connotations. For example, food that is *di* is sweet-tasting (as opposed to sour or bitter), or pleasant to eat. Depending on the context, to say that food is *nyi* may mean simply that it is edible, or else that it is wholesome, or ultimately that it is permissible to eat it (i.e., it is not prohibited by Islamic law). *Di* refers to aesthetic values, *nyi* to moral values. The same entity may be one without the other; medicine, for example, may be "bad-tasting" but "good" for you. Actions are or are not *nyi*; they are moral or immoral, but normally the notion of *di* would not be applied to them.[9] On the other hand, what is or is not *di* may be a question of personal taste, whereas in principle things are either *nyi* or not *nyi*. (This is not to say, of course, that individuals never disagree about what is or is not moral, but simply that such disagreement does not imply a position of moral relativism.) In short, an individual can say that something is *di* to him ("A ka di n ye"), a very common phrase, which means that he likes it, that it appeals to him personally. This is precisely the way my friend indicated his preference for the Tijaniyya as opposed to the Qadiriyya. The choice was purely aesthetic (*di*) and had no implications in moral (*nyi*) terms.

Another Tijani went even further in his attempts to explain to me why the Tijaniyya and the Qadiriyya were morally equivalent. Both, he claimed, were founded by the same individual, Ahmad Tijani Qadiri. One of his sons went on to found the Tijaniyya, another to found the Qadiriyya. Both orders were really identical, except that the litanies (*dhikr*) are recited aloud by Qadiris and silently by Tijanis. Historically speaking, this account is wildly inaccurate. The Qadiriyya traces its origins to 'Abd-al-Qadir al-Jilani, who lived in Baghdad in the twelfth century; the Tijaniyya was founded in the eighteenth-century Maghreb by Ahmad al-Tijani. There is at least a glimmer of historical truth in the story of Ahmad Tijani Qadiri; Ahmad al-Tijani was apparently initiated into the Qadiriyya order (among others) in Fez before founding his own order (Abun Nasr 1965: 17). However, the Dyula myth of Ahmad Tijani Qadiri goes much further than simply acknowledging that both the Tijani and Qadiri orders have common roots in the distant past. The Dyula story minimizes any and all differences between the two orders, reducing the whole issue to the question of whether the litanies are recited aloud or not, and furthermore attributing no special significance to the matter.

The question of the allegiance of *murid* to *shaykh* among Dyula Sufis is slightly more complex. In many cases, individuals are initiated by their teachers into one order or the other, and so it is necessary to attempt to separate out any allegiance a *murid* might owe to his *shaykh* from that which a pupil (*karamogo den*) owes to his teacher (*karamogo fa*). The teacher/pupil relationship is quite consciously modeled after the father/child relationship, and consequently the link is in principle a perpetual one, even when the pupil in turn becomes a teacher. A teacher may continue to exercise authority over his pupil for the rest of his life, and the pupil should always display deference to his teacher. Consequently, in those cases where individuals are intitiated into an order by their teachers, it is impossible to disentangle the extent to which authority is wielded by a *shaykh* per se, or whether this is simply an epiphenomenon of the teacher/pupil relationship. In this respect, the case of one particular Tijani scholar is instructive. This man's teacher is still alive, and he frequently visits him in Daloa, in southwestern Côte d'Ivoire, to consult with him; he regularly hosts members of his teacher's family whenever they visit Korhogo. His teacher did not, however, initiate him into the Tijaniyya, as he did not belong to either order at the time the scholar in question was a student. Indeed, when I inquired whether the teacher was now a member of either order, the scholar responded that he did not know, and did not for that matter seem to care, although the two men remain very close. He was initiated into the Tijaniyya by a man identified only as "Fama," who lives in another part of Korhogo. As the scholar rightly pointed out, it is impossible to join an order on one's own; one must be initiated by someone. However, he shows little interest in the man actually responsible for his initiation, although he lives only a short distance away, while he maintains very close ties with his teacher, who lives in another part of the country. In short, while the *shaykh/murid* relationship may reinforce a teacher's authority over his pupil, initiation by itself creates no binding or even enduring relationship. Needless to say, there is no acknowledgment, and perhaps little if any awareness, of higher levels of authority in either order, and neither did Tijanis or Qadiris consider themselves affiliated to any particular branches of the order. After all, if Tijanis and Qadiris are essentially the same, what sense does it make to belong to any particular branch?

Finally, neither Tijanis nor Qadiris display any sense of corporate identity as such among the Dyula of Koko. This is hardly surprising in the light of the absence of other "typical" features of West African Sufism. Since both acknowledgment of some common authority and the conviction that one order is fundamentally different from, if not superior to, the other are absent, they cannot serve as bases for the formation of any such sense of corporate identity. Yet even at the most elementary level, the orders never involve corporate activity in any form. In many societies, *dhikr* are often collectively recited by local members of an order, but they are always recited individually and privately in Koko. Such collective recitations do occur elsewhere in Korhogo, among immigrants whom the Dyula designate as "Malians," a generic label for Manding-speakers hailing from outside the country. Dyula Sufis consider that it would be desirable to hold such collective recitations, but they certainly do not participate in those of their "Malian" Sufi neighbors.

Sufism among the Dyula, it would seem, is characterized by the absence of features "typically" associated with Sufi orders in West Africa: no clear pattern of authority, no brotherhood rivalry, no sense of corporate identity, not even any collective recitations. What, one might well ask, is left? What does being a Qadiri or a Tijani among the Dyula entail? The answer, in the first place, is the private recitation of *dhikr*, aloud or in silence as the case may be. Under the circumstances, whether one is Qadiri or Tijani makes very little difference indeed.

In fact, the very legitimacy of the Sufi orders has been directly challenged: the Sufi brotherhoods are anathema to the Wahhabis. In a different vein, Sufism is alien to the religious sensibilities of the Western-educated in Koko, whether these be those members of the elite attracted to some form of secularism or the growing ranks who feel some affinity for the neoreformism of the AEEMCI and the Arab-trained scholars. Still, aside from the Wahhabis, no one condemns the orders in public. Nonetheless, Sufism is associated with scholars trained in the Suwarian tradition and with their followers, those I have broadly labeled neotraditionalists, who are still the overwhelming majority in Koko. The general consensus among these, the ordinary Muslims of Koko, is that joining an order confers religious merit. In spite of this apparent consensus, and to the consternation of members of both orders, very few Dyula ever join. Dyula Sufis point with some embarrassment to the "Malians" in town, who, they claim, have very high rates of participation. How can there be collective recitations of *dhikr* in Koko, they complain, if there are not enough members to attend? If only their fellow Dyula recognized the true merits of belonging to an order, they would flock to join.

In fact, the Dyula Sufis of Koko are hardly a random lot; for the most part, these are individuals for whom Arabic scholarship is at least a part-time profession. Most recognized scholars among the Dyula are either Tijanis or Qadiris, though it is important to stress that it is perfectly possible and generally admissible for a scholar to remain unaffiliated to either order.

Aside from scholars, virtually all other members are old men with a reputation for piety and a special interest in religious matters. Even among elders, relatively few ever join. In short, all Sufis are male and either scholars or senior elders.

These effective restrictions on membership are hardly imposed by members of the orders themselves. Admittedly, these Sufi scholars have not taken any aggressive steps (to put it mildly) to recruit new members. Still, the question remains: why don't other members of the community join? I asked one younger man whom I considered a priori a likely candidate. Though not a scholar by profession, he is as apparently pious as anyone else in his personal life and displays a keener than usual interest in Islam. A relatively poor man, he has one of the most extensive tape libraries of Muslim sermons in Dyula in the community and owns a cassette recorder, which he often uses to listen to them for his own edification. He confided to me that he did not feel that he was yet in a position to join one of the orders. Joining an order, he argued, amounted to a sacred pledge to recite all the necessary litanies at the appointed time. There are means for making up for lost prayers in extenuating circumstances, at least for ordinary Muslims, but this is a more serious breach for Tijanis or Qadiris. A working man does not always have the time to spare at any given moment to recite the obligatory *dhikr*; to pledge to do so and then neglect the promise is a far worse breach than to defer making the commitment. When his sons were old enough to support him and he no longer had to work for a living, then he would be in a position to join the Tijaniyya or the Qadiriyya. (Not surprisingly, he expressed no particular preference for either order.)

Taken at face value, this is a somewhat curious answer. It is certainly the case that individuals who hold salaried positions do not have absolute control over their work schedules. In Côte d'Ivoire, where Muslims are a minority, individuals can sometimes receive time off to perform regular obligatory prayers but would probably have difficulty convincing their superiors that they needed extra time to recite Sufi litanies. But the man in question, like many of his peers, does not hold a salaried job, is frequently unoccupied during the afternoon, when the requirements of work and worship are most likely to conflict, and is generally at liberty to manage his time as he sees fit. In any case, the notion that a man's sons will support him entirely in his old age is these days (and has perhaps always been) more of an ideal than a reality. It is by no means clear that elders really do have more time to devote to unremunerative activities, religious or otherwise. The crucial issue is symbolic, rather than real time, in terms of what it means to be a senior elder. A senior elder is stereotypically a man with grown sons (or other dependents) to "support" him. Such elders are expected to have time at their disposal and to act accordingly. An elder who must visibly devote all his time to earning his keep is not only unfortunate but, in a sense, a failure. On the other hand, a younger man who appears to have too much free time on his hands is, at worst, a good-for-nothing (if he uses his time for personal enjoyment), at best presumptuously behaving like an elder. Among younger men, only professional scholars can conspicuously devote their time to activities associated with Sufism; after all, this is their business, and not "spare" time at all.

The notion that only scholars and elders "ought" to have the time to engage in Sufi activities is closely related to general notions about standards of piety. Among the Dyula, it is obviously true that some individuals happen to be more pious than others. The point, rather, is that certain categories of persons are expected to be more pious than others, all else being equal. Gender and age distinctions are fundamental in this regard: males are expected to be more pious than females; the older people are, the more pious they are expected to be. In the most general terms, such piety is supposed to be reflected in the moral conduct of everyday life: praying five times a day, observing the fast at Ramadan (and indeed on optional occasions such as Kami Sun, the "fast of the guinea hen"), abstaining from alcohol, adultery, theft, and so forth. But there are also specific conventional signs of piety, both positive and negative. Certain acts are considered reprehensible for some categories of persons and tolerated for others, while other acts are expected of some categories of individuals and not for others. Dancing (*don*) and singing (*donkili*, literally "dance cry")[10] are acts that nowadays fall into the first category. Scholars in Koko argue that singing and dancing are displeasing to God, although only one scholar so far has taken any active steps to discourage them, and his success has been very modest indeed; he has managed to prevent his own wives and children from engaging in such activities, but the prohibition has not even been successfully implemented for the wives and children of his full brothers. Singing is almost exclusively a female activity. The exceptions to the rule are themselves revelatory. In the first place, men sing in accompaniment to certain *lo* society masquerades, hardly a very proper "Muslim" activity in modern Koko. Such an association only reinforces the notion that pious Muslim men should refrain from singing. Traditionally, there were no griots—professional bards—among the Dyula in the Korhogo region; Manding-speaking griots from other regions do visit town and sometimes take up residence there. However, two Dyula men do operate as professional singers and are, in certain respects, comparable to griots. The first is usually known by his nickname, "RDA."[11] An early supporter of what is now Côte d'Ivoire's ruling (and, until very recently, only) political party, he has been rewarded by becoming a quasi-official party "griot." His functions range from that of town crier to performing at funerals of local notables associated in one way or another with the party. In spite of his role—and I have seen him sing and dance at Senufo funerals surrounded by "pagan" *poro* masqueraders—RDA remains a respected member of the Dyula Muslim community. The same cannot be said of the other male professional singer among the Dyula, "Petit Sory." He hails from the village of Gbaminasso, and as such is a distant relative of an entire *kabila* of Koko, who regard him as something of a blot on the honor of the family name. Petit Sory's songs have an explicitly Muslim content, embodying Islamic moral maxims—perhaps a deliberate, if somewhat unsuccessful, attempt to win respectability among fellow Dyula. There are a number of reasons why RDA is both respectable and respected and Petit Sory is not. First of all, Petit Sory behaves much more like a typical griot; he shows up uninvited at weddings, funerals, and other such occasions in order to solicit money from all in attendance. RDA performs only by invitation of party notables and overtly solicits no gifts from the audience. More important, RDA occupies a historically unique niche. When he dies or retires, no one else will succeed to his position, and so his example defies emulation. Petit Sory's role, on the other hand, is not intrinsically unique, even if his performances are idiosyncratic. In short, he sets a bad example.

By and large, the exceptions of *lo* masquerading, of RDA, and of Petit Sory serve to prove the rule that singing is inappropriate behavior for pious Muslim men. Scholars argue that women should not sing either, but no one else seems to take this injunction seriously. Drummers are invariably male, except on certain occasions during Ramadan when women drum on inverted calabashes placed over a larger recipient filled with water. Males also dance, though both drumming and dancing are appropriate male activities only for *kambele* ("youths"; older men sometimes dance in *lo* masquerades, again an exception that proves the rule.) Otherwise, as a man marries, has children, and begins to assume the status of a junior elder, he is expected to leave drumming and dancing behind. The same rule does not apply to women, who at any age can and frequently do sing and dance. In short, while both singing and dancing are reprehensible in principle, abstaining from singing is only expected of men, and from dancing only of older men.

If singing and dancing are negative signs, designating certain categories of persons as less intrinsically "pious" than others, public prayer constitutes of a positive sign of piety. Nowadays, all Dyula are expected to pray regularly by the time they reach adolescence, though it still follows that the older the individual in question, the more serious the lapse. However, prayer can be performed in a number of different places: at the mosque; on the verandah or in front of the house; or inside the house. The mosque is a preeminently public place, just as inside the house is preeminently private and outside the public eye in the most literal way; praying in front of the house is an intermediate space, part private and part public. Older women will pray outside the mosque only on the occasion of the two great prayers of the Islamic calendar year, at the end of Ramadan and on *tabaski*. All adult men should attend these prayers at the mosque, and all married men are expected to attend the Friday midday prayer. The older a man is, the more often he will be expected to perform his other prayers at a mosque as well.[12] When he is at home, the male head of a household will frequently pray outside the house if he does not leave for the mosque. He will be joined by other senior males who happen to be visiting, if there are any. He may also be joined by older women, either visitors or members of the household. Most often, women pray inside the house until they are past the age of childbearing, males until they reach marriageable age. In this way, public prayers, as a conventional sign of piety, reinforces expectations that piety will vary with both age and gender.

Age and gender do not, of course, determine how pious an individual really is, but rather constitute a grid for evaluating his or her actual behavior, a way of determining which individuals actually go beyond what is expected of them or instead fall short. The *hajj* is connected with piety in a rather different way. Not only is it in principle a religious obligation for those who have the means to perform it, but it is also interpreted as an enduring commitment to lead an upright life once the pilgrim has returned. A *hajji* or *hajja* is expected to set an example and to live a life as reasonably beyond reproach as humanly possible. *Hajjis* and *hajjas* are entitled to wear specific items of clothing, which mark their special status, although, except for scholars, wearing such clothing too frequently is considered unduly ostentatious. Not surprisingly, standards of conduct are somewhat more stringent for men than for women who have made the *hajj*. *Hajjas* may sing and dance in public, and will even do so in their special attire on occasions such as weddings. For a variety of reasons, men are more likely to make the *hajj* at a younger age than women (and more likely to make it at all). Men who are wealthy enough to undertake the journey are usually polygynists, and it is often impolitic to pay for one wife's journey without bringing the others as well, a burden very few can afford. A few old women have accumulated enough earnings from petty trade to pay their own way. This is highly regarded as a token of unusual devotion, but it is also very rare, though I witnessed the departure of one such woman in 1985. More often, a son pays the way for his mother; unlike a husband, who has equal obligations to all of his wives, a son has a much stronger obligation to his biological mother than his father's other wives, although they are his "mothers" as well. But even men very rarely make the *hajj* before they reach middle age. One relatively young but highly paid civil servant once confided to me, only half jokingly, that he was too young to perform the *hajj*; with a twinkle in his eye, he added that he hadn't quite finished sowing his wild oats! (This admission was made in the course of a conversation about a *hajji* who had secretly married two additional wives behind his first wife's back, on the rather dubious grounds that, now that he had been to Mecca, adultery was quite out of the question; my friend expressed the opinion that such behavior was seriously reprehensible for a *hajji*, much more so than for an ordinary man.) The only younger men I know who have made the *hajj* are either professional scholars or serious aspirants to the profession of scholar. As an alternative to the *hajj*, there exists a ceremony that individuals may perform publicly, whereby they pledge to live uprightly for the rest of their lives. Such ceremonies were performed only by old men and women, and are, I am told, lapsing entirely now that the *hajj* is increasingly within the means of many townsmen. In any case, whether in the form of ceremony or in the form of the *hajj*, such commitments to living a strictly moral life reinforce the notion that piety is at least in part a function of both gender and age.

Yet there is one important category of exceptions to the rules regarding age, although not as regards gender. This is the case of younger scholars. Scholars are expected to practice what they preach and to set a moral example for the community. This explains, for instance, why younger scholars do not hesitate to perform the *hajj*; unlike ordinary individuals, their conduct is not expected to change after their return. In certain (though by no means in all) respects, scholars are considered to be like elders. Blessings (*duau*) are one example of how scholars and elders are alike. Blessings are a part of daily conversation among the Dyula. They tend to be rather formulaic utterances, of the sort "May God . . . ," and as such constitute certain of the figures of speech of ordinary politeness. For example, one says, "Allah nogoya ke" ("May God improve [your health]") to a person who is ill; "Allah i son" ("May God reward you") to someone who has offered a gift or a service; and "Allah hina a ra" ("May God take pity on him [or her]") in reference to someone deceased. Those to whom such a blessing is addressed must strike their foreheads with the right hand and reply, "Amina" ("Amen"). Virtually every adult, and even every adolescent, is likely to utter and to receive such blessings in the course of the day. However, on some occasions, blessings can be much more elaborate, and one individual may utter a whole string of more complex formulas at one time. Life crises—births, marriages, and deaths—are occasions when such elaborate blessings are de rigueur. An important visitor, or someone returning after a long absence, is likely to be treated to such elaborate blessings on his arrival. An elaborate blessing may also express exceptional gratitude, or even affection and esteem. Despite the fact that most blessings are purely formulaic utterances and that many are conventional acts of politeness, they are still petitions to God, from one person on behalf of another. One can never be absolutely sure which, if any, blessings will be truly efficacious. God is more likely to heed blessings uttered by persons He favors, and He favors those who are truly pious. However, God applies different standards of piety than humans, because He can judge a person's true intentions, whereas humans can only judge actions.

If anyone can utter a blessing, not everyone utters equally elaborate blessings. The blessings of young men and of most women tend to be perfunctory; middle-aged men and old women offer more extensive blessings; but the blessings of old men and scholars are the most elaborate of all. Younger individuals claim that their elders "know" how to bless more effectively, but given the formulaic nature of blessings, it is almost inconceivable that any one would be literally incapable of reciting such utterances verbatim. Rather, as one friend explained, the elders bless more effectively because they are "closer to God." Scholars, because of their commitment to religious learning and their higher standards of moral conduct, are in some respects even closer to God than elders; indeed, they claim that their blessings are the most efficacious of all, not least because it is their business to know how to address God in the most appropriate manner for each circumstance.

If I have elaborated at such length on the hierarchy of piety among the Dyula and on the different ways in which it is symbolically expressed, this is because it answers the crucial question of why membership in Sufi orders among the Dyula is so restricted. Those individuals who in fact join one order or the other—scholars and old men—are those at the apex of this hierarchy of piety. This symbolic hierarchy legitimates in Islamic terms certain social distinctions that underpin the fabric of the local community: between scholars and laymen, between men and women, between elders and juniors. By joining a Sufi order, one implicitly asserts that one is at the apex of this hierarchy. This is why it would be presumptuous for a younger layman, no matter how pious in actual fact, to join an order. This would amount to a public proclamation that he believes himself more pious than can rightfully be expected, a perfect example of the sin Dyula scholars call *yere bonya* ("self-aggrandizement"). Actions that seem to call others' attention to one's own exceptional piety are intrinsically impious, and consequently self-defeating. By a similar process of circular reasoning, the fact that joining an order constitutes a pledge to good behavior perhaps even more constraining than the *hajj*, and that consequently only scholars and old men do in fact join, legitimates the implicit hierarchy in the first place.

In short, Sufism among the Dyula serves to legitimate traditional social identities in terms of key distinctions such as gender and age. In other circumstances in West Africa, Sufism has served to legitimate the emergence of new social identities, in terms of ethnicity, class, or political loyalties. Paradoxically, the Islamic movement that has assumed such functions in Korhogo has been the Wahhabiyya, which is militantly anti-Sufi. In other words, changes in the practice of Islam in West Africa that have been attributed to the influence of Sufism may not be a feature of Sufi ideology at all. Under certain conditions, the Sufi orders may uphold rather than overturn "traditional" social distinctions, whereas anti-Sufi movements may exhibit some of those very features "typically" identified with Sufism. The pertinent question is not the extent of the influence of Sufi ideology, but rather those conditions under which Islamic movements, Sufi or otherwise, legitimize preexisting social distinctions or else seek to create new ones. The fact that, until recently, the Dyula of Koko were a Muslim minority with an established trade monopoly is salient in this regard; they had absolutely no vested interest in rocking the boat by establishing a new social order in the region, but were rather concerned with maintaining their relatively privileged position as it stood. When this monopoly was lost, the possibility of creating a new order was opened, and it was the Wahhabis rather than the Sufis who attempted to exploit it. However, most Dyula in Koko have resisted any such temptation to create a new order, and are in some respects even more defensive of their "traditional" identity. This is why they continue to extol the virtues of Sufism—and why they continue to avoid joining.

9

Sacrifices

The sacrificial meal was an appropriate expression of the
antique ideal of religious life, not merely because it was a
social act in which the god and his worshipers were conceived as partaking together, but because . . . the very act
of eating and drinking with a man was a symbol and a confirmation of fellowship and mutual social obligations.

W. Robertson Smith, *The Religion of the Semites*

Those Dyula friends of mine who are fluent in French consistently translate the word *saraka* as "sacrifice." I have always
found this translation puzzling. The words sound somewhat
alike, as if a vague homophony could make up for the vague-
ness of the synonymy. The idea of "sacrifice," in a religious
context, conjures up the image of an offering—typically,
though not exclusively, a blood offering—to a spirit or deity.
Dyula are quite familiar with blood sacrifices. They used to
be offered by *tun tigi* as part of *lo* society ritual. They remain
an integral feature of the religious life of those of their Senufo
neighbors—the majority, especially in the villages—who are
still "pagans." Dyula scholars lace their sermons with stock
stories from the Islamic repertoire about "idolatry": Ibrahim's
destruction of the idols; the wooden statue that miraculously
speaks only to ridicule its worshipers and to acknowledge its
impotence. By telling these stories, the scholars are somewhat complacently preaching to the convinced. The issue of
idolatry is one of the least controversial among Dyula Muslims in Koko. To the extent that such practices effectively distinguish "pagans" from "Muslims," the audience can be re-
assured that, ever since the *tun tigi* have renounced them,
they are all unambiguously "Muslim."

There is, of course, one obvious context where "blood sacrifice" is specifically associated with Islamic behavior. This is the annual slaughter of a ram during *tabaski*, the Great ʿId.[1] The event commemorates Ibrahim's (Abraham's) sacrifice of a ram instead of his son. It seems to me, however, that Dyula downplay this specifically "sacrificial" aspect of the *tabaski* celebration. Of course, since the ram's throat is cut in the name of God, the slaughter is, in a real sense, a sacrifice—but this is true of all animals slaughtered for their meat, and is hardly specific to the occasion. To the extent that Dyula—even in villages, and much more so in towns like Korhogo—typically obtain meat from professional butchers, such slaughter usually takes place away from the public eye. However, animals are publicly slaughtered during life-crisis rituals; most specifically, cattle are invariably butchered during wedding ceremonies. The bloodiness of the proceedings is bound to make a greater impression on European or American spectators who are not accustomed to witnessing the slaughter of animals than on Africans, for whom such events are hardly spectacular. The significance of slaughtering animals in God's name among the Dyula is inextricably tied to the fact that they are and have always been Muslims living amongst unbelievers. Only this kind of slaughter turns a live animal into edible food; animals who have died or been killed any other way are *jufaa*. Unbelievers, unlike Muslims, are willing to eat *jufaa*, even animals who have died naturally. The very fact that unbelievers who will willingly and knowingly eat unslaughtered animals also offer blood sacrifices to spirits contributes crucially to Dyula inclinations to distinguish the idea of "slaughter" from that of "blood sacrifice," rather than assimilating them.

If the slaughter of rams remains the pivotal moment of *tabaski*, this is rather because the act links two very different aspects, two dissimilar foci, of the celebration. The first focus is on the act of collective worship at the Friday mosque. It is on this occasion, and that of the Lesser ʿId marking the end of Ramadan, that all the Muslims of Korhogo are enjoined to worship together. Unlike at Friday prayer, the women come too, though they must pray separately, just outside the pre-cincts of the mosque. Men and women alike dress as splen-didly as possible. Prayer is an active celebration of the unity of the Muslim community of Korhogo as a whole, on both sides of the stream. But *tabaski* does not simply celebrate Ibra-him's sacrifice; it celebrates the *hajj*, the pilgrimage to Mecca. On this day, the pilgrims in Mecca will slaughter a ram to mark the culmination of their pilgrimage. On this occasion, Dyula are reminded very directly of all of their family mem-bers, friends, neighbors, and acquaintances who are per-forming the *hajj*. It is of them, and not of Ibrahim, that they invariably speak. Through the pilgrims, worshipers in Koko are linked to Mecca, and ultimately to the community of Muslims throughout the entire world.

When the prayer is over, Muslims stream home, in differ-ent directions, to slaughter their rams. This act, accom-plished in Koko as it is in Mecca and throughout Muslim communities around the world, is the culminating celebra-tion of the unity of the global Muslim community. But the act of killing the animal, in and of itself, is not the center of ev-eryone's attention but, on the contrary, a cue for a real shift in the emphasis of the festivities. Slaughtering the ram is straightforward. It is, on the contrary, its butchering that takes on significance, the cutting up and division of the meat. People keep for themselves only a relatively small portion of a sheep they kill. They are preoccupied, rather, with deciding to whom they will give meat, how much, and from which part of the animal. Kin of one sort or another, especially within the clan ward, are the primary recipients.[2] As one would expect, the protocol of seniority informs, if it does not entirely govern, the distribution of meat: for instance, one's elder brother ought to receive a hind leg, one's younger brother a foreleg; the *kabila tigi*, the senior person and head of the entire clan ward, must be given a relatively choice portion. Ties of friendship, as well as kinship, can be ac-knowledged by gifts of meat. As a result, all throughout the afternoon, children scurry back and forth throughout Koko carrying gifts of raw meat—often no more than a few mor-sels—from one person to another.

In this way, the slaughter of a sheep links Dyula Muslims in Koko with the global community of Muslims throughout the world, with Mecca, with pilgrims (especially from Koko) performing the *hajj* in any particular year, and finally with kinsmen and friends within the local community. It is the one occasion where the salience of membership in the global community and of membership in the local community are expressed more or less simultaneously. But it is only at the moment of slaughter that these two poles, the global and the local, come together for an instant. The collective prayer that leads up to the slaughter, as well as the elaborate division of the carcass that follows, each belong symbolically to one pole or the other. Rather than focus their attention on the moment of slaughter, as if to affirm the ultimate and transcendent identity of the "global" and the "local," Dyula pay more attention to the "before" and the "after," separating the global from the local in terms of context—different times, different places, sharply different moments of the same occasion.

In any case, *saraka*—"sacrifice"(?)—has nothing whatsoever to do with blood offerings. Rather, the word is the Dyula pronunciation of the Arabic term *sadaqa*, which "in the widest sense means a pious or charitable act; . . . in Muhammadan law it means a gift made with the object of obtaining merit in the eyes of God" (Fyzee 1964: 259). *Saraka* is a pious gift, as distinct from an ordinary gift (*son*). *Saraka* is also distinguished from *jaka* (Arabic *zakat*), the portion of one's wealth that every Muslim must, as a religious obligation, distribute to the poor each year.[3] Individuals distribute *jaka* on one specific day, of their own choosing, each year. On this day, they will be visited by those in the community who consider themselves needy, in the expectation of receiving a portion of the alms, which are distributed as the donor sees fit. Failure to offer *jaka* is a serious breach of religious obligations; one friend went as far as to assert that such failure invalidated whatever religious merit one might accumulate through prayer and even the *hajj*. By way of contrast, *saraka* is in no way a religious obligation, even though it constitutes a religious act.

Saraka might be translated as "alms," "charity," a free-will gift, rather than as "sacrifice." Such a translation is certainly more consistent with the standard texts of *fiqh*, but it comes no closer to exhausting the range of meanings *saraka* assumes, not only in the religious life, but also in the everyday life, of most Dyula in Koko. *Saraka*, as we have seen, is an integral part of life-crisis rituals—naming ceremonies, weddings, funerals—where its distribution is governed by an elaborate protocol that symbolically stresses the salience of age, gender, generation, free or slave status, kin group, and local community membership, as well as specific social ties between various participants. In addition, as we shall see, *saraka* can be offered for ends that are strictly this-worldly, and that seemingly have little to do with piety. All in all, *saraka* is an extremely complex notion. It invariably entails giving something to someone, but the different kinds, and above all the different contexts, of such prestations are more striking than any overall similarities. *Saraka* can be an individual and essentially private affair or a collective and highly public one. It is its very applicability in so many contexts—individual and collective, global and local—that makes it a key concept in Islamic practice among the Dyula of Koko.

Not surprisingly, some of the uses to which the notion of *saraka* is put have aroused the hostility of reformers. The Wahhabis argue that *saraka* is exclusively intended to be a charitable donation; as such, its use in life-crisis rituals, where recipients are not necessarily in any need of charity, is inappropriate. Moreover, Wahhabis disapprove of practices that might be called "magic," which most certainly includes prestations of *saraka* for purely this-worldly ends. The younger generation of reformers associated with the AEEMCI have been more circumspect in their criticism. They warn against excessive spending for life-crisis rituals, but who is to decide how much is "too much"? They inveigh against "charlatans," against "marabouts"—clerics—who prey on the credulous by selling spurious remedies. However, such invective can be construed in different ways. Skeptics may hold that all forms of "magic" are fraudulent, and that all clerics who dabble in such practices are blameworthy. However, individuals may be firmly convinced of the efficacy of "magic" and yet doubt the claims of certain practitioners. In other words, everyone agrees that charlatans are wicked. The problem is whether or not all practitioners of "magic" are frauds, and, if not, to know whose claims are genuine, and which ones are cheats. Younger scholars trained in the Middle East, along with certain—perhaps not all—of their followers probably disapprove of many of the ways in which *saraka* is offered. However, for the time being, this disapproval has been voiced in a sufficiently ambiguous manner, avoiding any confrontation over the issue, either with Suwarian scholars or with the laymen who resort to their services. As a result, *saraka*, in both public and private contexts, remains a common feature of everyday life in Koko.

The multifarious nature of *saraka* makes the concept ambiguous, even to Dyula scholars. Normally, as we have seen, the knowledge of *karamogos* can be classed relatively straightforwardly as *siru karamogoya*, "secret" knowledge to further private ends, or *bayani karamogoya*, "public" knowledge of religious obligations. Knowledge of written charms, of astrology, of lucky and unlucky days is clearly *siru karamogoya*. Knowledge of the proper techniques of prayer, of inheritance, the fast, the payment of *jaka*—*fiqh*, in short, but also *hadith*, *tafsir*, and so on—are all *bayani karamogoya*. Knowledge of *saraka* does not fit neatly or entirely into either category; it is, scholars told me, both *siru* and *bayani karamogoya*. It is not difficult to appreciate that gifts that are, in principle, pious donations fall within the purview of *bayani karamogoya*. The question is how such gifts also serve purely personal and this-worldly ends; how, in other words, they resemble the written magic charms whose production typifies the practice of *siru karamogoya*.

The use of written charms (*sebe*) is extremely common in Islamic "magic," not only in West Africa but throughout the Muslim world.[4] There are countless different formulas, though they all tend to correspond to a few general patterns. Their contents may include short suras from the Qur'an, laudatory prayers, names of angels or prophets, or even numbers arranged in the form of magic squares. Generally, the form of presentation as well as the content is fixed, most often in a simple geometric pattern of one kind or another. The patterns are quite simple, but the possible variations are virtually infinite, and both the form and the content of a particular formula must be reproduced exactly in order for it to be efficacious. Such formulas can be written on a piece of paper and, if necessary, sewn into a small leather pouch and attached to clothing, worn as a necklace, bracelet, or anklet, placed in a house (sometimes inside a wall, or under a door or roof, to protect one from intruders), and so forth. The formula may also be written on a wooden writing board and washed off with water, which is subsequently ingested or used for bathing or anointing a specific part of the body. Such formulas may even be written on leaves used as medication; the leaves are then boiled and the herbal infusion used as medication in whatever manner prescribed.

These formulas are not the monopoly of established scholars. On the contrary, most individuals with a rudimentary knowledge of reading and writing Arabic have their own private collections. Some formulas are readily sold or transmitted as favors from one individual to another, although others are closely guarded secrets. (One Dyula joke consists in asking someone if he has a magic formula for intelligence. The point of the joke is that he will invariably say no; anyone who possessed such a formula would obviously be too smart to let on!) Of course, one must not only know the formula, but also the specific rules for its use. Some formulas can be used for a variety of ends, while others—generally the most powerful and esoteric—have extremely specific purposes. This specificity accounts, in principle, for the seemingly infinite variety of formulas. As one *karamogo* explained, there are as many formulas as there are things that humans wish for, and human desires are boundless. Since knowledge of these formulas is transmitted piecemeal, one can never be sure who possesses the formula corresponding to one's precise needs, though obviously certain individuals, particularly but not exclusively established *karamogos,* enjoy a reputation for possessing a wide variety.

The question remains: why and how do these formulas work? One scholar's explanation is particularly suggestive. These formulas, he related, are essentially praises of God, of angels, and/or of prophets. Their work can be compared to that of *jeliba,* or griots. (Although griots are not indigenous to the Korhogo region, numbers of them have established residence in the modern town, and others visit the town and the surrounding region from time to time, where, it should be added, they are often considered a nuisance and of doubtful Islamic morality.) It is the griot's work to sing one's praises, and one is obliged to reward such praises appropriately; you have to give him money, even if you don't really want to. The praises embodied in written formulas work in the same way. If delivered properly, they place angels and prophets, if not God, under a moral obligation to come to one's assistance, interceding with God on one's behalf. In this scholar's view, the formulas use the idiom of reciprocity in order to create a moral obligation, if not with God, at least with privileged intermediaries. As with griots, this use of the idiom of reciprocity is morally ambivalent; in effect, it is a very thinly disguised form of coercion. With griots, and a fortiori with formulas, this coercion is never absolute. One who receives praise is never literally forced to reciprocate; moreover, if the praise is inappropriate or improperly delivered, the obligation is virtually nil. However, such praise, in the proper form, constrains if it does not absolutely coerce the recipient. God's will is obviously beyond the powers of human coercion, and so one can never be absolutely certain that formulas—or any other technique for imploring God's favor—will work. Nevertheless, these formulas attempt to manipulate the situation by seeking to create a relationship of moral reciprocity that works to the individual's advantage.

If the principle of reciprocity is implicit in the use of written charms, its significance might seem all the more apparent in the use of *saraka*. Nevertheless, the logic of giving is complicated by the fact that individuals use *saraka* as a means of communicating with God. *Saraka* is offered to God, and not, technically speaking, to any human recipient. Of course, the material possessions that constitute the offering, whatever they may be, must be delivered from one person to another. The problem is that it is doubly impossible for anyone to offer anything to God. In the first place, God is immaterial and consequently cannot literally "accept" a gift. Even more important, the material universe, God's creation, is already His; humans have, in this respect, literally nothing to offer. *Saraka* is not quite a gift to God, but it is not either, in an ordinary sense, a gift from one individual to another. An ordinary gift both symbolizes and serves to create or to perpetuate mutual obligations between persons or groups. *Saraka* does no such thing. Its human recipient is under no obligation to its donor; indeed, one must specify, when making such an offering, that it is indeed *saraka*, and no ordinary gift. The recipient need not even offer thanks, other than the standard blessing in such contexts, "Allah saraka mina" ("May God accept [literally, "catch"] the *saraka*").

In short, the reciprocity involved in *saraka* is somewhat skewed; one gives certain items to an individual in the expectation that God will grant some specific favor in return. It is no business of the human recipient to learn what the donor seeks; God knows, in any case. As a general rule, the more important the favor one seeks from God, the more valuable the offering is likely to be, though there need be no strict correspondence, if indeed such a correspondence were even literally possible. The value of the gift may be negligible—small change, a few kola nuts—or it may be considerable—a cow, an embroidered gown. The problem, as with other forms of imploring God's assistance, is the knowledge of what specific offering is appropriate for any specific purpose. As with written formulas, ordinary individuals have their own recipes, and need not always seek the advice of a specialist before making an offering. One lay friend of mine cited a tripartite division of offerings into white, red, and black objects. White offerings—a white chicken, white kola nuts, a white gown, a white cap, white sandals—were appropriate when one wanted to procure something desirable, in seeking good fortune. Red offerings, conversely, are intended as a way of avoiding or casting off misfortune; black offerings correspond to situations of uncertainty, where one is in doubt about an outcome and its consequences. He added that it was not always easy to find someone willing to accept a red offering. Such offerings are dangerous; the misfortune may be transferred in the process from the donor to the recipient. Such offerings are frequently made to a blind person, who cannot see what he is receiving, and is in any case rarely in a position to refuse what he is offered. Such a procedure is perhaps a little (but only a little) less cynical than it might seem. The Dyula consider blindness one of the worst possible afflictions, much worse than deafness, for example. The deaf are often surprisingly well integrated into the social fabric, whereas the blind are in important respects marginalized. The deaf, unlike the blind, can work at all sorts of tasks. A blind person has little choice but to accept the food he is offered; one can, my friend commented, put poison in a blind man's food right in front of his nose and he will not notice. The problem is not really, of course, that people go about systematically poisoning the blind. Rather, blindness reduces the afflicted to total dependence on those around them. At best, they depend entirely on the charity of their kin; at worst, reduced to the status of beggars, on the charity of strangers.[5] The misery of the blind is so great that a little more or less misfortune will not make much difference, whereas even a dangerous gift is likely to be appreciated. God is hardly likely to inflict further punishment unless it is in any case richly deserved. Although the blind may be the ideal recipients of such dangerous gifts, they are not always readily available. Another possibility is to try to fob the offering off on an unknown passer-by, someone to whom one can conveniently transfer misfortune without breaching any fundamental social obligation. Finally, and certainly most ethically, one can offer the red *saraka* to a scholar. Scholars know the proper techniques for averting any misfortune that such a gift might attract.

Such recipes are still relatively simplistic, and do not stipulate the precise nature of the offering. As one might expect, scholars are presumed to possess a more complete knowledge of *saraka*, and may stipulate not only the precise nature of the gift, but also the right category of recipient (e.g., a scholar, an elder, a blind person, a poor person, a stranger) although never his specific identity. They may stipulate, not only the color of the offering, but also the kind of material out of which it is made (iron, cloth, straw, etc.), the quantity, or whatever. The specifications are sometimes quite precise— say, a black hen with two white feathers—making the offering hard to procure, even if it is not valuable in and of itself. The kinds of objects prescribed tend to be limited—food, clothing, animals, household objects, money—but the possible variations and permutations are infinite. However, a scholar's advice on such matters is not free. Individuals may choose to decide on their own, either because the matter is relatively unimportant, because it is too urgent to wait, or simply as a first attempt; if such an attempt does not meet with success, a scholar can always be consulted later.

While one can decide for oneself what one wishes to obtain or to avoid, God may indicate the occasion for offering *saraka* directly by sending dreams. Dreams are considered to be messages sent directly by God to ordinary humans, and as such are taken very seriously. They may indicate events that are to take place in the future, but for better or for worse, these events are not inevitable. Good fortune predicted in dreams will not necessarily occur unless the beneficiary offers *saraka*; an offering of *saraka* can also avert predicted misfortune. Often, the events in the dream do not actually concern the dreamer, but rather a third party, and it is the dreamer's moral responsibility to convey the message to the person or persons whom it directly concerns. As an example, a local politician pointed to his Mercedes. A friend of his had seen the car in his possession in a dream at a time when the politician was out of favor and generally down on his luck. Such a tangible sign of prosperity was hardly a foregone conclusion, but the politician offered *saraka* and, lo and behold, the prediction came true. To underscore the point, he related yet another dream, in which a minister of state escaped from a plane accident where someone else was killed. The dreamer did not succeed in contacting the minister right away. A few days later, the minister's chauffeur was killed in an automobile crash. As the second example shows, the predictions in a dream need not be accurate in precise detail. As a result, it is hardly unlikely that many predictions from dreams will, in one way or another, be "verified" sooner or later, as the dream is reinterpreted ex post facto to fit the events it purportedly was intended to foretell. The circularity of the system is even tighter: if proper *saraka* is not offered, the predicted good fortune will not come to pass. (Even if *saraka* of one sort or another is offered, it may not be appropriate.) On the other hand, misfortune may be avoided through *saraka*. One way or the other, conventional wisdom dictates that such dreams ought not be taken lightly.

Even if the meaning of a dream is unclear, it may induce individuals to make an offering. One morning, as I was passing by the house of a friend, he pulled me aside and invited me to look into his bedroom, where I was treated to the sight of seven church candles, all lit and arranged on the bedroom floor as if (my friend explained) in front of an altar in a Catholic church. Having deliberately excited my curiosity, he proceeded to relate that he had dreamt of the burning candles in his bedroom the night before, and interpreted the dream as an injunction from God that he was to make precisely this kind of offering. He had no idea what kind of good luck this might be intended to bring, or what kind of evil it might ward off. He was obviously rather amused by the very unconventionality of the act, my own presence conveniently adding to the apparent incongruity of the whole situation. Nevertheless, he took the injunction quite seriously; one does not trifle with God's commands. For good measure, he also slaughtered a goat in his front yard, distributing the meat as *saraka* to assorted elders and, since I was present, to me—non-Muslims are perfectly eligible to receive *saraka*.

These uses of *saraka* have nothing to do with piety; their ends are purely this-worldly. Such practices—one might argue the practices of *siru karamogoya* in general—treat God rather like a political superior, to whom praises (written formulas) or gifts (*saraka*) may be offered in the hope of receiving some special favor or another. As with an important chief, it is crucial to know how, exactly, to approach Him. This is precisely what scholars claim to know better than ordinary laymen, although scholars cannot lay claim to any monopoly of such knowledge. This knowledge is essentially amoral. *Maraboutage*, in Ivoirian French, amounts to nothing less than sorcery, the deliberate use of Islamic magic to harm others. Such sorcery is no doubt associated more with written charms than with *saraka*. I do not know whether *saraka* may be offered with the deliberate intention of causing injury, but we have seen that certain offerings may place the recipient in danger, and that donors are sometimes prepared to resort to rather unscrupulous strategies in order to find someone willing to accept them.

The morality of such practices depends on the nature of the ends desired and means employed. It should be stressed that, for virtually all Dyula, wealth and material possessions are legitimate ends in themselves. Unlike their Senufo neighbors, among whom "it is not good to be too ill, nor is it good to be too well, too poor or too rich, nor even too 'normal' " (Sindzingre 1985: 55), Dyula hold that one cannot have too much of a good thing, provided that one's gains are licitly and honestly acquired. Material well-being is both desired and respected in itself. Dyula allude disparagingly to those Senufo whose wealth is only apparent on the occasion of their funerals, but who, during their lifetimes, ate, dressed and were housed as poorly as any of their neighbors. Indeed, the very profession of scholarship itself among the Dyula suffered from the general equation of prestige with prosperity. As one friend pointed out, scholarship these days affords most of its practitioners a scant living, hardly making it an attractive career for the most able or intelligent. No doubt, this situation contributes to the ambivalent attitude of Koko's residents to their scholars. Arguably, "learning" is valued more highly than the learned.

Of course, the licitness, indeed the desirability, of material prosperity and of well-being in general does not automatically justify the use of *saraka* as a means of attaining it. Indeed, I was told (admittedly by one of their staunch opponents, and not necessarily a reliable source) that some Wahhabis reject all resort to "medicine"—be it "traditional," Islamic, or "Western"; illness and health, riches and poverty are manifestations of God's will, to which the pious believer should submit, and which he or she should certainly not attempt—impiously—to manipulate. Such a position is indeed extreme, and implies a uniform and inflexible standard of piety as the only legitimate model of the relationship between God and His worshipers. For Dyula "neotraditionalists," we have seen that standards of piety are more flexible. While a single universal standard exists in principle, the degree to which individuals are expected to live up to that standard depends on whether they are male or female, juniors or elders, of slave or free origin, scholars or laymen. The same kind of flexibility applies to the use of *saraka* for personal ends. Such practices do not call into question the principle that God rewards the virtuous and punishes the wicked, nor that one's fortunes in this world, for better or for worse, are manifestations of His unquestionable will. However, this does not preclude attempts to establish an alternative mode of relationship with God, one based on reciprocity, even between oneself and one who is, in the final analysis, infinitely one's superior.

So far, we have opposed the use many Dyula make of *saraka* as a technique to obtain this-worldly ends with the practice of *saraka* as a pious donation. It must certainly not be imagined that such pious donations are unknown among the Dyula, and that *saraka* is always self-interested in the narrowest sense of the world. Otherwise, *saraka* would have nothing

to do with *bayani karamogoya*, but only with *siru karamogoya*.
Individuals do offer donations out of considerations of piety:
alms to beggars, gifts to scholars, contributions for building
or maintaining a mosque. Such gifts, unlike those whose primary purpose is curing an illness, passing an exam, finding
a job, or obtaining a Mercedes Benz, bring merit to the giver.
Yet this kind of gift is not entirely disinterested. Its purpose is
explicitly, like the kinds of *saraka* undertaken for this-worldly
aims, to obtain a reward from God. As one scholar explained
to me, precisely because God is just, He rewards all acts of
virtue, in the next life if not in this world, just as He punishes
all wickedness. Of course, all acts of charity are rewarded,
but not all such acts—quite apart from *jaka*, a religious obligation—necessarily constitute *saraka*. A gift is *saraka* if and
only if it is specified as such; it is, in other words, the intention of the gift that counts. Whether to obtain merit or to obtain some more specific and mundane benefit, *saraka* attempts to establish a moral relationship of one sort or another
between an individual and God through the medium of a gift
to a third party.

Saraka, it might seem, is essentially of concern to the individual and to God; the eventual (human) recipient or recipients of the gift appear of almost incidental importance. Yet
we have already mentioned a form of *saraka* that in no way
fits such a pattern: the public, indeed ostentatious, distribution of *saraka* during life-crisis rituals—naming ceremonies,
weddings, and especially funerals. Such *saraka* is offered, not
by individuals, but by collectivities. Typically, the core of
such a group is constituted by a clan ward (*kabila*), or sometimes a section (*gba*) of a large clan ward, the group to which
the newborn, the bride or groom,[6] or the deceased belongs.
However, contributions come from the kindreds of the individuals concerned, from relatives in other groups. *Saraka* is
offered *on behalf of* a baby, a couple, or a corpse, by their relatives, those most directly concerned with their welfare. It is
received, in turn, not by individuals per se but by representatives of various communities, groups, and social catego-

ries. Not infrequently, those who give in one capacity receive in another. Precisely because these occasions are so standard-ized, the attention of many participants focuses on the (ap-parently, but only apparently) minor variations: who gives how much to whom in what order. Such variations serve as a symbolic medium whereby groups and individuals may make claims about social relationships that have little, it would seem, to do with religion.

The religious component to such ceremonial distributions is expressed most tangibly by the uttering of blessings (*duau*) from those who have received *saraka*. In this instance, the blessings are not directed at the givers of *saraka*, but, more appropriately, to the newborn, the married couple, or the de-ceased. Symbolically, these blessings are uttered by the en-tire local community, each component part of which must be represented by at least one individual. These individuals will be offered *saraka*, not in their own capacities, but in the name of the collectivity they represent: for example, Cisseraka, "the people of Cissera [the Cisse clan ward of Koko]"; Wara-nieneka, "the people of Waraniene [a largely Dyula village a few kilometers from Korhogo]." The blessings, consequently, are symbolically offered by whole groups rather than by in-dividuals acting in their own capacity. Ultimately, the cere-mony enacts, in a dramatic form, the entire local communi-ty's concern with the critical events of the lives of its members.

But what is "the entire community"? In a sense, the an-swer is circular: the community is the aggregate of all those groups and categories represented in the ceremony. The community is in any case broader than Koko itself. Any such ceremony in Koko will involve representatives from "across the stream" in Korhogo, as well as from a host of Dyula vil-lages and village quarters from the general vicinity, and sometimes from well beyond. From ceremony to ceremony, the "community" symbolized, though broadly similar, is rarely if ever exactly identical. Specific villages may only be "concerned" with events in the lives of particular individuals or, more usually, kin groups, from Koko; obviously, specific ceremonies reflect the particular networks of groups and individuals in Koko. While the list of villages "represented" may differ from occasion to occasion, no ceremony ever takes place without a significant number of neighboring villages sending delegates, and the villages of Korhogo's immediate periphery—Kapele, Waraniene, Katia, Dyendana, to name a few—are almost invariably involved.

This variability does not only concern the "environment" of which Koko is a part, but even Koko itself. As mentioned before, the "Senufo" quarters of Koko—Tiembaraso, the neighborhood of the "Tiembara," the dominant group of Korhogo chiefdom; "Sonoso," the quarter of the Fodonon-speaking minority; as well as the quarters of "casted" artisans, Fonoso (the blacksmiths), Lokhonso (the brass casters), Kuleso (the woodcarvers)—are not necessarily invited. Ultimately, the ceremony does not just passively reflect the composition of the community. Rather, it constitutes an active recreation, a symbolic reconstitution, of the whole in terms of its constituent parts.

These ceremonies can be categorized in two apparently contradictory ways: while they may serve as a symbolic expression of the local community's collective concern for individual members, they are also characterized by a spirit of competitiveness and serve as a forum for the particular agendas of specific individuals and groups. Prestations are made publicly and ostentatiously; everyone can see who gives and how much. "Who," in these cases, is almost never an individual, except for politicians from "across the stream." Usually, *saraka* is offered by a group of some sort or other. In the days before the ceremony, such groups caucus, pooling their resources. The leading members attempt to induce as many others as they can to contribute as much as possible, and decisions are made about who will receive how much and in what order. How much such a group contributes is, in large measure, a statement about its wealth and its influence as a whole. However, this influence and prestige devolves particularly on its leaders, those whose effectiveness in holding the group together, as demonstrated by their capacity to persuade members to contribute as much as possible, is put to the test on each occasion. Indeed, groups and individuals compete, not only for prestige, but also by making implicit claims over dependent kinsmen and clients, those on whose behalf they bestow largesse. One might argue that the unity of the community, as symbolically expressed by the act of blessing, is only an "ideal," but, if so, why isn't the violation of that ideal, embodied in the thinly disguised competitiveness of the proceedings, considered inappropriate by most of the participants? More cynically, the affirmation of the community's unity might be portrayed as a "mask," an "ideological" denial of the competition lurking beneath the surface—but, if so, the mask is rather transparent.

On the contrary, there is no necessary contradiction between these two facets of the ceremony. It is precisely the nature and the existence of the local community that give meaning to the rivalries expressed in the course of the ceremony. In the first place, the local community is, both really and metaphorically, the audience. Even more important, the ceremony is about the status—in more ways than one—of its participants within the community at large. "Status" in one sense can be interpreted as prestige, as the respect individuals command within the local community. In another, but equally relevant, sense, "status" has to do with the nature of rights and obligations between various categories of persons. The respective "statuses" of groups and individuals, one way or the other, depend on the relevance—or the irrelevance—of such factors as kin-group membership, "caste," ethnicity, age, generation, and gender. The local community is the arena in which such issues are thrashed out, if not resolved. Indeed, as we have seen, the "community" cannot simply be taken for granted. The position of individuals within the "community" depends on the way in which the community itself is constituted. The symbolic identity of the community, expressed most powerfully through the act of collective blessing, does not deny the reality of competition among its members. On the contrary, it makes such competition not

only possible but meaningful, by providing the framework
where it takes place.

Even if we ignore the hidden agendas underlying the distribution of *saraka* in all these instances, the logic of exchange
remains a complex one. *Saraka* is being offered, not by individuals on their own behalf, but rather by collectivities on behalf of specific members. God is being implored to ensure the
well-being of a child, the success of a marriage, the salvation
of a dead person. The plea comes from the kin group to
which the individual belongs, and beyond that group to his
or her kindred as a whole, and sometimes beyond, to all who
in one way or another have a crucial "interest" in the person—patrons, clients, teacher, apprentices, friends, political
allies. The local community as a whole, as symbolized by its
representatives, witnesses this expression of collective concern, collectively accepts the offering on God's behalf, and in
turn bestows its own blessing. In this manner, the relationship between God and the individual or individuals on behalf
of whom the ceremony is performed is mediated, directly
and dramatically, by a cluster of social relationships, of agna-
tion, cognation and affinity, of seniority and dependence, of
patronage and clientship, which situate the individual within
the local community at large.

In a sense, one might oppose "private" and "public" *saraka*. Offerings individuals make to others for very specific,
this-worldly ends, while they are not necessarily secret, are
nobody else's business—not even the recipient's. Collective
offerings for the general well-being of individuals are, quite
literally, everybody's business. Of course, the pious offerings
individuals may make in order to accumulate merit are not
unambiguously public or private. In one sense, the offerings
are self-interested; they ultimately ought to benefit the giver.
On the other hand, the gifts themselves normally are of
some benefit—symbolic if not real—to the general community: alms to the poor, gifts to scholars, support for the
mosque, for example. Nothing intrinsically dictates the degree of publicity or secrecy accompanying the act of offering, but there is certainly no reason to conceal such gifts and

often advantage in making such an offering ostentatiously. In fact, life-crisis rituals provide an ideal forum, not only for the collective and virtually obligatory offering of *saraka*, but also for conspicuous pious donations, particularly to scholars, who are invariably present on such occasions. Broadly speaking, individuals are expected to give in keeping with their prosperity and their influence. Such offerings may be expressions of piety, but, as we have seen with respect to the Sufi brotherhoods, piety is itself a social construct and has as much to do with social expectations as with the qualities of individuals.

In any case, the public/private dichotomy is too crude, opposing the isolated individual in one instance to the community at large in the other. Yet individuals are members of Koko community as a whole only by virtue of their membership in specific kin groups, in localized, named clan wards (*kabilas*). These clan wards constitute yet another arena for the offering of *saraka*. At first sight, these instances seem to short-circuit the very logic of the gift; they are offered by the kin group to itself on its own behalf. The *saraka* invariably takes the form of a meal, of cooked food, of which all members of the kin group who are present in Koko must partake. The meal commemorates the collective ancestors of the group, and is, in a real sense, offered to them as well as to God. The ancestors are, in this particular context, intermediaries between their collective descendants and God.

I witnessed such collective meals on a few occasions, both in Koko and in the village of Kadioha. In principle, I was told, such *saraka* ought to be offered on a regular basis, once a year for example. Not surprisingly, actual practice is far more variable. The circumstances in which one such meal I attended in 1985 was offered are instructive. The meal was offered by the largest *kabila* in Koko. Not surprisingly, given its size, it included several quite prosperous members, as well as numbers of others who were relatively well-off. Moreover, it happens to enjoy proprietary rights over the office of imam for the town mosque. Because of these various factors, the *kabila* is quite influential in Koko as a whole. However, these same factors—size, wealth, and influence—foster jealousy, backbiting and factionalism, pitting not only other *kabilas* against them as a whole, but different members of the *kabila* against one another. This was the situation when they received an urgent message from one of their members in Abidjan, the capital. Apparently, the imam of one of the main mosques in the capital had dreamt of the ancestor of this very *kabila* in Koko. In the dream, the ancestor deplored the factional strife besetting his descendants, and explained that this was because the *kabila* had let the practice of offering communal meals of *saraka* lapse. They were instructed to offer such a meal as soon as possible, and to continue the practice regularly, in order to restore harmony within the group and ensure its prosperity. Strikingly, the imam in question is in no way related to the *kabila*, and is not even from the region of Korhogo. He has no direct, and not even a remote, interest in the affairs of the group, and the fact that the dream was experienced by an individual so geographically and social distant was held as proof positive of the urgency and validity of the message. As a result, the message was promptly heeded, and the members of the *kabila* were, at least for the time being, quite determined to resume the practice. A few days later, I attended another such meal, offered this time by one particular segment (*gba*) of the *kabila*. The logic dictating that one may petition the ancestors for the unity and prosperity of the *kabila* as a whole also suggests that one may legitimately do so on behalf of any particular segment. I was told that this had been the past practice of that particular segment, and that its members had been inspired by the *kabila's* meal to resurrect their own ceremony too.

In one sense, this kind of *saraka* is "public." The meals are consumed in the open, for everyone to see. Yet from another point of view, it is "private," of concern to no one outside the kin group sharing the ritual meal. Like the distribution of *saraka* during life crises, the ritual is collective, but the relationship between the offering and the collectivities involved is radically different. *Saraka* during life crises involves an offering from one collectivity to another of a different order. These collectivities are not fully predetermined, but to a certain extent defined, recreated, by the very occasion. One collectivity is the "kindred" of the individual on whose behalf the rite is performed; however, such links are not defined exclusively in genealogical terms, but rather in terms of the nature and depth of relationships. Those who offer *saraka* on one's behalf are those who are in one way or another concerned with the events of one's life, if not as kin, then as "hosts" or "strangers," patrons or clients, masters or apprentices, teachers or pupils. The act of contributing, and to some extent the amount offered, is a symbolic statement about the existence, the nature, and indeed the strength of the relationship. The rough outlines of such an ad hoc group are predictable on any occasion, but its precise form is a priori indeterminate. The same applies, as mentioned, to the "community" whose representatives receive the offering. If the local community is more or less the same on every occasion, its boundaries are constantly subject to shifting and even the nature of its constituent units may change over time. Admittedly, the same can be said of *kabilas*, of kin groups in general. However, the issue of what constitutes a *kabila*, or one of its segments, tends to be given symbolic expression during life-crisis rituals, in much the same manner as the wider "community." On the other hand, when *saraka* consists of a communal meal offered by a kin group to its members, living and dead, the nature and to a large extent the contours of the group are largely taken for granted. *Saraka* does not, in this instance, define the group, but rather seeks to maintain, if not to restore, its unity.

All in all, it is possible to identify at least four meanings of *saraka* in Koko:

1. A pious donation, conferring religious merit on the believer
2. A ritualized offering, for the purposes of attaining a specific, this-worldly benefit
3. The ceremonial distribution of food and/or money to the community at large in terms of its specified component parts, on behalf of specific individuals on the occasion of life crises

4. A ceremonial meal prepared and consumed by members of a specific kin group in order to promote or maintain harmony within the group and general prosperity

Saraka strikes us, in other words, by reason of its polyvalence. It is precisely this polyvalence that Wahhabis and other reformers find objectionable. For such reformers, *saraka* ought to be a category of action that falls within the purview of a universal moral code, an action that is meritorious without being obligatory for all believers. The vast majority of Dyula in Koko, those who perform *saraka* in a variety of contexts for a variety of ends, do not deny this aspect of *saraka*, but also acknowledge a very different aspect, involving the act of communicating with God. It is in this way that the translation of *saraka* as "sacrifice" makes sense; the act of offering is the means of establishing communication with the deity. *Saraka* is a way of asking God for "well-being," but "well-being," like *saraka* itself, means not one but many things. It is the material well-being of individuals, not only health and long life for themselves and their dependents, but material possessions, worldly success, even political power. It is also their spiritual well-being, particularly in the next life, when all sins will be punished and good actions rewarded. Such spiritual well-being is most obviously the aim of pious donations, but also of the *saraka* distributed at funerals, in order that God may have mercy (*hina*) on the deceased. Finally, and crucially, well-being is not only the well-being of the individual, but of the collectivity: the unity and prosperity of the clan ward (*kabila*) or one of its segments (*gba*).

In a perfect world, there would be no conflict between these different forms of well-being. The good would visibly be rewarded, and the evil punished; what is good for the individual would be good for the collectivity, and vice versa. However, Dyula are acutely aware of contradictory pulls in the world as it is. Piety and material prosperity do not always go hand in hand. An individual's prosperity gives rise to jealousy, and ultimately strife, within the kin group; in turn, the prosperity of any one kin group will foster opposition within the wider community at large. This is not to suggest that the collective sentiments symbolically expressed during life-crisis rituals are necessarily hypocritical (of course, they sometimes are); the collectivity, whether the kin group or ultimately the community as a whole, is really "concerned" with the well-being of its members. The prosperity of the group depends in many ways on the good fortune of some of its members: wealth, political influence, "connections" of one sort or another, know-how. Even so, there is a constant, if implicit, tension between the well-being of individuals, of particular groups, and of the "community" as a whole. It is appropriate that *saraka*, the ritual expression of the quest for well-being—whether spiritual or material, of the group or the individual—straddles the domains of *siru karamogoya* and *bayani karamogoya*, of self-interest and morality.

10

Universals and Particulars

The past has left signposts in the Dyula villages around Korhogo, and even in Koko itself, for those who know where to
find them. Such signposts include the graves of the *wali*, the
saints, those who, through their piety, earned the special
love of God. One may visit the graves of a *wali* with gifts (gra-
ciously accepted by the *wali's* descendants), imploring him
(or, exceptionally, her) to intercede with God on one's behalf
for one specific reason or another. Some *wali* are anonymous;
it stands to reason in old villages that some of the dead,
whose names may have been long forgotten, were once exceptionally pious. Some named *wali* have only a local reputation; some may be recognized as such only by a handful of
individuals, notably their own descendants. Others may be
well known throughout the region, or even well beyond, as is
the case of Muhammad al-Mustafa Saganogo of Boron,
whose grave has long been a site of pilgrimage. The most fa-
mous *wali* are, not surprisingly, the great scholars of past
times, those whose names recur again and again in the Suwarian *isnads*.

The *wali* are, in more ways than one, embodiments of the
Suwarian tradition. Most obviously, many of them were
scholars trained in the tradition who transmitted it to subsequent generations. More generally, they represent those of
past generations from the region, the village, and the kin
group, those whose exemplary piety still constitutes a
model, not to mention an additional basis for communicating
with God. Predictably, the Wahhabis reject the *wali*, or at
least deny their power to intercede on one's behalf with God.
The Wahhabis disapprove, on general principle, of all inter-

mediaries between God and the individual believer. In any case, the Wahhabis visibly reject the past, at least in the form of local religious tradition, specifically by rejecting the Maliki rite of prayer. Opponents of the Wahhabis invoke the past as a vindication. They will pray as their fathers prayed, and before that, their fathers' fathers, and generations before. The graves of the *wali*, of the holy dead, are, for those who acknowledge their sanctity and their power, testimonials to a Muslim past of which they can be proud.

Lo society groves constitute another kind of testimonial to another kind of past. Not infrequently, the abandoned groves have been left intact. The conviction that initiation societies and their associated activities are improper, if not immoral, does not necessarily entail the belief that *lo* spirits are powerless. It would be simplistic to assert that the abandoned *lo* groves represent the "bad" past and that the graves of the *wali* represent the "good" past. Some older men in Koko, not to mention the villages, speak quite nostalgically about the initiation societies; Dyula masquerading, in its occasional and attenuated manifestations, exerts a powerful fascination among Koko's youth. Even so, there is a general consensus that Islam as practiced in Koko is better, purer, morally superior now that the initiation societies have been abandoned, that Dyula now "know better" than to indulge in such activities. The widely varying—and often frankly ambivalent—attitudes in Koko to the renewal of masquerading in certain other communities demonstrate the extent to which individuals define themselves in terms of, or else in opposition to, specific aspects of the past. But this past, the past of the initiation societies, is over and done with. One may accept it or reject it, but one cannot really turn back.

The abandoned *lo* groves and the graves of the saints are, in any case, powerful symbols of what individuals reject in the past and of what they cherish and hold sacred. They embody the reality of a religious tradition, a continuity of practice throughout the generations, if not the conviction that the ancestors, those at whose tombs one seeks succor, were holier, more pious, and altogether better Muslims than people nowadays. Yet they also embody the reality of change, of the conscious abandonment of certain practices and the adoption of others, if not the conviction that Muslims today are more scrupulous, more pious perhaps, than the ancestors.

Muslims of Koko are acutely aware of both the continuity of religious tradition and the reality of changing religious practice. Where they differ is in their attitudes, ranging from a nostalgia for things past to an impatience with practices that seem, if not in error, then simply meaningless. I was struck by this awareness when I first came to Korhogo in 1972, and it was expressly in order to explore more fully the nature of this change that I returned in 1984. At the time, I was inclined to interpret the processes I had come to investigate in terms loosely derived from Robin Horton's (1971, 1975a, 1975b) theory of African conversion. To recapitulate briefly, Horton postulated that the extent to which individuals and communities were concerned with the social "macrocosm" as opposed to the "microcosm" corresponded to the extent of their religious concern with the creator—the monotheistic pole—as opposed to a polytheistic preoccupation with local spirits. Obviously, my concern was not with the conversion of the Dyula to a monotheistic religion. They were, after all, Muslims from their very arrival in the Korhogo region. Rather, I was at first inclined to place religious ideologies, within the broad scope of "Islam," on a scale ranging from particularistic to universalistic.

Interpreting the changes that have taken and are taking place in the practice of Islam in Koko in such terms is an easy enough exercise. What could be more particularistic than a Muslim community divided into two halves: "warriors" who initiated their youths into secret societies, and "scholars" who brought them up to recite, if not read, Arabic? Is not the concern for ritual exactitude, for the "correct" pronunciation of prayers in Arabic and the impeccable performance of ablutions, a manifestation of universalism, of a quest for religious conformity not only within the local community but among all Muslims as a whole? Seen in this light, "neotraditionalism," as I have awkwardly and inelegantly characterized Islam as practiced by the majority of Koko's residents, emerges as a "transitional phase," partly particularistic and partly universalistic.

In retrospect, I am now convinced that this kind of explanation, if not entirely on the wrong track, is both inadequate and misleading. In the first place, it is much too patly teleological, implying a clear and unambiguous movement in religious life and thought from particular to universal. If one rejects such a teleological vision, it becomes much more difficult, if not intrinsically absurd, to identify "transitional phases." It is not the notion of "transition," but the notion of "phase," to which I object. Islam, as historically believed in and practiced by specific groups and individuals at specific times and places, is always in transition. It is always possible to call into question what the majority take for granted, and by no means a foregone conclusion that such calls will fall on deaf ears.[1] Beliefs and practices are constantly shifting—subject to reevaluation, if not rejection—though not necessarily in uniform and entirely predictable ways.

But if we reject teleological explanations, must we abandon all reference to universalism and particularism? This need not really be the case. Particularism is the religious idiom in which involvement in the "microcosm," the "local community," is most adequately expressed; universalism stresses the importance of the "macrocosm," the "global community." It is a legacy of nineteenth-century social theory that we tend to see microcosm and macrocosm as polar opposites, as *Gemeinschaft* versus *Gesellschaft*; *societas* versus *civitas*; kinship versus territory. By implication, the extent of the individual's involvement in the microcosm is in inverse proportion to his or her involvement in the macrocosm. But microcosm and macrocosm, particularism and universalism, are not necessarily antithetical.

In any case, terms like "particularism" and "universalism," "macrocosm" and "microcosm," and indeed "local community" and "global community," are at best ambiguous and imprecise, at worst misleading reifications of a more elusive reality. We are dealing, not with pre-constituted entities, but rather with different modes of relationship. On one hand, there are face-to-face, multistranded relationships, based on a multitude of criteria including age, generation, and kin-group membership, but also the specific kin networks of individuals and their personal reputations. Such relationships are only possible within a relatively restricted arena where most individuals are personally known to most others, and consequently where identities are intrinsically complex. On the other hand, there are relatively impersonal relationships, where individuals are identified as representatives of one or another social type rather than in terms of a cluster of features that distinguish them from anyone else in a well-known, if restricted, universe.

The arenas in which these modes of relationship are relevant may, in one way or another, be situated in space: Koko, Côte d'Ivoire, the Muslim world. These "places"—some are admittedly easier than others to situate on a map—should in any case not be taken absolutely literally. Whether or not one belongs in Koko does not literally depend on which side of the stream one happens to reside. Yet the stream is a convenient metaphor separating the "local" from the "global" arena. Every member of the community of Koko is involved, to one extent or another, in both arenas. No one can choose, unambiguously, between particularism and universalism.

In any case, particularism and universalism do not really exist as such, in any meaningful way. There are only particularisms and universalisms. One cannot simply oppose "face-to-face" and "impersonal" types of relationships. The specific nature of the criteria individuals use to evaluate one another, in one arena or the other, are obviously of critical importance. At stake are the principles by which individuals identify and evaluate themselves and one another, principles that are implicitly or explicitly hierarchical: age, generation, and kin-group membership; wealth, education, and political connections; but also piety and the rigor with which one observes the Shariᶜa as one understands it.

Islam, after all, is intended to govern the whole of one's life, and not simply social interaction—in other words, in re-

ligious terms, morality—in one or the other arena, the global
or the local, the universal or the particular. Of course, a
purely particularistic Islam is a glaring contradiction in
terms, but one can also call into question the unambiguous
universalism of apparently universalistic ideologies. In very
different ways, both Wahhabis and secularists have had to
come to terms with the "local" arena of relationships. On one
hand, the Wahhabi insistence on a more completely uniform
(i.e., "universal") standard of piety has gone hand in hand
with forms of symbolic behavior that set the Wahhabis apart
as a separate Muslim community. It is no accident that their
detractors accuse them, rightly or wrongly, of exclusivism—
precisely the contrary of "universalism"; of establishing their
own, newly formed "local" communities in terms of their
common observance of supposedly "universal" norms. Individual Wahhabis are faced with the choice of renouncing
their membership in one kind of "local" community in favor
of another, or else of engaging in systematic and embarrassing hypocrisy, professing one set of beliefs among fellow
Wahhabis and practicing another in their home communities.
Secularists, in this respect, are at an advantage; they can
sometimes have their cake and eat it too. Yet I could not help
being struck by the spectacular and ostentatious participation of the rich and powerful in the public ritual life of their
home communities. The very wealthy cosmopolitan elite
have the luxury of reaping the fruits of success in both
spheres, the global and the local, but only a very few individuals command the resources to play at this game. The fact has
become painfully apparent to a whole younger generation of
Western-educated Dyula, and with this awareness, much of
the appeal of secularism has faded. Personal freedom, after
all, is sweetest to those who have the means to do as they
please, when and where they please. The choices that confront individuals are not between "particularism" and "universalism," but rather between allegiances to different local
communities, and between different "global" standards for
situating themselves outside the local community and for situating their local community with respect to the world
around them. Different ideologies of "universalism" must

either live side by side with particularisms or else generate
their own, in terms of new criteria of exclusiveness and inclu-
siveness, of hierarchy and authority, which regulate the morality of face-to-face interaction.

I have tended, in the course of this book, to present these
varying viewpoints as clear-cut alternatives, but this is only
sometimes true. My perception of religious differences in
Koko was conditioned by the fact that I first arrived in 1972
during what might be labeled the "Wahhabi crisis." The community was very definitely polarized—admittedly with overwhelming support for one pole against the other—and individuals whose loyalties were suspected of wavering were
very directly pressured to side against the Wahhabis. Yet in
many other respects, and even more emphatically a decade
later, religion was not strictly speaking "controversial." Religion mattered very much to a great many people in Koko. It
was a frequent, though hardly an obsessive, topic of everyday conversation. As with any topic of conversation, individuals would inevitably disagree openly from time to time,
though such disagreements did not always constitute arguments, and neither were all arguments necessarily bitter. In
the absence of controversy, of situations where individuals
are asked unambiguously to declare their support for one
side or the other, people are under decidedly less pressure to
keep their stated opinions, or for that matter their behavior,
fully consistent.

Such a state of affairs allows individuals to waver, and in
some respects to straddle positions that, in other circumstances, might seem irreconcilable: for example, by expressing their intellectual affinity to younger scholars trained
in Saudi Arabia without renouncing their close ties to
Suwarian-trained scholars who are their friends, kinsmen,
and neighbors. It frequently allows individuals to respond,
in terms of behavior or stated opinions, to specific circumstances, without worrying about contradicting themselves.
They may, for example, laud regimes that enforce strict standards of sexual morality by stoning adulterers, and yet apply
very different standards in resolving disputes about the

deeds and misdeeds of their own kin. In short, individuals can uphold a sort of double standard, committing themselves with equal sincerity to a relatively impersonal, "global"moral code of behavior and to a highly personal code governing face-to-face relationships in Koko. It is as if there were a tacit agreement in Koko to avoid confrontation on religious issues, to avoid publicly stating positions that would force individuals to make unambiguous public commitments one way or the other. In fact, such an attitude is fully consistent with one of the basic premises of face-to-face interaction in Koko—namely, that one should defer in public to one's seniors, to those in recognized relations of authority. To challenge scholars and elders openly is to call into question the hierarchy of piety (see chapter 8), the moral underpinnings of authority in Koko. The avoidance of confrontation and the semblance of unity that ensues are testimonials to the reality of Koko's existence as a moral community. But this unity is constantly threatened by the pull of the world across the stream, channeling its various members into different milieux, different sectors of economy and society, as bureaucrats and merchants, craftsmen, workers, or the unemployed, with different "interests" and, what is more to the point, different visions of what a "global" moral community ought ideally resemble.

There is a constant tension between the moral universe of Koko and the moral universe prevailing across the stream, between the kinds of particularistic ethos that can guide face-to-face relationships within a restricted arena and one or another of the universalistic codes on which one must rely when dealing with the world beyond. The principles governing relationships in Koko are clearly inappropriate, and usually simply irrelevant, once one crosses the stream. On the other hand, the consistent application of a global morality, with no concession to local particularisms, would spell the end of Koko as a moral community; it would become just another part of town. Most of the time, these tensions are only latent. Groups and individuals can deal with them on an ad hoc basis, or simply pretend they don't exist. From time to

time they erupt in crises, as with the abolition of the *lo* societies or the outcry over the Wahhabis. In each of these two
cases, the outcome has been reaffirmation of the moral unity
of the community, but there is no telling what will happen
the next time, if there is a next time.

These kinds of tensions are by no means peculiar to Koko.
In a very general sense, one might argue that these same
problems beset all small, close-knit communities in the modern world. However, I would suggest that these tensions are
experienced particularly acutely by Muslim communities. In
principle, Christianity is as universalistic a religion as Islam.
However, the Christian world has by now come to accept, if
sometimes begrudgingly, the reality of sectarianism. This
sectarian tradition, most markedly among Protestants, has
made possible, for example, the emergence of a whole variety of explicitly *African* Christian Churches.[2] The Christian
believer must adhere to one church or another. This is very
definitely the case in Côte d'Ivoire, where Catholics, evangelical Protestants, and, in some parts of the south, Harrists—
followers of the Liberian prophet William Wadé Harris—vie
with one another for followers. Under the circumstances, individuals cannot only—and perhaps do not even primarily—
identify themselves as "Christians," but as members of a particular church. The possibility of joining—and if necessary of
forming—a separate religious community provides an ave-
nue for resolving ideological tensions in the religious domain
that is not available to Muslims. This is arguably a very "Protestant" vision of Christianity, and seemingly of little or no
relevance to regions that are predominantly Catholic. I am
not sure this is entirely the case, however. The explicitly *ecumenical* and consequently "global" orientation of Vatican II
was accompanied by the explicit introduction of "local" particularisms—not least of which was the service in the vernacular—in the liturgy. Significantly, there is currently a debate
within the Catholic Church concerning the possibility of a
specifically African theology.[3] Moreover, the existence of an
ecclesiastical hierarchy that determines what is within and
what is beyond the pale serves, I would argue, to mediate be-

tween "global" and "local" facets of religion. No such hierarchy exists in Islam.

A Muslim "sect," on the other hand, is a contradiction in terms. The notion of an African Islam, an "Islam noir," is entirely a product of European scholars and administrators. Virtually all Muslims in Africa would deny the very possibility of a specifically "African" Islam, as opposed to the self-proclaimed African Christianity that clearly exists. Rather than a church, there exists the *umma*, the global, undivided moral community of Muslims. It must be stressed that the *umma* is real, in the same sense that Koko is real. Both are communities. It means a great deal to individuals that they belong to these communities, and membership in turn implies the existence of concrete rights and obligations. People may disagree about what such communities, global or local, are really like; about who really is or is not a member; but their ideas, their actions and reactions, are predicated on the salience of both kinds of community to everyday life.

The tensions experienced by Muslims in Koko are characteristic of members of small, face-to-face communities everywhere in a world whose horizons are such that interaction beyond a certain pale must inevitably be governed by some sort of relatively impersonal and "universal" code of behavior. These tensions are specifically (but not necessarily exclusively) experienced in religious terms. Questions about Islam are questions about the nature of communities and of their relationship to how individuals define their own identities and those of their neighbors. Of course, similar tensions, and similar questions, beset Dyula "villagers," many of whom are in any case living, temporarily or permanently, in towns. Like their cousins in Koko, villagers live a double existence in (at least) two moral communities, the face-to-face domain of "home" and the impersonal world outside. Yet there is some comfort to a universe where "home" and the "outside world" are separated at the very least by a bus ride. In Koko, these two communities are separated only by a little brook, which trickles under the road near the Friday mosque.

Notes

Preface

1. This ceremony, described in chapter 6, was the subject of my first publication about Islam among the Dyula (Launay 1977b). Parts of this article have been incorporated into chapter 6, but for the most part I have preferred to reformulate the discussion in somewhat different terms.

2. A version of chapter 4 (Launay 1990) is included in that volume.

Chapter 1

1. For accounts of the history of the idea of "totemism" and of its demise, see Lévi-Strauss 1962 and Kuper 1988.

2. Strictly speaking, it is quite conceivable that individuals identify themselves as "totemists." One African friend of mine proudly claimed to be an "animist." However, such cases involve the adoption by individuals, if not whole groups, of labels invented by outsiders; Islam is clearly in another category.

3. Such a position is explicitly adopted by Zein 1977; see Asad 1986 and Eickelman 1987 for critiques of it.

4. I have been as guilty of this practice as anyone else (Launay 1977b and 1982). By and large, such misuse of language has not been intended as the expression of an explicit theoretical position, but its very ambiguity reflects real conceptual concerns of anthropologists. It should be noted that many "anthropologists of Islam" who have used such phrases in the past have, like myself, publicly or privately recanted.

5. I certainly do not wish to imply that "traditional" religions are organic products of local communities, whereas "universal" religions are not. The pitfalls of the organic approach may be as great in the analysis of nonscriptural religions; they are simply less obvious.

6. Notable exceptions are Zein 1974 and, most recently, Holy 1991.

7. For example, Abner Cohen 1969, Amselle 1977, and Copans 1980, to cite only book-length studies.

8. The literature on West African jihad movements and the states they established is voluminous. Monographs on the subject include Last 1967, Hiskett 1973, Quinn 1972, and Robinson 1985.

9. Sufis and Sufi orders have also generated a massive corpus of scholarly writings. Again, purely by way of example, one can cite Behrman 1970, O'Brien 1971 and 1975, Coulon 1981, and Copans 1980 on Senegal alone, as well as Martin 1976, Paden 1973, Brenner 1984, and O'Brien and Coulon 1988.

10. Such emphasis on these particular themes is already evident in Trimingham's (1962) earlier survey. In many respects, Hiskett's and Clarke's books update Trimingham's information without calling into question the general framework.

11. Studies of societies characterized by the Suwarian tradition include Sanneh 1979, Hunter 1976 and 1977, Launay 1982, Ferguson 1973, Levtzion 1968, Wilks 1968 and 1989, Green 1984, and Handloff 1982.

12. See, e.g. Beidelman 1982.

13. The nature of the Iranian theocratic regime is quite exceptional in Islamic history; see Enayat 1983 and Arjomand 1987.

14. I certainly do not wish to imply that all Marxists subscribe to this kind of approach, by any means, though I would argue that it is consistent with the point of view of some Marxists. For a highly sophisticated Marxist approach to religion, one that confronts the problem of religion as "ideology" squarely, see Bloch 1986.

CHAPTER 2

1. See Launay 1978 and 1982 for a more detailed description of Dyula trade in Korhogo.

2. The issue of children born out of wedlock—*nyamogoden*—is a complex one. Technically, for instance, a child born to a couple who have eloped, before the marriage has been acknowledged by the woman's family, can be labeled *nyamogoden*, and could be claimed by the woman's descent groups as a member on these grounds. Of course, not least because the Dyula are Muslims, it is highly insulting to be called a bastard. Whatever "rules" might exist about who actually is a bastard and to which group he or she really belongs are systematically manipulated or violated. See Launay n.d.b.

3. See Launay 1979 on the "host/stranger" relationship among the Dyula.

4. See Bassett 1985 for a history and evaluation of cotton production in the region.

CHAPTER 3

1. See Lovejoy 1980 for a history of kola production and trade in West Africa.

2. Binger 1892 provides a detailed, firsthand description of Kong. For modern accounts of Kong's history, see Bernus 1960, Green 1984 and 1986, and Université Nationale de Côte d'Ivoire 1977.

3. On the chiefdom of Kadioha, see Launay 1988a and 1988b.

4. Bernus 1961, Ouattara 1977. However, Ouattara argues that these oral traditions reflect Dyula influences, and dates both Nanguin's reign and the foundation of Korhogo much earlier.

5. Ouattara 1977.

6. The identity of the Dieli language has been a subject of some controversy; see, e.g., Person 1964: 328 and Glaze 1981: 41. See Launay (n.d.a.) for a critical overview of theories about the Dieli's origin. In any case, their language is unintelligible to any other group in the region. The language is rapidly disappearing; many younger Dieli cannot understand it, much less speak it.

7. Louis Binger (1892: 298) noted a similar phenomenon in Kong, whose Muslim population he divided into three categories: (1) literate Muslims, (2) illiterate Muslims who nevertheless followed Koranic precepts reasonably strictly, (3) *dolo-* (i.e., beer-) drinking Muslims. Binger's beer-drinking Muslims are no doubt analogous to the *tun tigi* of Korhogo.

8. Strictly speaking, the term *banmana* was not used to refer to all unbelievers, but only to those living in the West African Sahel or the savanna. Forest dwellers such as the Akan or the Guro were called by other names.

9. This contrasts sharply with the celebration of Muslim festivities in various kingdoms of northern Ghana, such as Gonja (Goody 1967: 201–2) and Mamprusi (Brown 1975: 95–96, 98), where they were observed by Muslims and non-Muslims alike, and served to express political allegiance to chiefs, rather than membership in the religious community of Islam.

10. Cf. Abner Cohen 1971.

11. One Dyula informant asserted that the Milaga formerly ate dog flesh, proof positive of their staunch paganism; dog flesh, even more than pork, tends to symbolize forbidden meat (*jufaa*) among the Dyula. Whether or not such an assertion is true, it suggests a means whereby Dyula might symbolically distinguish the "pagan" Milaga from Muslim *tun tigi*, who, after all, drank beer and offered blood sacrifices to spirits.

12. See Goody 1968.

13. Ripert, cited in Marty 1922: 152. The story is situated in the Worodugu, a region with which the Korhogo Dyula maintained close contacts, and whose scholars shared with Korhogo the same "Suwarian" tradition (see Wilks 1968: 176–81).

14. See Triaud 1974 and Harrison 1988 for discussions of French attitudes and policy toward Islam, and of the context in which such declarations of support were solicited.

15. On the notion of "strangers" among the Dyula, see Launay 1979.

16. I would tentatively date the introduction of sermons to Koko to the late 1950s or early 1960s. Their introduction is generally attributed to al-Hajj Mustafa "Benkoro" Cisse, who is still active in Koko and is by no means an old man.

17. For a fuller discussion of Dyula sermons, see chapter 6.

18. In some contexts, the Dieli of Koko continue to stress their separate identity; they have become Dyula for most, but not quite all, intents and purposes.

19. See J. and M.-J. Dérive 1986.

CHAPTER 4

1. Sanneh 1979 argues for an earlier, thirteenth-century date for al-Hajj Salim Suware.

2. The phrase is that of Ivor Wilks (1984), to whom I am heavily indebted for his discussion of al-Hajj Salim and the Suwarian tradition.

3. For the career of al-Hajj Mahmud Karantaw, see Levtzion 1968: 147–51, Hiskett 1984: 168–70, and Wilks 1989: 100–103.

4. For a history of the "Wahhabi" movement in West Africa, see Kaba 1974 and Amselle 1988; see also Niezen 1990 for a description of a rural "Wahhabi" community in Mali.

5. See, e.g., Kaba 1974. Mervyn Hiskett (1984: 290) goes so far as to label them "the religious wing of the Rassemblement Démocratique Africain in West Africa."

6. On the role of rote memorization in other traditions of Islamic learning, see Eickelman 1985 and Santerre 1973.

7. Reichmuth 1989 describes comparable trends in Islamic education in Nigeria.

CHAPTER 5

1. This does not at all imply that ritual *only* expresses the nature of the moral community. It is senseless to attempt to reduce the "meaning" of ritual to any single dimension. Any analysis, much less any exegesis, is consequently incomplete at best. However, whatever else ritual is "about," it is a social act and thus has social ramifications. The examination of these ramifications, to the exclusion of other possible "meanings," is methodologically justifiable.

2. Although slavery was abolished in Côte d'Ivoire in 1908, and slaves were allowed to return to their home regions, many individuals remained with their former masters. As late as 1973 I knew a man who was a *san jon*, a slave who had been captured as a boy and

later was acquired by purchase. The status of *worosso*, a slave liter-ally "born in the house," that is to say, descended on both sides from slave parents, remains very common. In this, quite special, sense, "slaves" still exist in Korhogo today; see Launay 1977a.

3. "Senufo" masks were, in fact, either Tiembara, Fodonon, Fono, or Kule, and so forth. Before the colonial period, masks were unlikely to be conceived as "Senufo" per se, though the Dyula, as a minority, were much more conscious of their ethnic identity as such.

4. This was even true of funerals, at least the funerals of elders. The funerals of younger individuals were more uniformly solemn, but they were also far less elaborate.

5. Prouteaux 1925 describes the emergence of the *lo* masks in the old Dyula center of Kong. *Lo* masks would also dance at the funeral of important elders, *mory* as well as *tun tigi*.

6. On the chiefdom of Kadioha, see Launay 1988a and 1988b.

7. The word *saraka* has been borrowed by Senufo "unbelievers" to refer to certain sacrifices. However, such offerings would not be defined as *saraka* by Dyula. On the other hand, there are definitely occasions when "pagans" do offer *saraka*, notably when following the advice of a Muslim cleric about some personal problem.

8. Even nowadays, Dyula may refer to Muslim Senufo as *ban-mana*, "pagans."

9. Although much attention has been given to the issue of cross-ing or not crossing arms, it is most clearly the separatism of the Wahhabis that their detractors find most objectionable, and not the posture of prayer per se. One *hajji*, having observed that most Mus-lims in Mecca pray with arms crossed, chose on his return to adopt a mode of prayer that, at least superficially, resembled that of the Wahhabis. His behavior was tolerated as an idiosyncrasy.

CHAPTER 6

1. See, e.g., Fyzee 1964: 35.
2. Hallaq 1984.
3. For a detailed description of Dyula weddings, see Launay 1975.
4. For a more detailed discussion of the Ivoirian Civil Code and its impact among the Dyula, see Launay 1982: 139–45.
5. For reasons I do not understand, these lamb sandwiches seem to form part of the ceremony. The only other sermons I witnessed in which meat was distributed to the audience were during *donba*, a Muslim calendar holiday. However, *donba* sermons, unlike all other sermons (including wedding sermons), are an occasion for compet-itive ostentation in providing food for the audience.

6. The entire Saganogo *kabila* of Koko is an offshoot of the Saga-nogo of Kong, and consequently its members are all agnates of Mammadou-Labi. This certainly reinforces his links to the Dyula of Koko, though the fact is not relevant to the issue of wedding sermons as far as I know.

7. These names are all pseudonyms, except for Mammadou-Labi Saganogo. As he is a nationally known figure, and since his attempt to promulgate the new wedding ceremony was an explicitly public act, I see no reason not to give him the credit for it.

CHAPTER 7

1. This distinction, too, is hardly unambiguous; the term *mory* may also be used to refer specifically to the learned. Among the Mende of Sierra Leone, "morimen" are specialists in written Islamic magic, whereas *"karamokos"* specialize in the teaching of Arabic (Bledsoe and Robey 1986). Plausibly, the terms *mory* and *karamogo* were originally synonymous; through a process of semantic displacement, the distinction has acquired different shades of meaning in different local contexts.

2. Both *siru* and *bayani* are almost certainly borrowed from Arabic, but their specific derivations are open to question. J. R. Goody (1968: 236) derives the Hausa and Gonja equivalents of *siru* from the Arabic *sihr*, "magic" (cf. Eickelman 1985: 67). However, John Hunwick (personal communication) has suggested that these terms might derive rather from *sirr*, "secret," and *bayan*, "clear, evident," a term also associated with public speaking (Holden 1966, cited in Goody 1968: 224). Either derivation of *siru* is intrinsically plausible. Conceivably, the Dyula term collapses the meanings of both Arabic words.

3. I use the term *laymen* with considerable reservations to refer to individuals who are neither enturbaned scholars nor pursuing an advanced course of study that could eventually qualify them for the turban. It must be stressed that Muslim scholars are not the equivalent of the clergy in Christianity, as the use of the term *layman* might imply. Indeed, the Dyula have no word or expression to denote nonscholars.

4. The few exceptions are all young, unmarried, or very recently married men, who may yet choose to pursue their studies elsewhere if they are serious aspirants to the scholarly profession. The most advanced of these young men was in any case studying with his own father.

5. They are always given on a Thursday or Saturday night, technically "Friday" or "Sunday," holy and propitious days; nights are reckoned as parts of the following rather than the preceding day.

6. On the similar "ossiffication" of the *khutba* in early modern Egypt, see Gaffney 1987: 202.

7. It is perhaps relevant that this particular scholar happened to be a *worosso*, a person of slave status with license to joke obscenely (see Launay 1977a). Though the joke was not, strictly speaking, obscene, it might be considered too coarse for a scholar of "free" status. But it must be stressed that such "free" scholars, although they must avoid coarseness or excessive buffoonery lest they appear undignified, are by no means averse to using humor as a rhetorical device.

CHAPTER 8

1. This surge of interest in West African Sufi orders has spawned a literature far too vast to cite comprehensively. For an overview of the literature, see Hiskett 1984: 244–60, Levtzion 1986: 12–16, O'Brien 1981, and O'Brien and Coulon 1988.

2. Hiskett 1984: 258.

3. The term *recrudescence* is J. Spencer Trimingham's (1962: 155). He uses it with specific reference to the nineteenth century, but recent scholarship is increasingly turning to the eighteenth century for the social and ideological roots of the movements he describes.

4. Even more important, although Hiskett does not make this point, the "local patriotism" fostered by the Sufi orders and expressed in terms of allegiance to them may transcend or override traditional lines of segmentation or factional cleavage. Evans-Pritchard's (1949) analysis of the Sanusi order in Cyrenaica stresses precisely this aspect.

5. Hiskett stresses the links between the Sufi orders and various jihad movements in detail, but he also points out quite clearly that many Sufi leaders did not subscribe to the ideology of military jihad.

6. It is clear that at one time membership in various Sufi orders was not at all exclusive, and that individuals could be initiated into several of them. This is, by and large, no longer possible, and certainly not in West Africa.

7. Cohen 1969 has argued that this is the case among the modern "Hausa" of Ibadan. It might be argued that the Mouride order has played a similar role in the development of Wolof ethnicity in Senegal.

8. René Otayek (1988: 98) ascribes the absence of tightly institutionalized Sufism and of charismatic Sufi leaders in Burkina Faso to the "Mossi kingdoms' impermeability to outside influences." This kind of argument is an excellent example of the dangers of elaborating a "typical" model and of attempting to explain deviations. As noted, Sufism in Burkina Faso shares many features with Sufism

just across the border in northern Côte d'Ivoire—but the influence of the Mossi kingdoms is decidedly not one of them.

9. One exception to this rule is the phrase "A ka di Alla ye" ("It pleases God"). For obvious reasons, this is a special case. Somewhat similarly, persons in positions of authority—elders or parents—may wish to emphasize that they are personally pleased or displeased by the specific actions of others, especially subordinates.

10. While it might be labeled "singing" by Westerners, liturgical "chanting," either in Arabic or in Dyula, is never associated with dancing and is never referred to as *donkili*. It falls rather into the broad category of *kalan*, along with reading, reciting, studying, teaching, and delivering sermons. Unlike "singing," "chanting" is an exclusively male activity and confers religious merit.

11. RDA is in fact a Dieli from Koko. However, for most purposes, the Dieli community of Koko has been completely assimilated to the Dyula. It is interesting, though, that in most dialects of Manding, the term *dieli* denotes a "caste" of griots. Dyula of Koko use the term *dieliba* for hereditary griots, to distinguish them from their Dieli neighbors. RDA is often called a "griot" (using the French term), but never a *dieliba*. Perhaps his hereditary Dieli identity helps make his adoption of griot-like behavior more acceptable to the local Dyula population.

12. In Koko, this is usually the Friday mosque, which doubles as a local mosque for the quarter.

CHAPTER 9

1. Combs-Schilling 1989 provides an extended analysis of the symbolism of this specific "blood sacrifice" in Morocco.

2. Ties specifically with in-laws (including prospective in-laws) are stressed, not during *tabaski* but rather during Ramadan, where they invariably receive gifts of sugar. The symbolism is suggestive: "blood" ties are acknowledged through reciprocal, but asymmetrical, gifts of meat; affinal ties through unidirectional (husband to wife's parents) gifts of sweets.

3. Crudely, this amounts to one-fortieth of an individual's income. However, there are numerous qualifications (the prescriptions according to Maliki law are outlined in Qayrawani 1968: 126–39). Laypeople may need to consult scholars in order to determine the extent of their obligation.

4. Cf. Goody 1968.

5. In fact, I knew of no one from Koko reduced to begging, at least in a literal sense. However, Korhogo is very close to the borders of the much poorer countries of Mali and Burkina Faso, and conse-

quently attracts a certain number of beggars, including blind ones, from outside.

6. Frequently, bride and groom belong to the same group, given stated preferences for in-marriage (Launay 1975 and 1982).

CHAPTER 10

1. Cf. Brown 1972: 220: "Altogether, the intellectual events of the last decade of the fourth century are a reminder that controversies emerge not only when people have new ideas, but when they suddenly wake up to realize that they no longer have the old ones."

2. There is a vast literature on African sectarian churches. The pioneering monograph was Bengt Sundkler's *Bantu Prophets in South Africa* (1948). More recent studies include Peel 1968, Fabian 1971, Augé 1975, Jules-Rosette 1975, MacGaffey 1983, and Fields 1985.

3. See Mudimbe 1988: 161–75 for a review of the issues involved, from a philosopher's perspective.

Glossary

AEEMCI [Association des élèves et étudiants musulmans de la Côte d'Ivoire]: Muslim Student Association of Côte d'Ivoire, a quasi-official association with a platform of moderate reform

'alim (Arabic): see *'ulama'*

banmana (Manding): "refusers"; term generically applied to "unbelievers"—non-Muslim peoples of the Western Sudan (though not to peoples living to the south, in or toward the forest); in the Korhogo region, often used by Dyula to refer specifically to Senufo

bayani karamogoya (Manding): see *karamogoya*

dhikr (Arabic): "remembrance"; specifically, special litianies associated with each Sufi order

Dieli: an ethnic and occupational minority in the Korhogo region, formerly associated with leatherworking; their "native" language (which is rapidly disappearing) is distinct from any other in the region

donba (Manding): holiday celebrating the birth of the Prophet

duau (Manding, from Arabic *du'a*, petitionary prayer): blessing in the form of a petitionary prayer in someone else's behalf

Dyula: literally, "trader"; an ethnic category in northern Côte d'Ivoire referring to Manding-speaking Muslim minorities historically specialized in trade and weaving; nowadays, more broadly used in much of Côte d'Ivoire to refer to all Manding-speaking Muslims, if not all African Muslims in general

fijembele (Sienar): often called "castes"; members of hereditary minorities associated with various nonagricultural occupations

fiqh (Arabic): the study of Islamic jurisprudence

Fodonon: a dialect of Sienar, spoken as a native language by an enclaved minority within the chiefdom of Korhogo, as well as in other areas; also refers to native speakers of the language, except for members of "caste" groups

Fono: Sienar-speaking "caste" of blacksmiths

furu (Manding): marriage, to marry; also the name of a specific ceremony among the Dyula that finalizes the marriage

gba (Manding): hearth; recognized section of a large *kabila*

241

griot (French): professional musician or praise singer in West Africa, generally member of a hereditary "caste"

Hausa: a West African people (and the language they speak) from northern Nigeria and parts of Niger; Hausa is, like Manding, associated with a trading diaspora and is consequently a lingua franca in much of West Africa

hajj (Arabic): the pilgrimage to Mecca; al-Hajj, *hajji* (Manding *ladji*), is a title of respect accorded to those who have accomplished the pilgrimage

Hijaz: region of the Arabian Peninsula where the holy cities of Mecca and Medina are located

horon (Manding): a freeborn person

imam (Arabic): office designating the leader of prayer at a given mosque

isnad (Arabic): chain of transmitters of knowledge

jaka (Manding): see *zakat*

jihad (Arabic): "struggle," generally used to refer to violent conflict between Muslims and "unbelievers"

jinn (Arabic; Manding *jina*): a powerful and dangerous kind of spirit; among the Dyula, invariably associated with a specific locale in the "bush"

kabila (Manding; possibly derived from Arabic *qabila*): clan ward, a recognized residential section of a community associated with a specific patronym (*dyamu*), whose members either claim descent in the male line from a common ancestor or from a slave owned by a member of the group

kalan (Manding, probably from Arabic *qar'a*, "to recite"): to recite from a written text; to read; to study; *kalan ke*, "to make or do *kalan*," to read or recite from a written liturgical text on a formal occasion, or alternatively to deliver an extemporized sermon

karamogo (Manding): Muslim cleric, scholar; *karamogo fa*, "scholar father," i.e., teacher; *karamogo den*, "scholar child," i.e., pupil

karamogoya (Manding): scholarship; *bayani karamogoya*, "public" knowledge, specifically of religious duties; *siru* or *siri karamogoya*, "private" knowledge of written charms and other techniques applied to the pursuit of this-worldly ends

konyo mina (Manding): literally, "seizing the bride," an elaborate wedding ceremony performed only on the occasion of a woman's first marriage, associated with her transition from childhood to adulthood

Kpeem: Sienar-speaking "caste" of brass casters

Kule: Sienar-speaking "caste" of sculptors

lo (Manding): "secret" initiation societies among the Dyula *tun tigi*, similar to the Senufo *poro*; also refers to any mask associated with such societies, or to the spirits such masks personify *lon-ni-baga* (Manding): a learned person; i.e., the equivalent of the Arabic term *ʿalim*

madrasa (Arabic): school; in Côte d'Ivoire and neighboring countries, one that incorporates the Western model of classroom education but whose curriculum emphasizes Arabic language and Muslim religious instruction

Maliki (Arabic): one of the four "orthodox" Sunni schools of Islamic jurisprudence, based on the writings of Malik ibn Anas (715–95) of Medina, followed by the overwhelming majority of Muslims in the Maghreb and in West Africa

makafo or *makafu* (Manding): a loose association of several *kabilas*, one of which is usually "host" *(diatigi)* to the others

Manding: northern Mande language, widely spoken as a lingua franca throughout much of West Africa, and as a native language by Dyula as well as by other peoples, such as the Banmana (or Bambara), Maninka (or Malinke), and Marka

Mande: most generally, a family of West African languages; the term is often used to refer specifically to the Manding language as well as to Manding-speaking peoples, most of whom trace their origins to Manden, the heartland of the medieval West African empire of Mali

Milaga: a numerically small, Manding-speaking "caste" group in the Korhogo region, formerly specialized as blacksmiths

mory (Manding): "scholar," a Muslim cleric, but more usually referring in the Korhogo region to a hereditary category, as distinct from *tun tigi,* of *kabilas,* whether or not they specialized in Islamic scholarship, whose members did not initiate their youths into "secret" societies and who were expected to conform to "orthodox" Sunni standards of piety

Mouride: Sufi order based in Senegal, founded by Ahmad Bamba; from Arabic *murid* (see below)

murid (Arabic): disciple, particularly, in a Sufi order, the disciple of a specific *shaykh*

poro (Sienar): the generic name for the "secret" societies into which Senufo males are initiated

Qadiri (Arabic): an adherent of the Qadiriyya

Qadiriyya (Arabic): one of the oldest Sufi orders, tracing its origins to ʿAbd-ul-Qadir al-Jilani (d. 1166) in Baghdad

Ramadan (Arabic): month of obligatory fasting

RDA [Rassemblement démocratique africaine]: pro-independence political party in French West Africa, led by Félix Houphouët-Boigny in Côte d'Ivoire; after independence, the Ivoirian branch became the PDCI (Parti démocratique de la Côte d'Ivoire), until 1990 the only party in the country *salatu:* certain formulaic prayers or blessings in Arabic recited from a text on specific occasions, notably as part of funeral ceremonies on the third day after burial

san jon (Manding): a slave acquired by purchase, as opposed to a slave "born in the house" (*worosso*)

saraka (Manding, from Arabic *sadaqa*): technically, a nonobligatory pious donation; refers among the Dyula to a variety of prestations offered in different contexts to different ends

sebe (Manding): to write; a written charm or amulet

seri (Manding): the act of prayer, as performed five times daily; *seri ji*, "prayer water," the water used for ablutions before praying

sura (Arabic): a named section of the Qur'an

senambele (Sienar): term used to refer to all native speakers of Sienar except those of "caste" status

Senufo: used generally to refer to all the various Sienar-speaking peoples

shari'a (Arabic): Islamic law

sharif (Arabic; pl. *'ashraf*): a direct descendant of the Prophet

shaykh (Arabic): elder, leader; in Sufi orders, the individual who has initiated one and to whom one remains responsible

Sienar: the various dialects of a language, member of the Gur (or Voltaic) family of West African languages, spoken by peoples in northern Côte d'Ivoire, southeastern Mali, and southwestern Burkina Faso

silama (Manding): Muslim; *silamaya* "Muslimness," i.e., Islam

siru or *siri karamogoya* (Manding): see *karamogoya*

Sufi (Arabic): originally, a Muslim mystic; nowadays, usually refers to a member of one of several orders or brotherhoods (Arabic *tariqa*, pl. *turuq*), each based on the (more or less) esoteric teachings of the founder

sunna (Arabic): code of behavior modeled on the exemplary actions of Muhammad and his companions, as transmitted through authoritative traditions (*hadith*)

tabaski (Manding): Muslim holiday commemorating and reenacting Ibrahim's (Abraham's) sacrifice of a ram in lieu of his son, as well as the pilgrimage (*hajj*) to Mecca

tafsir (Arabic): Qur'anic exegesis

Tiembara: a dialect of Sienar, the native language of the chiefs and the majority of the population of the chiefdom of Korhogo; also used to refer to native speakers (except for "caste" groups) of the language

Tijani (Arabic): an adherent of the Tijaniyya

Tijaniyya (Arabic): Sufi order founded in the Maghreb by Ahmad al-Tijani (1737–1815)

tun tigi (Manding): "warriors," a hereditary category, as distinct from *mory,* of *kabilas* whose young men were initiated into "secret" *lo* societies and whose members were not expected to conform rigorously to "orthodox" Sunni standards of piety

ʿ*ulama*ʾ (Arabic, plural; singular, ʿ*alim*): learned individuals; specifically Muslim clerics

umma (Arabic): the global Muslim community

Wahhabi (Arabic): literally, a follower of the teachings of the Islamic reformer Muhammad ibn ʿAbd-al-Wahhab (d. 1791); in francophone West Africa, the term has been used, originally disparagingly by colonial authorities, to refer to adherents of "radical" Muslim reform

wali (Arabic): saint

worosso (Manding): a slave "born in the house," as opposed to a slave acquired by purchase (*san jon*)

yere (Manding): oneself; *yere bonya,* "to aggrandize oneself," to place oneself above others; *yere fo,* "to speak oneself," to boast

zakat (Arabic): a fixed portion of one's wealth or income that must, as a religious obligation, be distributed annually to the needy in the community; pronounced *jaka* in Dyula

Bibliography

Abun Nasr, Jamil. 1965. *The Tijaniyya*. London: Oxford University Press.

Amselle, Jean-Loup. 1977. *Les Négoçiants de la savane*. Paris: Anthropos.

——— . 1985. "Le Wahabisme à Bamako (1945–1985)." *Canadian Journal of African Studies* 19, no. 2: 345–57.

Arjomand, Said Amir. 1987. "Revolution in Shi'ism." In W. R. Roff, ed., *Islam and the Political Economy of Meaning*, pp. 111–31. Berkeley and Los Angeles: University of California Press.

Asad, Talal. 1985. "The Idea of an Anthropology of Islam." Center for Contemporary Arab Studies, Georgetown University, Occasional Paper Series.

Augé, Marc. 1975. *Prophétisme et thérapeutique*. Paris: Hermann.

Bassett, Thomas. 1985. "Food, Peasantry and the State in Northern Ivory Coast, 1898–1982." Ph.D. diss., University of California, Berkeley.

Behrman, Lucy C. 1970. *Muslim Brotherhoods and Politics in Senegal*. Cambridge, Mass.: Harvard University Press.

Beidelman, T. O. 1982. *Colonial Evangelism*. Bloomington: Indiana University Press.

Bernus, E. 1960. "Kong et sa région." *Etudes eburnéennes* 8: 239–324.

——— . 1961. "Notes sur l'histoire de Korhogo." *Bulletin de l'Institut fondamental d'Afrique noire*, série B (sciences humaines) 23(1–2, January–April): 284–90.

Binger, Louis. 1892. *Du Niger au Golfe de Guinée*. Paris: Hachette.

Bledsoe, Caroline, and Kenneth M. Robey. 1986. "Arabic Literacy and Secrecy among the Mende of Sierra Leone." *Man* 21, no. 2 (June): 202–26.

Bloch, Maurice. 1986. *From Blessing to Violence*. Cambridge: Cambridge University Press.

Brenner, Louis. 1984. *West African Sufi: The Religious Heritage and Spiritual Search of Cerno Bokar Saalif Taal*. Berkeley and Los Angeles: University of California Press.

Brown, Peter. 1972. *Religion and Society in the Age of Saint Augustine*. London: Faber & Faber.

Brown, Susan Drucker. 1975. *Ritual Aspects of the Mamprusi Kingship.* Cambridge: African Studies Centre.

Clarke, Peter B. 1982. *West Africa and Islam.* London: Edward Arnold.

Cohen, Abner. 1969. *Custom and Politics in Urban Africa.* London: Routledge & Kegan Paul.

————. 1971. "Cultural Strategies in the Organisation of Trading Diasporas." In Claude Meillassoux, ed., *The Development of Indigenous Trade and Markets in West Africa,* pp. 266–81. London: Oxford University Press.

Combs-Schilling, M. E. 1989. *Sacred Performances: Islam, Sexuality, and Sacrifice.* New York: Columbia University Press.

Copans, Jean. 1980. *Les Marabouts de l'arachide.* Paris: Le Sycomore.

Coulon, Christian. 1981. *Le Marabout et le prince.* Paris: Pédone.

Dérive, J., and M.-J. Dérive. 1986. "Francophonie et pratique linguistique en Côte d'Ivoire." *Politique africaine* 23 (September): 42–56.

Eickelman, Dale. 1985. *Knowledge and Power in Morocco: The Education of a Twentieth-Century Notable.* Princeton: Princeton University Press.

————. 1987. "Changing Interpretations of Islamic Movements." In W. Roff, ed., *Islam and the Political Economy of Meaning,* pp. 13–30. Berkeley and Los Angeles: University of California Press.

Eickelman, Dale, and J. Piscatori, eds. 1990. *Muslim Travellers: Pilgrimage, Migration and the Religious Imagination.* London: Routledge.

Enayat, Hamid. 1983. "Iran: Khumayni's concept of the 'guardianship of the jurisconsult.' " In J. Piscatori, ed., *Islam in the Political Process,* pp. 160–80. Cambridge: Cambridge University Press.

Evans-Pritchard, E. E. 1949. *The Sanusi of Cyrenaica.* London: Oxford University Press.

Fabian, J. 1971. *Jamaa: A Charismatic Movement in Katanga.* Evanston, Ill.: Northwestern University Press.

Ferguson, P. 1973. "Islamization in Dagbon: A Study of the Alfanema of Yendi." Ph.D. diss., University of Cambridge.

Fields, Karen. 1985. *Revival and Rebellion in Colonial Central Africa.* Princeton: Princeton University Press.

Fisher, Humphrey. 1973. "Conversion Reconsidered: Some Historical Aspects of Religious Conversion in Black Africa." *Africa* 43, no. 1 (January): 27–40.

Fyzee, Asaf A. A. 1964. *Outlines of Muhammadan Law.* 3d ed. London: Oxford University Press.

Gaffney, Patrick. 1987. "Authority and the Mosque in Upper Egypt: The Islamic Preacher as Image and Actor." In W. Roff, ed., *Islam and the Political Economy of Meaning,* pp. 199–225. Berkeley and Los Angeles: University of California Press.

Geertz, Clifford. 1960. *The Religions of Java.* New York: Free Press.

——— . 1968. *Islam Observed.* Chicago: University of Chicago Press.

Gellner, Ernest. 1981. *Muslim Society.* Cambridge: Cambridge University Press.

Gilsenan, Michael. 1982. *Recognizing Islam.* New York: Pantheon Books.

Glaze, Anita. 1981. *Art and Death in a Senufo Village.* Bloomington: Indiana University Press.

Goody, J. R. 1967. "The Over-Kingdom of Gonja." In D. Forde and P. Kaberry, eds., *West African Kingdoms in the Nineteenth Century,* pp. 178–205. London: Oxford University Press.

——— . 1968. "Restricted Literacy in Northern Ghana." In J. R. Goody, ed., *Literacy in Traditional Societies.* pp. 199–264. Cambridge: Cambridge University Press.

Green, K. 1984. "The Foundation of Kong: A study in Dyula and Sonongui Ethnic Identity." Ph.D. diss., Indiana University.

——— . 1986. "Dyula and Sonongui Roles in the Islamization of the Region of Kong." *Asian and African Studies* 20 (March): 97–117.

Greenberg, Joseph. 1946. *The Influence of Islam on a Sudanese Religion.* New York: Augustin.

Hallaq, Wael. 1984. "Was the Gate of Ijtihad Closed?" *International Journal of Middle East Studies* 16 (March): 3–41.

Handloff, Robert. 1982. "The Dyula of Gyaman: A study of Politics and Trade in the Nineteenth Century." Ph.D. diss., Northwestern University.

Harrison, Christopher. 1988. *France and Islam in West Africa, 1860–1960.* Cambridge: Cambridge University Press.

Hiskett, Mervyn. 1973. *The Sword of Truth.* New York: Oxford University Press.

——— . 1984. *The Development of Islam in West Africa.* London and New York: Longman.

Hodgson, Marshall. 1974. *The Venture of Islam.* 3 vols. Chicago: University of Chicago Press.

Holden, J. 1966. "Note on the Education and Early Life of Al-Hajj 'Umar Tall." *Research Review* (University of Ghana, Institute of African Studies [Legon]), 2, no. 2 (Lent).

Holy, Ladislav. 1991. *Religion and Custom in a Muslim Society: The Berti of Sudan.* Cambridge: Cambridge University Press.

Horton, Robin. 1971. "African Conversion." *Africa* 41, no. 2 (April): 85–108.

——— . 1975a. "On the Rationality of African Conversion, Part I." *Africa* 45, no. 3: 219–35.

——— . 1975b. "On the Rationality of African Conversion, Part II." *Africa* 45, no. 4: 373–99.

Hunter, Thomas. 1976. "The Jabi *Tarikhs:* Their Significance in West African Islam." *International Journal of African Historical Studies* 9, no. 3: 435–57.

———. 1977. The Development of an Islamic Tradition of Learning among the Jakhanke of West Africa." Ph.D. diss., University of Chicago.

Jules-Rosette, B. 1975. *African Apostles: Ritual and Conversion in the Church of John Maranke*. Ithaca, N.Y.: Cornell University Press.

Kaba, Lansine. 1974. *The Wahhabiyya*. Evanston, Ill.: Northwestern University Press.

Kuper, Adam. 1988. *The Invention of Primitive Society*. London and New York: Routledge.

Last, Murray. 1967. *The Sokoto Caliphate*. New York: Humanities Press.

Launay, Robert. 1975. "Tying the Cola: Dyula Marriage and Social Change." Ph.D. diss., University of Cambridge.

———. 1977a. "Joking slavery." *Africa* 47, no. 4: 413–22.

———. 1977b. "The Birth of a Ritual: The Politics of Innovation in Dyula Islam." *Savanna* 6, no. 2 (December): 145–54.

———. 1978. "Transactional Spheres and Inter-societal Exchange in Ivory Coast." *Cahiers d'études africaines* 18, no. 4: 561–73.

———. 1979. "Landlords, Hosts and Strangers among the Dyula." *Ethnology* 18, no. 1 (January): 71–83.

———. 1982. *Traders without Trade: Responses to Change in Two Dyula Communities*. Cambridge: Cambridge University Press.

———. 1988a. "Sabati-Ba's Coup d'etat: Contexts of Legitimacy in a West African Chiefdom." In R. Cohen and J. Toland, eds., *State Formation and Political Legitimacy*, pp. 45–67. New Brunswick, N.J.: Transactions.

———. 1988b. "Warriors and Traders: The Political Organization of a West African Chiefdom." *Cahiers d'études africaines* 28, nos. 111–12 (3–4): 355–73.

———. 1990. "Pedigrees and Paradigms: Scholarly Credentials among the Dyula of Northern Ivory Coast." In D. Eickelman and J. Piscatori, eds., *Muslim Travellers*, pp. 175–199. London: Routledge.

———. N.d.a. "The Dieli of Korhogo: Identity and Identification." In D. Conrad and B. Frank, eds., *Status and Identity in West Africa: The Nyamakalaw of Mande*. Forthcoming.

———. N.d.b. "Illegitimacy in an African Muslim Community." In Susan Greenhalgh, ed., *The Social Construction of the Family: Anthropological Contributions to Fertility Theory*. Forthcoming.

Lévi-Strauss, Claude. 1962. *Le Totémisme aujourd'hui*. Paris: Presses universitaires de France.

Levtzion, Nehemiah. 1968. *Muslims and Chiefs in West Africa*. Oxford: Clarendon Press.

———. 1973. *Ancient Ghana and Mali*. London: Methuen.

MacGaffey, W. 1983. *Modern Kongo Prophets*. Bloomington: Indiana University Press.

Martin, Bradford G. 1976. *Muslim Brotherhoods in Nineteenth-Century Africa*. Cambridge: Cambridge University Press.

Marty, P. 1922. *Etudes sur l'Islam en Côte d'Ivoire*. Paris: Ernest Leroux.

Miner, Horace. 1953. *The Primitive City of Timbuctoo*. Princeton: Princeton University Press.

Mudimbe, V. 1988. *The Invention of Africa: Gnosis, Philosophy and the Order of Knowledge*. Bloomington: Indiana University Press.

Niezen, R. W. 1990. "The 'Community of the Helpers of the Sunna': Islamic Reform among the Songhay of Gao (Mali)." *Africa* 60, no. 3: 399–424.

O'Brien, Donal Cruise. 1971. *The Mourides of Senegal*. Oxford: Clarendon Press.

——— . 1975. *Saints and Politicians: Essays in the Organisation of a Senegalese Peasant Society*. Cambridge: Cambridge University Press.

——— . 1981. "La Filière musulmane: Confréries soufies et politique en Afrique noire." *Politique africaine* 4: 7–30.

O'Brien, Donal Cruise, and Christian Coulon, eds. 1988. *Charisma and Brotherhood in African Islam*. Oxford: Clarendon Press.

Ouattara, T. 1977. "Les Tiembara de Korhogo, des origines à Peleforo Gbon Coulibaly (1962)." Thèse de doctorat de 3ᵉ cycle, Paris.

Otayek, René. 1988. "Muslim Charisma in Burkina Faso." In Donal Cruise O'Brien and C. Coulon, eds., *Charisma and Brotherhood in African Islam*, pp. 90–112. Oxford: Clarendon Press.

Paden, John. 1973. *Religion and Political Culture in Kano*. Berkeley and Los Angeles: University of California Press.

Peel, John. 1969. *Aladura: A Religious Movement among the Yoruba*. London: Oxford University Press.

Person, Yves. 1964. "En quête d'une chronologie ivoirienne." In J. Vansina et al., eds., *The Historian in Tropical Africa*, pp. 322–38. London: Oxford University Press.

——— . 1968. *Samori: Une Révolution dyula*. Vol 1. Dakar: Institut Fondamental d'Afrique Noire.

——— . 1975. *Samori: Une Révolution dyula*. Vol 3. Dakar: Institut Fondamental d'Afrique Noire.

Piscatori, James. 1986. *Islam in a World of Nation-States*. Cambridge: Cambridge University Press.

Prouteaux, R. 1925. "Divertissements de Kong." *Bulletin du Comité d'études historiques et scientifiques de l'Afrique Occidentale Française* 8, no. 4 (October–December): 609–50.

Qayrawani, ibn abi Zayd al-. 1968. [written in 996]. *La Risala*. Translated by Léon Bercher. 5th ed. Algiers: Editions populaires de l'armée.

Quinn, Charlotte. 1972. *Mandingo Kingdoms of the Senegambia*. Evanston, Ill.: Northwestern University Press.

Reichmuth, Stefan. 1989. "New Trends in Islamic Education in Nigeria: A Preliminary Account." *Die Welt des Islams* 29: 41–60.

Richter, Dolores. 1980. *Art, Economics and Change: The Kulebele of Northern Ivory Coast.* La Jolla, Calif.: Psych-Graphic Publishers.

Robinson, David. 1985. *The Holy War of Umar Tal: The Western Sudan in the Mid-Nineteenth Century.* Oxford: Clarendon Press.

Sanneh, Lamine. 1979. *The Jakhanke.* London: Oxford University Press.

Santerre, R. 1973. *Pédagogie musulmane d'Afrique noire.* Montreal: Presses de l'Université de Montréal.

SEDES [Société d'études pour le développement économique et sociale]. 1965. *Région de Korhogo: Etude de développement socio-économique.* Vol. 1, *Rapport démographique.* Abidjan: Ministère des finances, des affaires économiques et du plan.

Sindzingre, Nicole. 1985. "Healing Is as Healing Does: Pragmatic Resolution of Misfortune among the Senufo (Ivory Coast)." *History and Anthropology* 2: 33–57.

Smith, W. Robertson. 1972. [1889]. *The Religion of the Semites.* New York: Schocken Books.

Stewart, Charles. 1973. *Islam and Social Order in Mauritania.* Oxford: Clarendon Press.

Sundkler, Bengt. 1948. *Bantu Prophets in South Africa.* London: Lutterworth Press.

Triaud, Jean-Louis. 1974. "La Question musulmane en Côte d'Ivoire (1893–1939)," *Revue française d'histoire d'outre mer* 61, no. 225 (4): 542–71.

Trimingham, J. Spencer. 1959. *Islam in West Africa.* Oxford: Clarendon Press.

———. 1962. *A History of Islam in West Africa.* London: Oxford University Press.

Université Nationale de Côte d'Ivoire. "Table ronde sur les origines de Kong." *Annales de l'Université d'Abidjan,* série J (traditions orales), 1.

Wilks, Ivor. 1962. "A Medieval Trade-Route from the Niger to the Gulf of Guinea." *Journal of African History* 3, no. 2: 337–41.

———. 1968. "The Transmission of Islamic Learning in the Western Sudan." In J. R. Goody, ed., *Literacy in Traditional Societies,* pp. 162–97. Cambridge: Cambridge University Press.

———. 1984. "The Suwarians: Laissez-faire, laissez-nous faire?" Paper presented to the Conference on Islam in Africa, Northwestern University, Evanston, Ill.

———. 1989. *Wa and the Wala.* Cambridge: Cambridge University Press.

Willis, J. R., ed. 1979. *The Cultivators of Islam.* London: Frank Cass.

Zein, Abdul Hamid M. el-. 1974. *The Sacred Meadows.* Evanston, Ill.: Northwestern University Press.

———. 1977. "Beyond Ideology and Theology: The Search for an Anthropology of Islam." *Annual Review of Anthropology* 6: 227–54.

Index

'Abduh, Muhammad, 86
Abidjan, 42, 46, 94, 216
AEEMCI (Association des élèves et
étudiants musulmans de Côte
d'Ivoire), 72–73, 74, 95–97, 123–
24, 186, 200
Al-Azhar, 86, 90, 92, 97, 100
Alcoholic beverages: abstention
from, 63, 64, 109; consumption
of, 55, 57, 58, 62, 116, 117, 233
n. 7
Arabic (language), 2–3, 77, 93, 112;
literacy in, 56, 77, 92–95, 117–
18, 150–51, 160, 179, 202; pronunciation of, 94–95, 117–18; in
sermons, 170, 171, 174–75
Artisans. See "Castes"

Bamako, 86, 88, 89, 92
Beggars, 74–75, 205, 238–39 n. 5
Begho, 49
Blessings, 119, 120, 193–94, 205,
211, 213
Blindness, 205, 238–39 n. 5
Borno, 17
Boron, 80, 220
Bouake, 86, 88, 89, 90, 94, 134, 140
Burkina Faso, 21, 43, 47, 65, 182,
237–38 n. 8, 238–39 n. 5

"Castes," 89, 100, 122; in Koko, 40,
43, 51–53, 213. See also Dieli;
Fonombele; Kpeembele; Kule-
bele; Milaga
Catholics in Côte d'Ivoire, 72–75
Christianity, 25–28 passim; African
Churches, 26, 228–29, 239 nn. 2,
3; compared to Islam by Mus-

lims, 8, 23, 74–75; as competitor
of Islam, 72–75
Clan wards: associations of
(*makafu*), 41, 69, 70, 112, 119;
divisions of Dyula communities,
40–41; economic specialization,
54; and factional politics, 144–
45; and "host/stranger" relationship, 41, 44, 66, 232 n. 2, 234
n. 15; in-marriage within, 11,
40, 239 n. 6; rights to office, 45,
54, 71, 158, 215; sections of, 90,
210, 216
—and ritual, 89, 111–13 passim,
120, 128–31 passim, 210; collective *saraka*, 215–17; ownership of
masks, 109–10; representation at
life-crisis rituals, 69–70, 119,
211, 213
Class, 29; and different conceptions
of Islam, 30–31, 34, 129–31
Clerics. See Scholars
Conversion, 23–24; to Christianity,
23–24, 73–74; Horton's theory
of, 24–27, 104–5; to Islam, 15,
16, 57, 62–63, 66, 73–74, 113–14
Côte d'Ivoire, 1, 8, 21, 36–47 passim, 51, 58–75 passim; Civil
Code, 138–39; 235 n. 4; education, 47, 91; elites, 127–28, 139;
government and politics, 45,
72–73, 95, 97, 144; plantations,
42; precolonial trade, 49–50;
urbanization, 42–43
—national religious communities:
Catholic, 72–75; Muslim, 68,
71–75, 124, 131; Protestant,
72–75
Cotton, cultivation of, 47, 232 n. 4

253

Compositor: BookMasters, Inc.
Text: 10/12 Palatino
Display: Palatino
Printer and Binder: BookCrafters, Inc.